BOSNIA BY TELEVISION

BOSNIA BY TELEVISION

Edited by

James Gow, Richard Paterson, Alison Preston

BRITISH FILM INSTITUTE

bfi

BFI PUBLISHING

Published in 1996 by the
British Film Institute
21 Stephen Street
London W1P 2LN

Copyright © British Film Institute 1996

The British Film Institute exists to promote
appreciation, protection and development of
moving image culture in and throughout the whole
of the United Kingdom. Its activities include the
National Film and Television Archive; the
National Film Theatre; the London Film Festival;
the Museum of the Moving Image; the production
and distribution of film and video; funding and
support for regional activities; Library and
Information Services; Stills, Posters and
Designs; Research; Publishing and Education; and
the monthly *Sight and Sound* magazine.

British Library Cataloguing in Publication Data
A catalogue record for this book is available
from the British Library

ISBN 0-85170-611-8 hbk
     0-85170-612-6 pbk

Cover design: Romas Foord
Cover image: Courtesy of ITN

Typeset by Fakenham Photosetting Ltd,
Fakenham, Norfolk
Printed in Great Britain by
St Edmundsbury Press
Bury St Edmunds, Suffolk

Contents

Acknowledgments

The papers collected here come from two activities co-ordinated by the British Film Institute's Research and Education Division: *Turbulent Europe*, a major international conference; and an international research project on news reporting about the conflict in Bosnia.

In July 1994 the BFI organised a European Film and Television Studies Conference, *Turbulent Europe: Conflict Identity and Culture*, at the National Film Theatre in London. The conference was multi-disciplinary and considered the transformation of Europe after 1989, and television and film's role in these times of change. The event took place at a time when the prospects for peace in Europe had been decisively cut across by war and conflict in the former Yugoslavia and a resurgence of nationalism, and where uncertainty above the future of political and economic integration had emerged following the Maastricht Treaty on European Union. There were four themes in the conference: conflict, war reporting and news management; the public sphere, democracy and the media; religion and the media; and identities and nationalism, and more than eighty papers from twenty-five countries were discussed. Some of the most challenging debates at the conference focused on the media's role in Yugoslav War of Dissolution and a selection of those papers is included in the first three parts of this book.

We would particularly like to express our thanks to the other members of the Conference Advisory Committee for their help in organising the event: Ian Brough-Williams, Nicky North, Duncan Petrie, Kevin Robins, Esther Ronay, Philip Schlesinger, Colin Sparks, Judith Squires, Janet Willis and Tana Wollen. Especial thanks go to Jacintha Cusack, the conference director, for her administrative skill, adroitness and efficiency in co-ordinating the whole event and making it such a success.

The conference benefited from financial assistance from a number of sources without which this volume would have been impossible to produce. We wish to thank the Soros Foundation, the Foreign and Commonwealth Office, the British Council, the British Association for Central and Eastern Europe, Channel Four Television and BBC Worldwide for lending us their valuable support.

The papers in Part Four are drawn from a separate but parallel BFI initiative. In May 1994 the BFI co-ordinated a major research exercise to examine one week's television news coverage of Yugoslavia in countries across Europe and its periphery. It is a testimony to the commitment of the researchers with whom we worked that we succeeded with no direct financial support in completing this ground-breaking research, and we are grateful to all of them and their host institutions for making this study possible. In addition, in the UK we are grateful to Reuters Television, ITN, Sky News and the BBC for their assistance.

Richard Paterson

Notes on Contributors

Asu Aksoy, researcher based in Istanbul, Turkey

Anantha Babbili, Department of Journalism, Texas Christian University, USA

Klime Babunski, Institute for Political, Sociological and Juridical Research, University of Skopje, Macedonia

Sandra Bašić-Hrvatin, Faculty of Social Sciences, University of Ljubljana, Slovenia

Ian Brough-Williams, Dartington College of Art, UK

John Burns, St Cross College, Oxford, UK

James Gow, Department of War Studies, King's College London, UK

Nik Gowing, Diplomatic Editor Channel Four News until 1996; since, presenter BBC World, UK

Brigitte Hipfl, Institute for Educational Technology and Media Studies, University of Klagenfurt, Austria

Klaus Hipfl, ORF, Austria

jan jagodzinski, School of Education, University of Alberta, Canada

Zohra Khandriche, University of Alger, Algeria

Milena Michalski, School of Slavonic and Eastern European Studies, University of London, UK

Zdenka Milivojević, Argument, Belgrade, Serbia

Richard Paterson, Research and Education Division, British Film Institute, UK

Alison Preston, British Film Institute/University of Stirling, UK

Walter Schludermann, Institute of Educational Technology and Media Studies, University of Klagenfurt, Austria

Marie-Claude Taranger, Department of Film and Audiovisual Studies, University of Provence, France

James Tilsley, Department of War Studies, King's College London, UK

Antonia Torchi, freelance media researcher, Bologna, Italy

Roza Tsagarousianou, Centre for Communication and Information Studies, University of Westminster, UK

Hrvoje Turković, Academy of Dramatic Art, Theatre, Film and Television, Zagreb University, Croatia

Jože Vogrinc, Department of Sociology, University of Ljubljana, Slovenia

Map of the former Yugoslavia

1	LJUBLJANA	8	Tuzla	15	Mostar
2	ZAGREB	9	BELGRADE	16	Dubrovnik
3	Sisak	10	Srebenica	17	PODGORICA
4	Osijek	11	SARAJEVO	18	Priština
5	Novi Sad	12	Pale	19	SKOPJE
6	Bihac	13	Goražde	20	Vukovar
7	Banja Luka	14	Split		

Introduction

JAMES GOW, RICHARD PATERSON AND ALISON PRESTON

The Yugoslav War of Dissolution was a major focus for the international news media in the early 90s. The conflict was mediated through multiple prisms, leaving a variety of images and details, several archives of records and unresolved debates on essential 'truths', both specific and incidental. The relative lack of information and the sheer number of 'authors' involved in each medium were such that often no more than fractured accounts, unreliable narratives and partial (often in both meanings of that word) analysis emerged.

As a study, this volume derives from two fields and aims to be of relevance in both: media studies and policy and strategic studies. From a perspective combining the two, the volume is an attempt to understand the variability of influential media reporting across national boundaries, the importance of the media for policy and strategy, and the influence on policy-making or on public concern. This multiple focus of analysis has powerful repercussions. It focuses on the influences brought to bear on journalists and editors, involving questions of representation and the difficulties which journalists face in addressing audiences so that they can comprehend as citizens able to act and influence the actions of their governments. It emphasises the need for a journalistic ethics. It brings into focus the influence and counter-influence of politicians and journalists in offering accounts of the war in their own 'professional' terms.

It was a war often regarded as incomprehensible and blurred, in some cases, and clear-cut and simple, in others. In both human and military–political terms, international media coverage got the essence of the war in Bosnia right, even if dispute remains over its origins and causes, its conduct and character. The war was complex, with fault all around, but with the overwhelming burden of responsibility falling on the Serbian side.

However, it is important to understand not only what happened in any situation, but how the interpretation of events was affected by the embeddedness of reports within different national political–cultural contexts, as well as the significance of the ways in which modern media reporting influenced government policy.

It should be made clear that from the outset, given the competition for truth over the Yugoslav war, that some of the detail contained in the following chapters should be treated with caution: in a few places where it is known to the editors to be wrong, where amendment was suggested, but not made, the material appears as the authors wished to present it. This is done to reflect the ambiguity surrounding issues of accuracy and so as not to open to accusations of exercising a prejudicial editorial policy on any particular version of an event, even where there is unchallengeable alternative information. Throughout the volume, the issues of 'truth' and distance will be important motifs, although the collection as a whole reflects a diversity of approaches and themes that extends beyond these.

Interpretation

What this collection of essays reveals is that the 'reality' of the war presented to television audiences in different countries was affected by a range of discourses. These derived from dominant historical memories, or followed particular ideological emphases reflecting past and current national involvement. In this respect the fears of European politicians during and after the more distant Gulf War of a future homogeneity of reporting of major international events dominated by CNN did not take place.

'The first casualty when war comes is truth', said Sen. Hiram Johnson in 1917.[1] A recurrent theme in studies of the media in war has been that war reporting leads to partiality and distorts the reality it is claiming to present.[2] It ignores a wider perspective, relative in its focus, which unpacks any overeasy notion of what that 'truth' is. This approach reveals the partialities which are trapped in journalistic (and wider national) discourses and, though thereby not underplaying the importance of journalistic endeavour and the aim of informing the citizens in a well-functioning democracy, creates an awareness of grounded differences. Narratives were employed in most news regimes which were typically constructed using well-established conventions which underpin any continuing story. But the narrative 'truths' of this conflict were not singular and their complexity was beset by contradictions of purpose, of diplomacy and compassion, of cynicism and idealism.

Policy Influence

The conflicts in Bosnia focused frustration at the limits of international diplomatic action.[3] Although the media rarely affected decisions, it sometimes placed those in the policy field under great pressure. In the absence of the clear and strong international, particularly Western, policy that there had been over the Iraqi invasion of Kuwait, policy was characterised by indecision and a lack of cohesion. In the absence of policy, there was debate, and much of that debate was held in the news media. In part, it was because of the proximity to Europe and the graphic awfulness of what was happening.

In an earlier period this conflict would have received less attention. Whereas in 1938, British Prime Minister Neville Chamberlain had been able to explain appeasement of Nazi Germany by characterising Czechoslovakia as a 'far away country of which we know little', his successors in the 90s had to contend with an environment in which modern media communications meant that too much was known for it to be impassively dismissed. However, that same environment was also one in which, however much was known, even more still was not. Thus, the truth surrounding particular events might be discussed, contributing either to the confusion or clarification on the greater truths of the war. This had salience for policy-makers.

Technology

The degree in which the war was double-mediated was a function of late twentieth-century technology and mass communications. The work of international negotiators was facilitated by rapid air travel and by the omnipresence of telephone and radio communications, especially involving satellite relay, as well as, in some cases, hand-me-down information from military intelligence gathering and managing capabilities.

Agents of international diplomacy were also aided and goaded by the work of international media which, itself, often depended on up-to-date technology. It was the reality of the satellite dish in a war theatre, with its possibility of immediate 'real-time' transmission, and the universal presence of the hand-held camcorder which gave the Yugoslav conflict its status as the most comprehensively media-documented war ever. This made it the first true television war.

The camcorder was the instrument by which many Yugoslav witnesses to disintegration and destruction could keep their own record and attempt to tell their own story. Unlike any previous war – possibly any future war – the Yugoslav War of Dissolution had the inevitable fog of war both clarified and further clouded by immediate and widespread visual chronicles. Ultimately, however, they also began (and are likely to continue) to be a major resource for reconstructing an accurate picture of what actually happened – as can be seen in such programmes as *The Death of Yugoslavia*.[4]

It was the advent of the camcorder which had perhaps the most significant impact. Where the Crimean and Boer wars had marked the importance of journalism, something carried through into the First World War where photography also came into its element, the Second World War saw the predominance of radio and newsreel. By the time of the Vietnam War filmed reports were opening the way for 'television' war. That phenomenon was taken a step further in the Gulf Conflict which was marked by video images and instant reporting using the portable satellite dish to uplink from the battlefield (or Baghdad). The Yugoslav War proceeded further in terms of instant reporting than the Gulf Conflict and added the personal report from someone, somewhere, with a video-camera, making it the most recorded and reported of all conflicts. Former Yugoslavia's proximity to Western Europe permitted frequent freelance travel in a way that other wars did not; the camcorder enabled Western individuals to become adventurers and to seek to make their career in the unique world of war reporting, alongside the print and photographic journalists.[5]

Journalists

The quality of texture and text in *The Death of Yugoslavia* was partly due to the astonishing amount of video material that was available. This was a manifestation of the technical revolution which had taken place in the 80s: personal video-recorders meant that anyone keeping a family or personal archive would have material. The nature of the war added to this quantum leap in conflict reporting to create a situation in which personal commitment became highly important. With ethnic cleansing and siege (whether Dubrovnik, Vukovar, Sarajevo or Srebrenica) competing for the status of central image of the war, the common understanding was clear: if war was hell, Bosnia was on its lower levels. Events in former Yugoslavia impelled a strong and emotional response from those reporting on it. As Paul Harris observed, even with the 'war tourist' distance of not being actually involved,[6] 'once you become personally aware of what is happening it is difficult to ignore, to turn your back.'[7]

The Yugoslav War was dangerous for journalists since they could reveal the truth to the outside world. In the eyes of the Serbian side, for most of the war, this made them spies,[8] especially if they were carrying cameras. This danger was not peculiar to journalists: it was fear of being killed which made the Dutch troops serving with UNPROFOR destroy, or 'lose' their videotape recordings of events at Srebrenica in

July 1995, when several thousand Muslims disappeared. The imperative of television in the lightweight video and satellite age added to the danger. As John Simpson noted, the 'trouble is, television is nothing without pictures'.[9] Getting pictures means that those taking them must expose themselves – getting out of a vehicle, or standing in the open pointing the camera. Guilty soldiers wanting to prevent their murderous activities from being reported, therefore, may be prepared to kill. Personal danger can only increase personal commitment.

Reporting of the Yugoslav War appears to indicate that personal involvement is important, if integrity can be preserved. Being present is an important aspect, it seems, of TV news. This was undoubtedly true of the reports by Penny Marshall and Ian Williams for ITN in the summer of 1992: it was the images they provided of brave and intrepid reporters interviewing camp detainees and confronting those who imprisoned them, as well as the horror which flashed around the world as one emaciated Bosnian Muslim by the camp fence recalled images of events fifty years before.[10] More than anything else, it may be that the personal report to camera, from the right face, is what has impact.

Agencies

However, as important as the camcorder has been, the continued power of the television news agencies to define much of the news agenda from the war itself, through available pictures and a preliminary mediation of their meaning is notable. That this actuality footage was constrained in scope by the dangers of war reporting away from UNPROFOR, and that it was complemented by coverage emanating from the combatants and the UN, was one of the innovative features of the media stories from this war.

The apparent lesson to be learned from much of the reporting on the Yugoslav War is that where international diplomacy is present, journalists will follow (even if they do not follow the official line). The clearest manifestation of this phenomenon was the way in which most of the international press corps in Bosnia tended to travel with the British battalion serving with UNPROFOR (the United Nations Protection Force) in Bosnia. This was because BRITBAT was able to provide both accomplished assistance to journalists and protection in dangerous areas. As a result, the greatest part of international, not simply British, TV (and other) reporting on the war in Bosnia that did not come from Sarajevo was focused around the British contingent.

An additional set of lessons follow from this. Where TV journalists are present, there will be news – sending reporters is far too expensive not to have something to show. Where there is a TV journalist of established integrity present, then a news story and its accompanying images will establish personal contact and reach into homes. It is probably the reporter's presence at the scene which contracts the distance between the viewer and the event and can turn Bosnia from a far away country of which little is known into one which is familiar and about which much is understood, often to the irritation of policy-makers.

Bosnia by Television

This collection of diverse studies based on research in a number of countries shows the importance of mediation through both the personal and the broad national political agendas available. Jože Vogrinc in Chapter 1 shows how Slovenian TV, once Slovenia had gained independence, effectively put distance between their own country and the rest of former Yugoslavia, especially war-torn Bosnia. The ratio of time devoted to a subject (the war in Bosnia) was linked to the presence of an on-site reporter. For the most part, Slovenian TV did not have reporters in Bosnia, therefore coverage was limited to formal studio presentation, or commentary over pictures obtained from elsewhere. The cumulative effect was to reduce Slovenia's proximate concern with the war – although people could not cease to be affected by it.

The relevance of on-site transmission for establishing contact also emerges in the contribution by Antonia Torchi. Torchi uses an account of an initiative by one Italian television station, Italia 1, to stimulate opinion by broadcasting live from Sarajevo for a fifteen-day period. This provided a direct link between Sarajevo and the Italian audience – crucially, at the time of the Sarajevo market massacre in February 1994. The immediacy of this type of reporting provides an 'audiovisual truth', which brings the war to an audience in new ways and with greater insight and understanding.

Ian Brough-Williams, in reviewing the phenomenon of *Bloody Bosnia*, a week of themed programming on the conflict by Channel Four TV in the UK, reveals the striking importance of the personal dimension. For the most part, the programmes with the biggest impact (*Sarajevo Diary, Frontline* and *The Unforgiving*) all had a distinct personal dimension. In contrast, one of the critically least-successful elements in the season, *The Essential Guide*, was disliked precisely because it was made in the impersonal, disposable style of the MTV generation.

The difficulties of reconciling personal involvement with professional objectivity, at the heart of so many debates on coverage of the war in Bosnia, appear in the discussion offered by Brigitte Hipfl, Klaus Hipfl and jan jagodzinski in an unusual contribution in the form of a discussion between a brother and sister, moderated and reported by a third party. Built around Klaus Hipfl's experience as a documentary film-maker in the former Yugoslavia, they consider the reaction of the audience to the work they have completed, as well as the tension between objectivity and emotional motivation, with her favouring purist detachment and his believing that emotional commitment is the only honest approach. 'The reporter is closer to the war than the viewer is at home', they write, so the reporting itself becomes 'part of the war's "reality"; that part that can be caught with the cameras at a reasonably safe distance'.

The need for 'action footage' – gained only by working alongside troops close to the front line – in news reporting, leaves the bulk of that which is shown – 'the sadness, the plight of refugees, the burnt and destroyed villages' – as social, rather than war reporting in many minds. The difficulties and contradictions which are of interest in this chapter by Hipfl et al. are central to understandings of truth and distance in war: the truth of war is more the suffering than the action scenes. Moreover, it is the suffering of the innocent which poses the greatest challenge to the integrity of the would-be objective journalist: which act of integrity is greater, to resist the emotional dilemma in telling the unvarnished truth, or to be true to the subjects used in making films through a personal commitment to help make the viewers care?

The issue of journalistic objectivity is at the core of John Burns's contribution. Burns sees the Yugoslav War as one in which numerous international journalists have lost their objectivity and have become purveyors of inaccuracy and untruth, with a view to shaping international policy towards the war. He maintains that international policy was shaped by one-sided, advocacy journalism which 'pressured' Western policy makers into directions which were not the most appropriate. In this situation, Burns charges, the space for dissenting voices was narrow, or non-existent, and the foundation for the decisions made was shaky.

To support this thesis, he adduces a number of examples to show that the war was more complex than some simplistic accounts might admit and that there were occasions on which, he maintains, stories were simply incorrect. There can be no doubt that he is right to note the complexity of the war, nor that many mistakes were made. However, his case is weakened (or possibly strengthened, depending on the point of view adopted) by errors in his own account. For example, he asserts that most international coverage of the early phases of war in Croatia was derived from Croatian government media management, whereas it has been noted by some of those involved that one of Zagreb's failings in the initial part of the war was its absence: there was 'no press centre, a shortage of background literature for foreign journalists and a less-than-accommodating attitude to the media'.[11] More critically, one of his central claims on the question of inaccuracy is to report Serbian rumours that the emaciated figure whose image at the camp fence in the Marshall and Williams ITN reports was not a Muslim, but a Serb called Slobodan Konjević: in fact, the individual in question was a Muslim, as was generally understood, called Fikret Alić.[12]

Another dimension is added to discussions of objectivity and commitment in journalism, as well as to those on accuracy, truth and distance by both Sandra Bašić-Hrvatin and Hrvoje Turković. Central to both is the place of the 'public sphere' and the degree to which audiences are homogenised and, in a sense, see and hear what they want to see and hear. Both contend that the media was a vital instrument in shaping 'national' consciousness. In Chapter 5, Bašić-Hrvatin assesses the degree to which the audience in both Serbia and Croatia had become nationally homogenised. She notes ways in which national identity is reinforced by TV simplifications which highlight differences. TV in Croatia and Serbia establishes public discourse and sets agendas. However, in doing so, it is important to understand that TV may be the 'cathedral' of the nation. As such, with a popular diet of popular programmes in both countries based on folk culture and music, religious practices, folk customs or national history, however manipulative the media is, it may be satisfying a need.

This is clearly the perspective of Turković in Chapter 6. He notes that, although the content of Croatian TV was significantly propagandistic, this should not be understood, as is conventionally the case, as a matter of top-down manipulation. It is important to realise, first of all, that those working in the medium share the objectives of their political masters: moreover, not only was the work of those in Croatian TV voluntaristic, in a time of crisis and war, he argues, it was their 'professional and civic obligation'. This, he argues, is not due to the government's agenda, but to the requirement to satisfy mass needs. Thus, the dilemmas raised for Western journalists, are irrelevant in Turković's radical view of the situation in Croatia which goes one step beyond Bašić-Hrvatin's assessment, by moving from observation to an explanation of commitment: the media's role is to reinforce the government's position.

Thus the sensibilities on objectivity and influence on governments promoted by John Burns and Brigitte Hipfl have no place in Turković's world. Indeed, in contrast to Burns, there is no question of the media influencing government. Burns is not alone in his interest in the question of media influence on the policy of governments. It is shared by Nik Gowing in Chapter 7. However, where Burns argues that influence is considerable, Gowing challenges this view, broadly held by others, including many in the media. Instead, Gowing discovers, governments are resilient in the face of intense media pressure and, in general, do not alter policy to meet demands. However, Gowing's research revealed exceptional occasions when policy was changed as a result of media pressure. These were only when the governments in question were caught off-guard and unprepared for what emerged in the media – the most significant example of this was the ITN reporting on Bosnian Serb concentration camps in the summer of 1992.

Although governments did not shift policy to respond to media influence, other than in exceptional circumstances, it is nonetheless the case that governments and their bureaucracies felt great pressure. One reason for this may have been in the absence of a clear policy: as a consequence, there was no clear media management programme to shape media discussion on policy; in the vacuum left, and in view of the brutality of the Yugoslav War, the media, therefore, shaped its own agenda. Over the Gulf Conflict of 1990–91, there had been a clear policy agenda and a clear commitment; these gave rise to a more or less comprehensive media management campaign which not only played a role in generating and maintaining support for the international military effort, but also in providing disinformation for Iraq.[13] The absence of a clear and comprehensive strategy with regard to the Yugoslav War of Dissolution left a gap which was filled by the media.

This emphasises the need in modern warfare for efficient and effective management of the media to complement strategic purpose. This is the fundamental aspect for students of war and diplomacy to grasp. In the contemporary period, without television, a military–political campaign will be under-armed. The extent to which this is the case is outlined in Chapter 9, where James Gow and James Tilsley identify the strategic imperative of media management, arguing that propaganda was a vital element in the conflict. In modern war, media-strategic synergy and marketing may be the single most important factor. Otherwise, the success of a campaign will be jeopardised and unhelpful and contradictory media coverage, with its cacophony of truths, of the kind discussed by Nik Gowing, may emerge. This leads back to a focus on the media. In Chapter 10, Alison Preston examines the narratives of distance and proximity in the UK media's description of the war in Bosnia. She analyses the ways in which the media and the government perceived these discourses about the purpose of television news.

In the final section of the book, authors from the BFI co-ordinated research project analyse the data gathered when coverage across thirteen countries in a one week period was studied. Such a study can only begin to identify the elements of context and issues at stake in reporting the Yugoslav War. The aim was to test out a number of hypotheses: that coverage in all countries was dependent on a limited amount of available footage; that the interpretations varied and that these might be explained in a number of ways relating to contemporary involvement and historically embedded cultural understandings of the Balkans; that the role of the United Nations would be variably perceived. The findings confirm the fractured nature of accounts, the multiple prisms through which the war is understood and the importance of recognising the unavoidable variety of war reports, as well as the different ways in which media coverage may have influence. As such, the BFI study and the volume as a whole provide some empirical and analytical raw material on the diversity of perspectives on media coverage of the Yugoslav War of Dissolution from which further study might follow.

Ultimately, this volume is about the ways in which the war in former Yugoslavia was reported, the influence that coverage had, the conflicting personal and political pressures which emerged, and the competition for truth. This last aspect, in particular, underlined the reality that media coverage of the Yugoslav War of Dissolution was both challenging and challenged. From the media studies perspective, the war presents a rich empirical reservoir for investigation and comparison. European television news programmes in the early 90s covered a range of issues bearing directly on the future political, social and cultural order of the Continent in the wake of the collapse of the Soviet Union. Coverage of the Yugoslav conflict in many ways gives the most telling message of disharmony and the problems of the wider aspirations for political unity in Europe.

By combining the interests of policy and strategic students with those of their media counterparts and by offering the first academic volume on an otherwise much discussed topic, this collection also marks an analytical starting-point for subsequent study. It is no more than a beginning.

Notes

1. Quoted in Phillip Knightley, *The First Casualty* (London: Quartet, 1982).
2. Some academic analysis of the role of the media in the Gulf War concluded that the mass media had colluded with government to provide a distorted view of the war. Evidence of the ways in which the military managed news through the media pool system, military briefings and disinformation strategies was used to show that the reported reality was different to the actuality to a degree that severely undermined the public's ability to understand the conflict. See, for example, Douglas Kellner, *The Persian Gulf TV War* (Boulder, Co.: Westview, 1992).
3. See Nik Gowing (Ch. 7) below and Nicholas Hopkinson, *The Media and International Affairs after the Cold War* (Norwich: HMSO, 1993).
4. *The Death of Yugoslavia*, Brian Lapping/BBC, 5 programmes, 1995.
5. Paul Harris, *Somebody Else's War: Frontline Reports from the Balkan Wars, 1991–92* (Stevenage: Spa Books, 1992) pp. 13ff, provides an authentic and sensitive account of what it meant, especially for freelance journalists to go into the Yugoslav war zones.
6. The term 'war tourist' was coined by P. J. O'Rourke.
7. Harris, *Somebody Else's War*.
8. Harris, *Somebody Else's War*, pp. 17–18.
9. John Simpson, 'A Joke, a Shot, a Pool of Blood', *The Independent*, 15 August 1995. Simpson, BBC TV News Foreign Affairs Editor, wrote this after the murder by Croatian soldiers of John Schofield, working for BBC Radio. Simpson points out that John Schofield was travelling with others, including a TV cameraman, and suggests that it was the presence of the camera, including the need to stop and stand to obtain footage, which resulted in the fatal incident.
10. Penny Marshall has insisted that they were unaware of the particular image and its potential (*Forty Years of ITN*, ITN, 1995).
11. Christopher Bennett, *Yugoslavia's Bloody Collapse: Causes, Course and Consequences* (London: C. Hurst, 1995) p. 162.
12. See *Washington Post*, 25 September 1994, for interview with Steve Coll.
13. *Forty Years of ITN*, ITN, 1995.

PART ONE
Witnesses to War

Close Distance

Dilemmas in the Presentation of the War in Bosnia in the Daily News Bulletin of TV Slovenia

JOŽE VOGRINC

An obvious reason for the significance of reporting on Bosnia in Slovenian TV news is that Slovenia and Bosnia are both former 'fraternal republics' (to use Titoist terms) of Yugoslavia. But while their positions are similar *in abstracto* – both are newly independent small states in the same region of the European continent, the prices they have been paying for independence and their respective situations *in concreto* are clearly dissimilar. The reporting of the Bosnian conflict on the most popular television programme in Slovenia, the daily news bulletin *TV Dnevnik*, offers a case study of the practices and dilemmas of journalists coping with a situation that is strongly emotional and highly ambivalent for both programme producers and viewers.[1]

The following paper is not, however, a psychological study, a content analysis or an attempt to unveil the secret mediations of 'high' politics in the daily drama of TV news. Slovenian Television, TVS, officially a public service broadcaster, is a virtual monopolist in the supply of information to the inhabitants of Slovenia in the Slovene language. No wonder that, in a country with a plethora of mostly shortlived and inexperienced parliamentary parties, such a newscasting organisation is inclined to prefer consensual themes and to elaborate them with the purpose of strengthening and naturalising consensus.

Whether Slovenia's relationship with Bosnia actually is a consensual matter, or why this should be the case, is less clear. We will start with an undoubtedly ideological and simplified 'answer' to this problem: it is an answer from a 'native' point of view, but one that will serve as a 'horizon of expectations' in subsequent steps of the analysis. The place of reporting on Bosnia, the ways and means of presentation it uses and those it shuns, will be analysed in comparison with the usual running order and presentation rules and techniques of *TV Dnevnik*. In this way we hope to isolate those inadvertent programme-specific 'grasps' – rather than 'mechanisms' – which enable TVS news-makers to establish a consensus regardless of the actual events in Bosnia and the reporting thereof. In order to contextualise reporting on Bosnia, it is necessary to explain briefly the overall broadcasting climate in Slovenia, the place TVS holds within it, the importance of *TV Dnevnik* both for TVS and for Slovenia in general, and, of course, the usual structure and rules of presentation of the news programme in question.

What, then, makes Bosnia 'distant' from a Slovene point of view? The skirmishes of June/July 1991 that led to Slovenia's independence may not seem a particularly traumatic experience in comparison with the subsequent wars in Croatia and in Bosnia and Hercegovina. But the events of the 1991 'War of Independence' have already grown to mythical proportions as the founding act of Slovenia. Widely shared feelings of relief that Slovenia has been – at least for the time being – spared the fate of its former 'fraternal' republics, together with growing impatience at the slow pace and high price of the process of 'rejoining' Europe, have mentally displaced 'trouble in the Balkans' into an indefinite but inaccessible distance (or, rather, a distance from where *we* would be inaccessible).

But the war is in reality too close to avoid: it is only about 35km from the Slovenian bordertown of Metlika to Serb-held positions in Croatia by the main road through Karlovac, or about 85km to the Muslim enclave in north-west Bosnia. Some parts of the Croatia–Krajina demarcation line are less than 15km air distance from Slovenian territory; shelling can easily be heard and Yugoslav army missiles are capable of reaching anywhere in Slovenia. Slovenian fears about Bosnia are therefore in a sense fears of contagion and relapse. 'We're glad we're out, but we're terrified at the very thought that someone might want to put us into this mess again' – such statements would be an appropriate expression of the prevalent feeling.

While Slovenia is sharply divided politically into a moderate ruling coalition and a nationalist opposition, the differences between both sides vis-à-vis Bosnia and the former Yugoslavia are insignificant. The nationalists generally want to restrict citizenship for non-Slovenes from the former Yugoslavia as far as possible, and to get rid of war refugees quickly. However, both they and the Liberal-Democrat/Christian-Democrat/ex-Communist coalition agree on trying to detach Slovenia from any political context or arrangement in which it could be treated as a part of Yugoslavia or the Balkans, or even the Eastern European complex. Instead they wish to attach Slovenia in every imaginable way, directly or indirectly, to the European Community. Such a choice results in Slovenia showing a total lack of initiative in the peace process, contrary to its potential role as a non-involved but well-informed mediator between the sides in direct conflict. While relations with Belgrade are, as might be expected, frozen, those with the newly independent republics are surprisingly only lukewarm: there are disagreements with Croatia and, with the latter exhausted by war, a growing gap in their respective standards of living; there is less disagreement but less, too, in common with Macedonia; low-key economic co-operation but avoidance of any commitments of alliance with Bosnia.

Broadcasting systems in Belgrade, Zagreb and Ljubljana began to develop independently in the 1920s and were never integrated beyond the level of means of transmission. Radio broadcasting in Slovenia after 1945 was a monopoly effectively in the hands of bureaucrats at the level of the republic. When in the late 1950s regular television programming started, its centralisation at a Yugoslav level was rejected in Ljubljana and Zagreb. Instead, Slovenia and Croatia settled for a regular exchange of programmes, notably the evening news, produced from the outset in each of the three capitals in turn, for broadcast throughout Yugoslavia. With the rapid decentralisation of most state prerogatives after 1971, RTV Ljubljana (later to be renamed Radiotelevizija Slovenije: Radio Slovenije and Televizija Slovenije) discontinued the practice of rotating *TV Dnevnik* and, using its timeslot, title and usual choice of themes and running order, began to transmit its own daily news bulletin, exclusively in the Slovene language. Increasing reliance on self-sufficient programming produced in Ljubljana (and, of course, in the Slovene[3] language, which is incomprehensible to the majority of the Yugoslav audience) resulted not only in the reduction of TVS's audience but also in its homogenisation, owing to a gradual but steady reduction of the contribution by other Yugoslav TV studios to its output. Its audience, too, tended to consist increasingly of Slovenes addressed as such, i.e. as Slovene-speaking members of the Slovene nation. In other words, Slovenes had come to constitute for TVS its exclusive 'imagined community' (Anderson 1983) long before there were any visible signs of the disintegration of Yugoslavia.

Thus pre-prepared, TVS had no need to change the structure of reporting or its modes of address in the course of the so-called 'process towards independence' between 1988 and 1992. The first pluralist parliament in Slovenia (then still a constituent part of the Yugoslav Federation) was elected in spring 1990. It left the broadcasting system intact, except for the control of TVS which was given the status of a public service, but with the members of its overseeing council named by parliament without the participation of an organised civil service. This resulted in an excessive struggle for influence by the political parties in the council itself and in TVS. In the legislative transition period, commercial radio and TV broadcasters, as well as cable and satellite operators, emerged. All continue to be financially weak and almost totally dependent on imported programming, but they have already had a strong impact on viewers' range of choice.[4]

The supply of programming must, however, be considered against the background of the share and structure of domestic programming production. TVS transmits on two channels, TVS 1 and TVS 2.[5] Although the amount of domestic programming far exceeds half of the total time on both TVS 1 and TVS 2, both channels rely heavily on imported material for the most popular types of programming, such as serials, films and documentaries. Many programmes produced by TVS also typically consist of either compiled or re-edited foreign footage put into a new discursive context. Examples include pop music programmes featuring Slovenian DJs presenting Anglo-American pop, or Slovenian experts commenting on ITN-shot film, or simply introducing and summarising reports in their original form, with added subtitles in Slovene. The most prestigious programmes from the point of view of the TVS Council, which treats TVS as the disseminator of national culture, are watched by only a few: it is hardly a surprise that an hour of poetry in prime-time TV attracts only 1 or 2 per cent of potential viewers. On the other hand, top ratings are won not by imported series but by home-grown quizzes and variety shows. Number one in the ratings, however, is invariably *TV Dnevnik*, which regularly scores a rating of over 50.[6]

TV Dnevnik begins at 7.30 pm and lasts approximately 23 to 24 minutes. It is transmitted simultaneously on both channels, TVS 1 and TVS 2.[7] It is preceded by a gameshow at 6.45, a cartoon (7.10–7.15) and a block of advertisements. It is immediately followed by a weather report, a short sports news and another block of advertisements (until 8.05–8.10). Its central time slot and the fact of that it is the only programme carried by both channels at the same time underscore its central position on Slovenian television. Its dominant ideological function and position are clear: it holds the exclusive privilege of addressing its viewers with information supposedly relevant to Slovenia in the Slovene language, as Slovenes, by Slovenes.

Each bulletin presents its material compartmentalised by items into a few 'given' thematic fields, sequenced hierarchically with the more important at the beginning and those of less importance following. It is well known that compartmentalisation of news into a small number of 'naturally' given generalised categories, possibly with a 'permanent' running order, is actually an arbitrary discursive strategy serving to stabilise the frame of 'objectivity' of news discourse (Fiske and Hartley 1978, Hartley 1982, Fiske 1987 etc.). It is always problematic for an analyst to name and categorise these thematic fields – precisely because they are neither concepts (i.e. established through analysis, although possibly non-existent for a journalist) nor fixed directives, but rather a fluctuating result of the division of labour in news departments.

TV Dnevnik practises two basic modes of organising thematic fields: 1. clustering items by paradigmatic relatedness; and 2. applying implicit and loose but nevertheless strict rules of priority between certain thematic fields. Thus, 'foreign news' may be divided into two clusters: one deemed the most important news of the day and placed at the top (on Monday, 11 January 1994, for example, there was a cluster consisting of two themes: a NATO summit in Brussels, and the war in Bosnia), the other placed after news from Slovenia (consisting of four unrelated news items from different parts of the world, read by a newsreader in the studio, different from the presenter). On other days, 'domestic news' may precede 'foreign news'. Hierarchy is preserved by never placing 'economy' or 'health and social security' before 'high politics', never placing 'ecology' or 'education' before 'economy' or 'social security', never placing 'culture' before 'ecology', and so on.[8]

In the analysis of TVS news output, a 'theme' would best be defined as an item, or a cluster of items, treating the same event in any particular *TV Dnevnik*. A theme (NATO summit, siege of Goražde, a session of parliament in Ljubljana) can comprise very different journalistic 'genres' or means of presentation. Its limits are fluid, as there can be items connecting two themes, or which overflow from one theme into another. Furthermore, events regularly reported over several days or more raise the question of the identity of any theme. However, there is no event *per se* in any news; there are only constant reconstructions of it in news discourse and these reconstructions are central to this analysis.

Ten years ago news from Belgrade or from the other Yugoslav republics was still treated as 'domestic' news. It was in a different category from foreign news, but separated nonetheless as a thematic field from 'news from Slovenia', except in those more and more frequent cases where the issue was, for instance, the position of Slovenia versus the federal state. TVS had its own reporters in every republic or autonomous region and it frequently used sources like the federal news agency TANJUG or reports produced by TV studios in other republics, subtitled in the Slovene language. In the moments of crisis during the dismantling of Yugoslavia at the end of the 80s, news bulletins grew longer and tended to consist predominantly of Yugoslav news. Large amounts of time were dedicated to reports from other studios, but, at the same time, quite a lot of effort was spent countering these with commentaries and reports in the news bulletins and in special current affairs programmes in order to recontextualise and defuse their message. With the official independence of Slovenia in 1990/1991 the amount of space in *TV Dnevnik* dedicated to the rest of Yugoslavia was sharply reduced. News from the former fraternal republics was categorised as 'foreign news' and preferably reported by TVS resident correspondents.

During the escalation of war in Croatia TVS relied heavily on its own special reporters from the front line, as well as resident correspondents. When in spring 1992 the war in Bosnia broke out and the already heavy toll of death, injury and intimidation of reporters and their teams grew worse, TVS reversed its previous policy and, even though there were no fatalities to TVS staff, recalled its reporters from Bosnia as well as from Kosovo.

Since then the pattern of reporting from Bosnia has been strongly influenced by the absence of resident TVS reporters in Bosnia. At the moment (1994), TVS only has resident reporters in Zagreb and Belgrade covering the whole territory of former

Yugoslavia, which means there is virtually no coverage from Montenegro, Kosovo or Vojvodina and Skopje. However, these reporters' contribution to *TV Dnevnik* is relatively small – on average two or three appearances a week, each about one minute long for the reporters from Zagreb and Belgrade, and only an occasional call, less than one a week, from Skopje. In striking contrast, there is no bulletin without at least a chronicle of the dead and wounded in Bosnia, its cease-fires and the Security Council resolutions, and it is normal for the theme of Bosnia to occupy between three and eight minutes of a programme. In spite of such generous treatment, in none of the bulletins does a Slovenian reporter appear on location in Bosnia, as a supposed direct witness of the events.

Let us examine a thematic cluster on Bosnia transmitted on Thursday, 6 January 1994:

00:10 (00:00=7.30 pm) [Presenter in studio, mid-shot.] After welcoming the viewers, the male presenter summarises the report that will follow: the Pope's pastoral letter on the occasion of the Epiphany, coinciding with Christmas in the Serb Orthodox religious calendar.

00:41 Reporter from Rome (by phone) summarises the Pope's message, stressing his call for peace in Bosnia. [Unidentified footage, presumably shot at the event reported.]

01:50 Presenter [mid-shot] briefly describes two new peace initiatives, a Croatian one, and a German one [footage of German diplomats]. He introduces [mid-shot] the war with a question: 'And what are the reports from the front lines today?'

02:25 A chronicle about the last twenty-four hours in Bosnia, compiled in the studio. Reader/compiler is routinely identified with a subtitle, '*pripravil* ('made ready by', 'compiled by') *Jani Rojina*'. The last sentence refers to the announced replacement of the commander of UNPROFOR in Sarajevo, General Francis Briquemont, by General Sir Michael Rose. [Footage from various unidentified sources, showing familiar scenes of war.]

04:00 Reporter from London gives a biography of Rose, then proceeds by explaining the current British standpoint concerning Bosnia. [Film compiled from footage, identified as 'TVS archive', showing first Rose, then war scenes from Bosnia and finally the British Foreign Minister.]

Each chronicle is a compilation with a duration of between 60 to 120 seconds. It usually consists of an enumeration of losses, a description of the situation at critical points, citing local authorities, UN officials, ordinary people. Footage is used from different sources, mainly Western, such as ITN, CNN, Sky etc., and this is usually combined so that the film source corresponds to one or two sentences of the compiler's text. Identified original reports are very rarely used, either in full, or in part.

As we have seen, these compiled chronicles from the studio are not normally used alone and, when this does happen, are never used without being properly introduced by the news presenter. No matter what motive TVS had for withdrawing reporters from Bosnia in 1992, this pattern of reporting has serious consequences, and it strongly inflects the discourse of *TV Dnevnik*.

First, because TVS 'is not there', because it has no representatives at the heart of the matter, by virtue of its monopoly of representation of Slovene viewers, *Slovenes are not directly involved*. Scenes from Bosnia, as seen by viewers in Slovenia, have been shot and edited by Western television crews for their own audiences. The commentary, applied to those scenes, is also largely based on the agency reports, accompanying the footage. Occasionally, however, the editors enrich the compiled information with their own commentary, expressing their – and presumably their viewers' – feelings, most often of grief and frustration at the course of events. 'When will Europe do something?', they sigh once in a while. Are not these feelings of helplessness to a large extent structured precisely by the disengaged procedure of TV, which merely recombines others' news reports from afar?

Secondly, because the spoken text and the film are compilations of fragments, they leave the impression, when viewed day after day, of utter incoherence. Furthermore, the everyday chronicle is usually preceded and/or followed by another item connected with Bosnia. As TVS is absent from Bosnia, its reporters feed viewers with up-to-date perspectives on the peace process from abroad, from Belgrade, Zagreb, Moscow, New York, London, Bonn etc. It can safely be said that the 'Bosnian chronicle' is so securely embedded that there is no danger of its crashing into anything fragile and smashing it. For Slovenian television 'War in Bosnia' is invariably a 'foreign news' theme, always aligned with another 'foreign news' theme to form a cluster, no matter whether it is the first theme in a bulletin, or if it is in the middle of a programme. It is not allowed to interface with any theme concerning Slovenia, although, at first glance, it might appear otherwise.

On Sunday, 2 January 1994, the last day of the Christmas–New Year holidays in Slovenia, and a snowy day too, the bulletin began exceptionally with a weather report and a warning to drivers. Immediately after that, the presenter associated the difficulties of UN convoys to Muslim enclaves with cars on Slovenian roads and so introduced the regular Bosnian chronicle. It was followed by items on 1993 in Bosnia, and a railwaymen's strike in Serbia. The following Saturday, the 8th, the bulletin began with a short feature about a World Cup giant-slalom in Kranjska Gora, which was followed by Bosnian news, with the presenter explicitly introducing it neutrally as 'news from abroad'. The situation was similar the next day: after a report from Kranjska Gora and a commemoration of a battle with the Germans in 1943, the presenter invited the viewers to 'take a look abroad', and after informing them that Mr Izetbegović is in Bonn while Mr Silajdžić is in Pakistan, looks at Bosnia.

Any events in Slovenia which are allowed to be aligned with the war in Bosnia are not political events, and where they are, there is no trace of a possible connection. On Friday, 22 April 1994, for instance, *TV Dnevnik* began with a report from the parliament in Ljubljana (the session had just finished) and continued immediately with the anchorwoman's invitation: 'And now to Goražde, where fighting has been going on for 25 days ...' Paradigmatic relatedness enabling this syntagmatic contiguity of both events is as generalised and as neutral as possible: mere *importance* of both.

The prohibited contact is not, then, contact of an item, categorised 'Bosnia', with an item, categorised 'Slovenia'; rather, it is impossible to *question the relation of Bosnia to Slovenia*. This attitude is totally different to the circumstances that justify inclusion of a report from Zagreb, Belgrade or Skopje: they appear in a bulletin when there is any trouble in mutual relationships. In the first quarter of 1994 the topics of reporting from these locations were: the supposed unwillingness of Croatia to pay for electricity from a power station in Slovenia; the refusal of Belgrade to compromise on former Yugoslav property abroad; Slovenian import taxes on wine imported from Macedonia; the refusal by war refugees lodged provisionally in holiday homes owned by Slovenian trade unions, in resorts on the Croatian coast, to vacate their temporary abodes before the tourist season.

To be sure, there are no known disagreements between the Slovenian and Bosnian governments, but what is at stake is the question of Slovene identity. It is 'impossible' to 'relate' to Bosnia at all, because then Slovenia would be *involved*.

It is significant that *TV Dnevnik* never reports on Bosnian war refugees in Slovenia as an integral part of the war in Bosnia theme. When all is not quiet, refugees are placed and treated at the same time as local health or pollution problems: they don't want to be moved from a holiday home to a refugee centre; a humanitarian relief convoy has just arrived as a gift of a friendly regional government in Germany, etc. In short, they are treated as an obstacle. Most often, they are not even seen, on TV or anywhere else.

Finally, it is necessary to consider another aspect of news presentation in Slovenia. The bulletin is presented by an anchorperson[9] whose role in the show is pivotal. She or he not only 'acts as a link between different parts of the programme and maintains contact with people and reporters in other studios' (COBUILD 1987: 47b) or, as a presenter, 'introduces the separate parts' (COBUILD 1987: 1133a), but also acts as personification of the TV institution she or he represents – in linking, framing and summarising fragments of discourse (Brunsdon and Morley 1978) into a hierarchically ordered narrative, with typified scenes and characters resembling soap opera (Fiske 1987: 281–308), if not *commedia dell' arte*.

It is not enough to conceptualise the hierarchisation of speakers in news discourse as an objectifying strategy of containment with institutional control over news values as its purpose (Fiske 1987: ibid.); such a control was perfectly attainable within a now-forgotten tradition of reading news directly to camera and/or voicing over film footage. Considering the anchor as different from newsreader allows us to integrate into news presentation the authenticating and immediate effects of such reporting practices as live coverage, talking to camera on location, and the insertion of interviews with experts, witnesses and victims in close-ups.

The presenter's key task occurs at the beginning of the programme: it is not enough that she or he addresses the supposed viewer 'directly', mimicking eye contact, just as if the viewer was right there in the studio; the viewer is welcomed and invited to be the presenter's guest. The offer simply 'can't be refused' because the viewer is immediately engaged. Whenever the presenter is again presented in standard mid-shot frame during the programme, he or she is binding together the items in such a way, that any other speaker in the programme can only address the viewer 'directly' after having been introduced, and by the same token relayed, mediated to the position of 'direct' address. And at the end of the show it is absolutely necessary for the presenter to thank the viewer for his/her effort and to 'dismiss' him/her (or, rather, to direct her/him to the next programme).

The presenter is invested as the representative of the programme/television with the power to address the viewer directly, and to present the other persons in the programme. The viewer becomes susceptible to the presenter's discourse. This is not another version of discursive determinism, but a reminder that the objectified and unified discourse of a news bulletin is *ipso facto* made a person-to-person address through the presenter's interventions.

By not having someone with a microphone speaking into camera in the Slovene language in the middle of Sarajevo, TVS refuses to relay to its viewers a witness's account of what is going on. It doesn't take chances because it would endanger and contradict its strategy of non-involvement. The Slovene viewer is – through the contents of TVS chronicles, if not otherwise – quite aware how ITN, CNN, Sky News, and others report from Sarajevo. Live from Sarajevo in the Slovene language would be completely different; it would be substantiated by the official stance of TVS regarding its viewer, relayed from the presenter in Ljubljana to the reporter in Bosnia. TVS and its viewers would become involved.

'We are not involved' is the fundamental meaning of the practices deployed by *TV Dnevnik* to inform people in Slovenia about the war in Bosnia. This is mere wishful thinking: 'We act as if we were not involved, because we know we are involved, but we don't want to be involved.' Slovenia is most definitely part of Europe: it acts like Europe, it daydreams like Europe.

Notes

1. Programmes analysed below were transmitted from January to April 1994, but the trends described are valid for a longer period, approximately from the middle of 1992 on.
2. TVS = Televizija Slovenija/Slovenia Television/, a part of RTVS = Radiotelevizija Slovenija. Its former name was Televizija Ljubljana. To avoid unnecessary confusion, TVS is used throughout the text.
3. The possibility of choice between *Slovene* and *Slovenian* is exploited here to refer to ethos and to language as *Slovene* and to what pertains to the country or its inhabitants, regardless of their ethnic identity, as *Slovenian*.
4. Geographical dispersion of viewing choices is very uneven. In urban centres like Ljubljana or Maribor it isn't unusual for a household to be able to watch 25 to 30 different channels in six or more different languages, while in the Adriatic littoral most people watch Italian TV anyway. On the other hand, houses in thinly populated areas on the rugged terrain prevalent in Slovenia often do not have access to more than one or two channels.
5. The main difference between TVS 1 and TVS 2 is in viewers' access. TVS 1 is receivable everywhere in Slovenia except in a few pockets in mountainous areas, while TVS 2 is not. TVS usually transmits programmes of national importance (in its judgement) and broadly popular shows and games on its first channel. The second channel is deemed to be more suitable for high culture and generally for types of programming catering to the tastes of 'urban' viewers.
6. TVS originated data for internal use are based on regular telephone questioning of a random sample of respondents at fifteen-minute intervals. Curiously, the question what (if anything) viewers watch when they don't watch TVS is *not* posed. So relative *shares* of TVS viewers at any moment are anybody's guess. They could be significantly higher than respective ratings, considering the very limited choice of a substantial part of the Slovenian audience.
7. The early (5 pm) and the late (beginning, depending on the length of preceding programmes, around 10.20) news bulletins are shorter and transmitted only on TVS 1, along with a short news at 1 pm. TVS 2 has no news programmes of its own. News on commercial channels is either local in scope or limited in range.
8. 'Importance' is of course the symptom of arbitrariness of the hierarchy of thematic fields: at the top, anything goes, as long as it can be made to seem 'naturally' the news of the day.
9. Presenting *TV Dnevnik* had been an entirely male domain until the early 80s when the first anchorwoman was introduced. Nowadays male and female presenters alternate, one person presenting usually three consecutive bulletins. (More recently, after this paper was completed, a *pair* of hosts – a male and a female – was introduced. Ed.)

References

Anderson, Benedict (1983) *Imagined Communities*, London: Verso.
Brunsdon, Charlotte, and Morley, David (1978), Everyday Television: 'Nationwide', London: BFI.
COBUILD (= *Collins COBUILD English Language Dictionary*) (1987), London and Glasgow: Collins.
Fiske, John (1987) *Television Culture*, London: Methuen.
Fiske, John, and Hartley, John (1978) *Reading Television*, London: Methuen.
Hartley, John (1982) *Understanding News*, London: Methuen.

War Without End?

The *Bloody Bosnia* Season on Channel Four

IAN BROUGH-WILLIAMS

Introduction

> Watching the news, we come to feel not only that the world is blowing up, but that it does so for no reason, that its ongoing history is nothing more than a series of eruptions, each without cause or context. The news creates this vision of mere anarchy through its erasure of the past and its simultaneous tendency to atomize the present into so many unrelated happenings, each recounted through a series of dramatic, unintelligible pictures ... And so we have the correspondent, solemnly nattering among the ruins, offering crude 'analysis' and 'background', as if to compensate us for the deep bewilderment that his medium created in the first place. (Miller 1988: 367–8)

War is a staple in the diet of television current affairs. Since cameras first served up the daily events in Vietnam to an incredulous American public, many conflicts around the globe have been granted the epithet 'Television War' and received blanket coverage from the world's media, coverage that arguably reached its apotheosis in the Persian Gulf in 1991, a 'Television War' par excellence. Since its outbreak in 1991, the conflict in the former Yugoslavia has been subject to almost the same level of scrutiny by an electronic media hungry to repeat the successes of the Middle East, and to relay the drama in 'real time' by satellite to an expectant viewing public back home.

The Yugoslav crisis, however, proved a far more difficult proposition. Although unencumbered by many of the reporting restrictions imposed in the Gulf, foreign correspondents were faced with a new, and perhaps more intractable, set of problems in trying to provide a context for domestic consumption. As they, and the international community, have found to their cost, the questions of geopolitics, religion and ethnicity raised by the conflict are immeasurably more complex than those at play in Iraq. In attempting to solve these problems news organisations have tended to employ two (largely contradictory) strategies in their attempts to conceptualise antagonisms and contain the war. On the one hand, they have tried to relay the plethora of internecine skirmishes in their totality, but have done so at the expense of background analysis and a wider perspective – conveying the confusion of a complex sequence of events but leaving the viewer at home bewildered as to their origin, repercussions and possible outcome. Conversely, and in time-honoured

19

fashion, they have framed the tripartite oppositions between the warring factions in terms of a civil war between two clearly delineated combatants, thus superimposing onto events an interpretative grid which adequately facilitated readings of the Gulf War and previous conflicts, but which did not (and could not) adequately contain the situation on the ground in this instance.

As a result, the multiple conflicts of what may be called the War of the Yugoslav Succession have either been unwittingly portrayed as being too complicated to understand fully (thus allowing the Western Powers to continue to adhere to a policy of non-intervention) or vastly over-simplified and reduced to a blur known as the Bosnian War. The gradual political disintegration of the League of Communists of Yugoslavia and the significance of the earlier wars in Slovenia and Croatia have largely been passed over by the world's media in favour of a Balkan war fuelled by ancient, unfathomable hatreds, with a beleaguered, fledgling Bosnian presidency (embodying Western ideals of democracy and cosmopolitanism) bravely resisting the expansionist aims of a draconian Serbia stuck in outdated Communist dogma, and Croat involvement often appearing as an adjunct to the 'main event'.

This is in no way intended to belittle the role of the many journalists who, often at considerable personal risk, have striven to alert the world to the horrors perpetrated against civilian populations in the name of ethnic unity and to retain a sense of balance while working in difficult conditions that often test their journalistic credentials to the limit. But in attempting to 'construct meaningful totalities out of scattered events', television news, by the very nature of the medium, operates under considerable constraints on time and other resources and, by selecting, constructing and framing these events for our consumption, tends to 'endow past events with artificial boundaries' (Ricoeur 1981, cit. Bird and Dardenne 1988: 70). In conveying the reality of modern warfare, the message, however laudable, is often sacrificed to the immediacy of the image; in Bosnia, as in other wars, the news has tended to 'concentrate on the symptoms of the conflict rather than the cause' (Ashdown, *The Sunday Times*, 20 March 1994) and, while amplifying the call for 'something to be done', has often done so without specifying just what that 'something' was, why it should be done, and what its possible efficacy was likely to be.

Conscious of such deficiencies in their coverage, the networks, to their credit, have evolved strategies to overcome the constraints of the news bulletin. The drawn-out nature of war in the former Yugoslavia and critical viewer reaction to the mixture of 'live feeds' and 'expert speculation' that came to typify Gulf War coverage have drawn them to the realisation that, at least in the British context, the '... viewer is willing to forgo immediate information for a broader vista of understanding. The viewer does not, in other words, wish for unfiltered "news" ...' (Morrison 1992: 25). The BBC has complemented its news output with a number of documentaries (most notably the Martin Bell report for *Panorama*) as well as *Sarajevo: A Street under Siege*, a series of short 'video postcards' depicting life under siege in the Bosnian capital, broadcast daily (then weekly) over a number of months and which helped to foster the sense of continuity so often absent from fragmented news reports.

The most ambitious and extensive coverage, however, has appeared on Channel Four. In August 1993, to mark the anniversary of the discovery, by ITN journalists, of the first concentration camps at Omarska and Trnopolje, the Channel devoted a week's special programming of the conflict, provocatively entitled *Bloody Bosnia* – a title that not only encapsulated the continuing carnage of the war, but also echoed the increasing climate of exasperation and apathy in the West's reaction to events. Intended as an awareness-raising exercise by Channel Four, the Season's stated aims were the following:

- To provide the wider historical and political context needed for public under-standing of the war;
- To examine the success (or lack of it) of diplomatic efforts made by the international community in the attempt to end the bloodshed;
- In the absence of a peaceful resolution, to alleviate the suffering through an appeal to viewers for humanitarian aid.

This paper offers a case study of that week's television.[1] To this end, I outline the reaction of media and public to the Season and, through a series of interviews with Channel Four personnel, attempt to gauge a sense of their estimations of the series' impact, the value of 'themed' seasons in the current television climate, and their future in the Channel's public service role.

Organisation and Content
Organisation
The *Bloody Bosnia* season was broadcast on Channel Four between 1 and 8 August 1993. Programmes were transmitted every night of the week during peak/late-night hours (7 pm to 1 am) with the vast majority falling between 8 and 11 pm, the highest-profile programmes being scheduled around the 9 or 10 pm slots. Program-ming (in terms of the number of items aired) was most heavily concentrated on Thursday and Monday, the lightest days falling on Friday and Saturday. The mix of programming was extremely diverse, ranging from video diary/cinéma vérité accounts of the war's effects, through documentary/critical investigative reporting of its causes, factual presentation of the region's history, appeals programmes for refugees and 'opinion slots', to arts programmes and fiction. (See Appendix 1 for a full description of scheduling, viewing figures and a brief synopsis of each pro-gramme.)

Content
How does this mix of programmes frame the conflict and what impressions of it do we carry away from them? In attempting to gain an overview of the series, it is useful to form groupings according to the way in which programmes satisfy Channel Four's three stated aims. In so doing, a picture emerges in which the Season is over-whelmingly weighted towards the first strand or modality, that is, providing a wider historical context. Only one programme, *Diplomacy and Deceit* by Nik Gowing (*Channel Four News* Diplomatic Editor), is exclusively devoted to the diplomatic role of the West, while appeals for aid occupy the spaces at the end of the credit sequences of the four short *Refugee Stories* (personal exposés of refugees' experiences and their subsequent lives in exile) and the six *Artists for Bosnia* slots. This first strand is concentrated around five 'flagship' programmes, three of which attempt to explain Yugoslav history and the process of descent into war, while the remaining two deal with its consequences in human terms for the various populations affected by the fighting.

Societies and Peoples Affected by the War – 'Urbicide' and 'Ethnic Cleansing'
Bloody Bosnia does not over-emphasise, either qualitatively or quantitatively, the military operations of the war, or the 'human interest' value of its victims' suffering,

nor does it reduce them to a symbolic set of icons, as many news reports have done, in montage title-sequences which embody the stereotypes of the conflict and thus serve as a sort of shorthand for the war (e.g. the skeletal frames of Omarska internees, the gutted tower blocks of Sarajevo, mosques, mass burials and elderly peasant women in mourning). The two programmes that do address the human effects of war (*A Sarajevo Diary, The Unforgiving*) do so in far more subtle ways and provide useful counterpoints to one another by highlighting the dichotomy between the plight of sophisticated, cosmopolitan Sarajevo and the more brutal realities of 'ethnic cleansing in the rural hinterland' (Vulliamy 1994: ix).

In Western media coverage, the plight of Sarajevo has come to function metonymically for the plight of Bosnia as a whole, its demoralised people fulfilling television's demand for 'groups [of victims] whom it can sentimentalise' (Miller 1988: 371). More significantly, the media has characterised the three warring parties as Serb, Croat and Muslim, '... thereby accepting in terminology what has been in essence one of Karadžić's main war aims' (Borden: 1993). This semantic division of the combatants only adds to the physical division of Yugoslavia; labelling multi-ethnic Sarajevo and Bosnia as Muslim denies its population an identity as citizens of a state and reduces them to the status of religious followers, while unifying Serbs and Croats under the banner of homogenous statehood. Why are Bosnians labelled as Muslim and Serb and Croats not called Orthodox or Catholic?

These are the issues foregrounded in *A Sarajevo Diary*, a video diary account in which British academic Bill Tribe, a citizen of Sarajevo for twenty-six years, returns to the city from which he was recently forced to flee, to find out what has become of the home and friends he left behind. In the course of the programme, very different pictures of Sarajevans emerge than the ones we are used to seeing on the news. The 'urbicide', or mass slaughter wreaked on the city by its besiegers, does not form the main substance of the account and, although the programme does contain some extremely graphic footage (the mortaring of a bread queue and cemetery, a man being shot by snipers), the resilience, solidarity and resourcefulness of Sarajevans is emphasised over the suffering through which they came to depend on such qualities. These qualities are emphasised in a series of episodes which frame the population in communal, domestic settings (a New Year's Eve party, numerous family dinners by candlelight in the absence of electricity) or trying to preserve a sense of normality amid the destruction (chopping wood, pulling supplies through the snow, producing the local newspaper, *Oslobodjenje*, in sub-zero temperatures in a bombed-out office). The interaction and cohabitation of the various ethnic groups is repeatedly stressed in these episodes, the nonsense of trying to separate the ethnic mélange evolved over centuries of intermarriage exposed by 'mixed' friends, families and couples, but also by Tribe himself, in personal, angry addresses to camera, or voiceovers in which he attempts to correct the warped perspectives of Sarajevans offered to the outsider by the international media:

> The world's media have colluded in this (myth of national identity) by accepting the ethnic categories laid down by the nationalists and labelling the warring sides accordingly. There are 50,000 Serbs inside Sarajevo, who are resisting the onslaught of their fellow Serbs, but in the media Sarajevo and its government are nearly always referred to as Muslim. How are the Bosnian Serbs in Sarajevo to be labelled? How are the thousands born from mixed marriages to be categorised? How are you going to sort and file a city where, even now, Muslims, Serbs and Croats still intermarry and will continue to do so as long as sanity survives?

The urban cosmopolitanism and largely secular character of Sarajevo is a world away from the rural front lines around Srebrenica in Serb-held eastern Bosnia, where religion, nationalism and the experience of atrocity on all sides have hardened the attitudes of fighting men and civilian victims of the violence, fuelling the climate of rumour, suspicion, fear and mutual hatred between the three ethnic groups. This climate pervades *The Unforgiving*, Clive Gordon's war documentary, which gained unprecedented permission to film without restriction behind Serb lines and which patently illustrates not only the fact that '... atrocities are not the preserve of one side or another ...' (C4 press release) but also the way in which the mythology of Yugoslavia's past has been resurrected alongside the new propaganda, in order to demonise the combatants (with the generic labels of Chetniks and Ustasha revived in response to the Serb branding of Muslim fighters as Mujahadin). This remarkable observational documentary largely employs a 'vérité' style in following a Serb couple's search for their murdered child, combining strictly denotive sequences of their quest with the personal testimonies of Muslim and Croat refugees who experienced the 'cleansing' at Omarska and the differing account of their treatment by the camp commandant. Although the film features accounts of savagery on the part of Serbs, Croats and Muslims, the viewer comes away with the impression that the Serbs have committed more than their fair share; this is not stated explicitly in the diegesis but the juxtaposition of the commandant's statement that '... there was no physical contact between those questioned and the inspectors ...' and horrific accounts by former internees of the factory efficiency of 'killing in shifts night and day' and recreational savagery of competitions to kick prisoners to death with the least number of kicks wholly undermines on moral grounds any credibility the viewer might otherwise lend to his explanations.

Causes for Conflict – The Historical Background to the War
In attempting to trace the origins of the present conflict, it soon became clear to journalists that '... history dominates every interview in the Bosnian war. The answer to a question about an artillery attack yesterday will begin in the year 925, invariably illustrated with maps. Eventually you realise that what is so important to the participants in the war has to be important to any understanding of it' (Vulliamy 1994: 5). If we take this premise to its logical conclusion, it should follow that if you are able to navigate the tortuous path of Yugoslavia's past, the reasons behind and motivations for today's conflict will become self-evident. This has led many observers to the conclusion that the recent troubles are not isolated occurrences, but instead form part of the continuum of what is really a thousand-year-old civil war between the three Yugoslav peoples, the latest incidence of tribal warfare in an ancient, mythic cycle of violence, and thus somehow inevitable because of the deeply ingrained nature of ethnic hatred in their respective national psyches. Although attractive, this causal interpretation is over-simplistic and largely misses the point – the significance of history in the current Yugoslav context is *precisely* the process by which opportunistic, unscrupulous nationalists in Serbia and Croatia have mythologised the past (and, by extension, revived historical insecurities relating to national identity and geography) in order to build power bases for themselves in the political vacuum following Tito's death and the attendant climate of insecurity over Yugoslavia's future as a federation of ethnic states. By exploiting perceived historical injustices, which would otherwise have had little relevance to the current conflict, they have elevated them to a central, mythic place in the newly constructed national conscious-ness in order to justify the cynical theft of territory in Bosnia–Hercegovina as the

legitimate righting of ancient wrongs, and it is therefore the *manipulation* and not the *substance* of the various mythical histories that is significant when combatants invoke the past in an attempt to explain their current actions.

This process is clearly exposed in the documentary *The Roots of War* and in the *Frontline* investigative report by *Guardian* journalist Maggie O'Kane. The former chronicles, through the use of historical commentary, contemporary footage and previously unseen film from the Yugoslav archives, the political disintegration of the federal system, the rise of nationalism and the start of unrest as early as 1981 (by ethnic Albanians in Kosovo), illustrating the gradual slide into war over a decade, rather than as a sudden explosion of violence. Similarly, the Maggie O'Kane report, albeit in a less objective, more confrontational series of encounters with the main 'players' in Serbian politics, highlights the way (particularly in the case of Slobodan Milošević) in which they used the media in order to consolidate their own power base and later prepared the Serbian people for war, disseminating nationalist propaganda and a message of ethnic hatred on state-controlled television.

Where *Bloody Bosnia*'s account of Yugoslav history really falls down, though, is in the way that the series of three high-speed *Essential Guides* completely contradicts these messages in suggesting that Bosnia's troubles can be reduced to its geography, resting as it does on mythical, seismic 'fault-lines', liable to open up at a moment's notice and plunge the region (and the rest of the world if it is not careful to avoid intervention) into violent and bloody conflict. The series, reflecting the current vogue for dramatised history, is a highly accomplished feat of visual pyrotechnics and, although visually stunning, presents the viewer with so much information that it is hard to remember the points it was hastily trying to make. The procession of computer-animated graphics, picture within picture, archive footage, stills and moving images proceeds at such a frenetic pace that the three 15-minute episodes, intended as an introductory history for the non-expert of the 'MTV Generation' (C4 press release) has the same effect as the music videos that its visually sophisticated audience supposedly watches – it is entertaining while it lasts, soon over, easy to forget and ultimately disposable. These programmes cloud the history they seek to elucidate, employ a welter of jargon in attempts to be populist (in references to 'tribal gridlock', Serbia's historical quest for 'mergers and acquisitions' and the political ambitions of 'Slobo' Milošević) and essentially portray the Yugoslav peoples as a superstitious eastern 'other' rather than as rational Europeans, as victim to 'political ghosts' and 'dark myths', and (by implication) best left alone in the constantly recurring tragedy of their Balkan melting pot.

The Diplomatic Process – Peace Negotiations.

The chief examination of political attempts at ending the violence are encompassed within Nik Gowing's *Diplomacy and Deceit*, the 'inside story of how the West bungled in the Balkans' (C4 promotional trail), and an illuminating insight into how policy agreements between Washington and Brussels, as well as increasing divisions within the European Community itself, have led to a rash of inadequate, hastily prepared diplomatic initiatives wholly unable to keep up with the rapidly changing nature of the war in Bosnia.

Framed by the increasingly jaded Western ideals of the New World Order on the one hand, and the duplicity of 'the old Communist ways and dirty tricks' of Milošević on the other, the film is as equally damning of the cynical calculation of EC ministers as it is of Balkan politicians' blatant duplicity, repeatedly emphasising the tendency of the Twelve to choose largely cosmetic policies based on 'the least worst option' or 'watered down to the lowest common denominator', in order to prevent further internal division at a time when a great number of political futures were riding on the success of European unity and the ratification of Maastricht.

The discursive mechanisms used to achieve this are numerous. The programme repeatedly constructs images of normality and contrasts them with an impression of underlying duplicity and threat; images of the calm surface of a lily pond are juxtaposed with shadowy goings on inside the European Parliament and in the title sequence footage of the main political figures arriving at the London Conference (overdubbed with a menacing synthesiser soundtrack) is thrown into sharp contrast with pictures of an oblivious public sunbathing in a nearby park. The frank admissions by a number of international politicians of the litany of policy failures add to the indictment, as does the pinpointing by Gowing of the nodal moment of failure as the EC, under immense pressure from Germany, recognised Croatia in spite of repeated warnings by Lord Carrington that '... this could be the spark that sets Bosnia–Hercegovina alight'. The end result is that Europe has sent, in the words of UN special envoy Herbert Okun, a clear message to the Serbs that it was unwilling to use force and 'that when the chips were down, unity came first', thereby giving them a free hand to pursue their policy of genocide in the ethnic enclave carve-up of Bosnia.

Alleviating the Effects of War – Appeals for Humanitarian Aid
In a strictly technical sense, the *Bloody Bosnia* season did not contain any specific appeals programming for humanitarian aid, but relied instead on brief announcements at the end of a series of personal *Refugee Stories* and short performances by *Artists for Bosnia*. While the reconstructed accounts of refugees' experiences, both before and after leaving their homes for Britain, were largely successful in alerting the general public to their plight, they did tend to rely on the kind of stereotypical images of elderly peasant women the rest of the Season had tried hard to avoid and, through repeated use of a mournful voiceover and of studio sets representing once happy, then shattered, domestic scenes (complete with substances not unreminiscent of tomato sauce to signify blood), often strayed perilously close to trite sentimentalisation. This said, they were at least scheduled at times likely to have an effect on viewers' sympathies, which was certainly untrue of *Artists for Bosnia* programmes, usually relegated to the ghetto hours beyond midnight, with little or no explanation of their relevance to the appeal or to the Season as a whole, appearing as little more than 'the whiff of self-congratulation' of a handful of tortured aesthetes (Allison Pearson, *The Independent on Sunday*, 8 August 1993).

Reaction to the Season – The Media and Public Response
Critical reaction to the *Bloody Bosnia* season was, at least in the national press, extremely positive, with praise being reserved for what was generally seen as a selfless act on Channel Four's part in risking the loss of ratings (and therefore of revenue, now that the Channel is selling its own advertising space) in order to raise public awareness of a war in danger of slipping from the headlines. Programmes that incurred the greatest number of negative notices were *The Essential Guide* and *Artists for Bosnia*, while *A Sarajevo Diary* and *The Unforgiving* received the most frequent praise. Other negative comments generally centred around perceptions of the Season as an example of '... the vogue for deliberately creating a TV Event through themed programming, a C4 speciality ...' (Peter Lewis, *The Sunday Times*, 1 August 1993) or of the way it was used to break up the schedules: 'It's like a version of war – short

bursts of action, followed by long periods of *Brookside* ...' (Giles Smith, *The Independent*, 4 August 1993). The most serious charge levelled at the Season, though, was that it would undoubtedly exhibit bias and contribute to the media's 'wanton demonisation of the Serbs' by overlooking the Croat detention camps in Split and atrocities in areas too inaccessible to camera crews in search of 'award-winning footage' (Con Coughlin, *The Telegraph*, 31 July 1993). Although this was fair comment of the news media in general, this was something of a pre-emptive strike at *Bloody Bosnia*, in light of the actual content of *The Unforgiving* which had not yet been broadcast.

Television and public response to the Season, and to news coverage of the Yugoslav crisis in general, was limited to a *Right to Reply* special, broadcast on Friday 6 August, in which viewers, both Yugoslav and British, confronted a panel of media practitioners responsible for bringing them images of the war. The general consensus of the studio audience and panel was that, while *Bloody Bosnia* did achieve some success in addressing the need for a wider context in current affairs in general and war reporting in particular, television coverage was still too simplistic and that the wider contextual perspectives desired by the public were mainly to be found in the print media. One member of the studio audience said:

> The important thing about TV is that images take over ideas, so you flick from image to image and it's like a pop video, the coherence is lost of news items ... you have snapshots, and it's the time of soundbites. For someone who reads the paper, the Bosnian war comes across as *very* different from someone who watches television – I do both, and I can see the difference in reporting ... there is something inherently flawed in TV because it deals only with images, and hence it's very important to put ideas behind those images, and put opinions behind those images and show the reality in that way.

It would seem, therefore, that television still has some way to go in satisfying an unfulfilled public desire for wider analytic perspectives as part of its current affairs coverage, and that seasons like *Bloody Bosnia* are only a first step in this direction.

In the world of commercial television, the ultimate audience response is, of course, not reflected in terms of critical notice but in the viewing figures a programme receives. The television audience, like any other, will vote with its feet (or at least with its remote control) when dissatisfied. In terms of *Bloody Bosnia* overall viewing figures ranged from a low of 118,000 for *Artists for Bosnia* (Sunday, 1 August) to a high of around 1.1 million for the third *Essential Guide* on Thursday, 5 August, the Season achieving a rather low share of 4 per cent of total terrestrial viewing (Source: C4 Research) and giving the Channel '... its lowest 1993 peak-time viewing share' (*Broadcast*/BARB, 27 August 1993: 18). Thus, although several programmes achieved a modest level of success, others were abject failures, and overall audience share remained low. In addition, not all the programmes Channel Four publicised most widely hit their targets. Of the three most widely trailed programmes during the series, only *The Unforgiving* registers in the top five list of most highly rated programmes (see Appendix 2), with *A Sarajevo Diary* and *Diplomacy and Deceit* registering eighth and tenth respectively. Of the other most highly rated programmes, two of the glossy *Essential Guides* featured prominently, as did *Frontline*, but the inclusion, at number three in the list, of *Tourist Sarajevo 93* (a parodic city guide for the would-be Western tourist) comes as something as a surprise.

'Themed TV', Channel Four and Public Service Performance

Obviously, owing to the difficult subject matter of the Season, the Channel was not expecting astronomical ratings but, conversely, '... audience size must be some indicator of performance, so low figures cannot be shrugged off as the price paid for public service.' (Peter Fiddick, *The Guardian*, 31 May 1993.) Subject matter is not, however, the only factor to guarantee a programme's success or failure with the audience; scheduling, particularly in relation to competitors (in Channel Four's case, and in the context of current affairs, BBC2) is of equal, if not greater importance. In respect of both scheduling and content, Channel Four seemed to have made considerable efforts to ensure the success of *Bloody Bosnia*. With the notable exception, as I have already indicated, of *Artists for Bosnia*, programmes received high-profile slots in the key peak-time hours between 8 and 10 pm over an otherwise quiet week in terms of the other channels' output and which, according to the Channel's press office was chosen to '... maximise their appeal when the other two channels were largely screening repeats'.

Channel Four attributed the Season's rather low overall audience share to the phenomenon of compassion-fatigue and the Bosnian war as a target of media overkill, where intensive CNN-styled news coverage, with its emphasis on person-alised reporting, has subjected the viewer to a '... constant barrage of media coverage where he is kept up to date with almost every occurrence in Bosnia (wittingly or unwittingly)' (C4 Research). It is not clear whether the general public's feeling of having a 'duty to watch' often unpleasant or violent actuality on the news, within the general responsibility of keeping the self informed of world events (Millwood Hargrave 1993: 16), extends to documentary/current affairs programming; what is clear is that, while in theory the public values Channel Four's commitment to 'public issue' programming and themed seasons as *the* particular vehicle to achieve this, theoretical support for the Channel's mission does not seem to have been borne out by viewing practice in this instance. Responses to a questionnaire submitted to RSGB's weekly omnibus survey of 2,000 adults between 11 and 15 August would seem to highlight this dichotomy between theory and practice: 88% of those who had heard of *Bloody Bosnia* agreed that it was important to keep up to date with world events, 69% agreed that this type of programming helped them to understand the complex issues involved in this conflict, and 68% agreed that a dedicated series of programmes on one subject was 'a good idea'. However, 54% felt that they found out enough about Bosnia by watching the news (Source: C4 Research). In *Keeping Faith? Channel Four and Its Audience*, Docherty, Morrison and Tracey encapsulate the situation thus:

> In a fascinating and curious way the public appears to believe in Channel Four in the way that it believes in some abstract concept like 'truth'. People continue to tell lies despite holding truth to be an ultimate value and they want Channel Four to be committed to the culturally and politically disenfranchised even though the majority will never watch such programmes. ... in a very profound way, the public believes in the Channel as an expression of the need for television to challenge, renovate and, occasionally, disturb. (cit. Jivani 1990: 27)

Where does this leave Programme Heads at Channel Four in relation to themed seasons and the public consumers of them? At present, they are not too worried about *Bloody Bosnia's* below-par performance. As previously stated, audience figures for individual programmes do not accurately reflect the cumulative repercussions of a season of this kind, or the role that it plays in fostering a collective impression of

Channel Four in the minds of the general viewing public. Although Channel Four cannot compete with the huge peak-time audience figures of the ITV companies, it is not invisible in the minds of the television audience and has concentrated on competing in those areas where it can directly challenge its rivals, so much so that, in the daytime schedules at least, it is actually eroding their audience share through imaginative and genuinely alternative programming. If we take into consideration the fact that '... on a typical day, between a third and a half of the nation tune into C4 at least once ...' and '... that over a week nearly all of us do so ...' (*Broadcast*, 20 August 1993: 22) then the cumulative awareness-raising effects of a season like *Bloody Bosnia* far outweigh those of the single documentary. Around 18.8 million people (35.6% of the population) tuned in for at least part of the Season (Source: C4 Research) and in spite of the disappointing share of peak-time viewing, a picture emerges of the Channel actually increasing its year-on-year share (around 11.2% in August 1993) with the result that, during the Bosnia week as a whole, '... daytime potency kept C4's overall share safely in double figures' (*Broadcast*, ratings section, 27 August 1993: 18).

Thus, although 'themed' seasons are not able to compete head-to-head with more commercial fare, security in other sections of the schedule perhaps allows the Channel greater flexibility than its competitors in staging riskier ventures like *Bloody Bosnia*. In the conversations I had with commissioning editors at the Channel, I noted the sense of pride in Channel Four's *modus operandi* as a 'devolved federal system' which, by drawing on the resources of the independent sector, was able to mobilise ventures of this kind more quickly than the BBC and thus, having identified a topic for treatment, could get it on air as a response to current events rather than as a retrospective look at them (in the event *Bloody Bosnia* was put together in about twelve weeks). Despite depleted ratings, it was felt that the Season 'did the Channel a huge amount of good' because of the way such vehicles help foster perceptions of Channel Four as being committed to addressing the more difficult questions surrounding public debate of contemporary issues, and so distinguish the Channel from its rivals in the minds of the audience. Although useful as such a 'distinguishing device', there are limitations to the number of viewers that can be sacrificed to image building, and Channel Four, while committed to maintaining a healthy output of quality factual programmes in its peak-time schedules, may have to increase the more populist aspects of other sections of its programming if it wishes to continue to enjoy room to manoeuvre in protecting and projecting its minority remit.

Conclusion

In summing up, what overall picture emerges of Channel Four as a public service broadcaster, and of *Bloody Bosnia* within that remit? In fulfilling its three 'main aims' for the Season, it can be said that the Channel achieved a respectable, if modest, degree of success in awareness-raising, through the examination of a number of complex issues surrounding the wars in Bosnia–Hercegovina, most notably the ways in which the conflicts have been wrongly conceptualised by television for the viewing public, and of the shameful appeasement by the European Community of the Serbs' wanton aggression. In addition, appeals broadcast during the Season raised around £150,000 for humanitarian aid to ease the suffering of the war's victims (Source: C4 Press Office). While the deployment of seasons of this kind is still largely at the experimental stage (the other most notable example to date being *Gimmee Shelter* – on homelessness – which was successful in holding audiences share) there remains the feeling that, if Channel Four is to function in the more rarefied atmosphere of commercial competition, a more cautious approach may dilute the Channel's tendency towards risk-taking in seasons of this kind:

> Before the start of last year ... it was in some ways easier to be internationalist, it was easier to be experimental because we weren't paying for it, the ITV companies were paying for it. Now we're on our own, when we make these decisions, we have to think carefully about them ... How do we support it by other efforts in the schedule to keep the figures up? Because if we can't keep the figures up, we can't afford the shows ... (Peter Salmon, Controller for Factual Programmes).

Whether subsequent series will continue to be as hard-hitting and as uncompromising remains to be seen, but it is clear that the Channel is enthusiastic about their deployment. At present the picture of Channel Four programming is one of a '... peaktime schedule which has increased its commitment to serious programming ...' (Barnett and Lansley, *The Guardian*, 17 January 1994), and so, supported for the moment by buoyant viewing figures in the daytime arena, the Channel can continue to air projects such as *Bloody Bosnia* (and even afford to transmit a follow-up series at Christmas) secure in the knowledge that its overall audience share remains healthily intact. The experience of this Season, however, may mean that in future, and as pressure on the Channel to deliver commercially increases, the amount of 'themed TV' of this kind will either consist of the more popularly packaged programmes that did well in *Bloody Bosnia*, or more sure-fire audience attractors like *Dinomania* (a *Jurassic Park* tie-in) or *The French Connection*, another season of special programming to coincide with the opening of the Channel Tunnel. While the latter seasons currently offset the commercial risk of screening the former and help build favourable audience perception of Channel Four as the genuine alternative to the other two channels, one cannot help feeling that their over-use in the schedules may become self-defeating and hackneyed, and that Heads of Programming will ultimately curtail or even cancel their use in order to secure share of increasingly fragmented audiences, constantly channel-surfing the airwaves in the search for something new.

Note

1. Only those programmes most widely trailed by Channel Four and/or which received the highest viewing figures are covered here, in an attempt to highlight the themes they foregrounded, the perceptions of war they fostered and the way in which they fostered them. By examining this subject-specific period of broadcasting it is also possible to go some way in assessing Channel

Four's performance as a public service broadcaster, in fulfilling the goals set out for the Season above.

References

Ashdown, Paddy, 'A Melting Pot Brought to the Boil', review of *Bosnia: A Short History* by N. Malcolm, *The Sunday Times*, 20 March 1994.

Barnett, Steven and Lansley, Stewart, 'Heavyweight Contenders', *The Guardian*, 17 January 1994.

Bird, Elizabeth S., and Dardenne, Robert W. (1988) 'Myth, Chronicle and Story: Exploring the Narrative Qualities of News', in James W. Carey (ed.), *Media, Myths and Narratives: Television and the Press*, London: Sage.

Borden, Anthony (1993) 'War of Words and Pictures', in Noll Scot and Derek Jones (eds), *Bloody Bosnia: A European Tragedy*, London: The Guardian/Channel Four Television.

Coughlin, Con, 'How Bosnia's Demons Were Made', *The Telegraph*, 31 July 1993.

Docherty, David, Morrison, David E, and Tracey, Michael (1988) *Keeping Faith? Channel Four and its Audience*, London: John Libbey/Broadcasting Research Unit.

Fiddick, Peter, *The Guardian* (Media Research), 31 May 1993.

Jivani, Alkarim (1990) 'Making a Difference: The Impact of Channel Four', in J. Willis and T. Wollen (eds), *The Neglected Audience*, London: BFI.

Lewis, Peter, 'Watch the Big Idea', *The Sunday Times*, 1 August 1993.

Miller, Mark C. (1988) 'How TV Covers War', in Alan Rosenthal (ed.), *New Challenges for Documentary*, Berkeley, CA: University of California Press.

Millwood Hargrave, A. (1993) *Violence in Factual Television*, London: John Libbey.

Morrison, David E. (1992) *Television and the Gulf War*, Academia Research Monograph 7, London: John Libbey.

Pearson, Allison, *The Independent on Sunday*, 8 August 1993.

Phillips, William, 'Small Steps on the Fourward March', *Broadcast*, 20 August 1993.

Phillips, William, *Broadcast* (ratings section), 27 August 1993.

Smith, Giles, 'Pieces of the Action', *The Independent*, 4 August 1993.

Vulliamy, E. (1994) *Seasons in Hell: Understanding Bosnia's War*, London: Simon and Schuster.

Appendix 1: The *Bloody Bosnia* Season

Date	Time	Programme	Description	Thousands of viewers
1.8.93	20.00–20.30	*Opinions*	Personal opinion of Hungarian-born financier George Soros	608
	20.30–21.00	*Frontline*	Investigative report by *Guardian* journalist Maggie O'Kane on the rise to power of Slobodan Milošević and the Serbian political figures responsible for the war	913
	23.55–00.10	*Artists for Bosnia*	First of nightly artistic performances as part of a charity appeal for aid. Excerpt from the ballet *Manon Lescaut*	118
2.8.93	19.50–20.00	*Refugee Stories* (Part 1)	Refugees recount their experiences of fleeing their homes and their lives in exile	488
	21.00–21.15	*The Essential Guide*	First of three 'high-speed' histories of the region, explaining the background to the current conflict: the Medieval Age to 1918	870
	21.15–22.00	*Diplomacy and Deceit*	Report by Nik Gowing, Channel Four Diplomatic Editor, on diplomatic blunders in the Balkans and the West's policy of inaction	619
	23.00–00.05	*The Roots of War*	Account of Yugoslav history this century, chronicling the region's political landscape, the failure of federalism and descent into war	430
	00.05–00.25	*Artists for Bosnia*	Ute Lemper and Bruno Fontaine present wartime songs from Europe's past	514
3.8.93	19.50–20.00	*Refugee Stories* (Part 2)	See above	591
3.8.93	21.00–21.15	*The Essential Guide*	Second in the three-part series, 1918–1945	713
	00.20–00.35	*Artists for Bosnia*	Patrick Hughes on his picture *The Shadow of War*	652
4.8.93	19.50–20.00	*Refugee Stories* (Part 3)	See above	421
	21.00–22.00	*A Sarajevo Diary*	Personal 'video diary' account by honorary Bosnian Bill Tribe, of the suffering, resilience and solidarity of Sarajevans under siege	676
	00.05–00.20	*Artists for Bosnia*	John Williams and Paco Peña play guitar duet	178
	24.20–24.55	*Everything is under Control*	Slovenian black comedy about an army skirmish at a Yugoslav border post	279
5.8.93	19.50–20.00	*Refugee Stories* (Part 4)	See above	550
	21.00–21.15	*The Essential Guide*	Conclusion of the series: establishment of the Federal Republic to the present day	1144

Appendix 1: The *Bloody Bosnia* Season (cont.)

Date	Time	Programme	Description	Thousands of viewers
	21.15–22.45	*True Stories: The Unforgiving*	Clive Gordon's documentary, filmed behind Serbian lines, follows a Serbian couple's search for their murdered child and details instances of atrocities on all sides	1043
	22.45–23.00	*Tourist Sarajevo '93*	Parodic, surreal tourist guide to surviving Sarajevo by its beleaguered inhabitants	952
	00.55–00.10	*Artists for Bosnia*	Slovenian dancer Istok Kovak	122
6.8.93	19.50–20.00	*First Reaction*	'Words of War'–analysis of origins and use of the euphemism 'ethnic cleansing' by *Independent* journalist Thomas Sutcliffe	493
	20.00–20.30	*Right to Reply Special*	Debate between broadcasters and public on the Western media's role in covering the war	689
7.8.93	19.00–20.00	*The World This Week*	International affairs series examining the week's news, with special reports from Bosnia	531
	22.45–25.00	*After Dark Special*	Open-ended discussion programme examining issues arising from the war	186
8.8.93	19.00–20.00	*Disappearing World: We Are All Neighbours*	Debbie Cristie's portrait of an ethnically mixed Bosnian village which disintegrates from friendship into suspicion, fear and violence as the war approaches	600
	20.00–20.30	*Opinions*	Avant-garde film-maker Dušan Makavejev	380
	23.35–23.50	*Artists for Bosnia*	Extract from Ariel Dorfman's play *Death and the Maiden*	336
	23.50–01.15	*Plastic Jesus*	Yugoslav feature film directed by Lazar Stojanović. The film was banned in 1971 and its writer–director jailed for three years	301
Average				549

Sources: Channel Four Research; Channel Four Press Release

Appendix 2: Analysis

Top Five Programmes in terms of Viewing Figures

Date	Time	Title	Thousands
5.8.93 Thurs	21.00–21.15	*The Essential Guide (Part 3)*	1114
5.8.93 Thurs	21.15–22.45	*The Unforgiving*	1043
5.8.93 Thurs	22.45–23.00	*Tourist Sarajevo '93*	952
1.8.93 Sun	20.30–21.00	*Frontline*	913
2.8.93 Mon	21.00–21.15	*The Essential Guide (Part 1)*	870

Source: Channel Four Research

Top Three Programmes in terms of Publicity Trails

Date	Time	Title	Thousands
5.8.93 Thurs	21.15–21.45	*The Unforgiving*	1043
4.8.93 Wed	21.00–22.00	*A Sarajevo Diary*	676
2.8.93 Mon	21.15–22.00	*Diplomacy and Deceit*	619

Source: Bloody Bosnia

Documentary Films and the Bosnia–Hercegovina Conflict

From Production to Reception

BRIGITTE HIPFL, KLAUS HIPFL, JAN JAGODZINSKI

Reflections on the Newscasts of the Bosnian Conflict – Klaus Hipfl

General Concerns regarding the Reported War Discourse

Even after two years of newscasts about the war in Bosnia, there still seems to be a wide gap between the cruel, absurd reality of the war and the televised images the public is able to see. For the reporter, there is a feeling that this gap is impossible to close. She or he is unable to use the whole mass of collected information, or its summary, to convey that reality to the viewers, and therefore is liable to feel guilty that the television viewer is given such a fragmented view of the events in former Yugoslavia. I am referring here, not to the selections made by the chief editor, but to the process by which the reporter has already internalised what is expected – in terms of both the choice that is to be made from the wealth of information available and the necessity of ignoring certain events while elevating others as important and meaningful.

Among journalists there seems to be something like a general agreement, or tacit understanding, that reports of the war should be characterised by frantic language, hectic cutting and sensational commentary, all strategically set against an exciting background where bombs explode and the sound of machine-gun fire can be heard. These are the elements which are said to make up 'good' war coverage. It is assumed that viewers expect such reports and hence there is competition among commercial broadcasters to present war on this 'experiential level', making it necessary for every journalist to do the same. This is generally not seen as problematic if the reporter is in the war zone where there appears to be no gap between report and action. But this is not the way it is. If a reporter is to work professionally in a war zone, a base station has to be maintained that offers a minimum of civilised working conditions and that is not under fire. However, around such a base station, e.g. Sarajevo's television station, there may not always be a lot of action. The main part of the TV story may be the totally untypical minutes of the day when grenades explode more or less close enough to where the reporter is staying, and of which the crew is lucky enough to get footage. For the other 23 hours and 50 minutes, the viewers have no clue as to what has taken place. Is this a distortion of reality or is it its legitimate condensation in the sense of the *pars pro toto* principle – the part representing the whole?

The reporter is closer to the war than the viewer is at home, but the reporter is not a soldier. The reporting takes place in a restricted or reduced part of the war's 'reality', the part that can be caught with the cameras at a reasonably safe distance. Many journalists are dissatisfied with this contradiction and choose to be in the thick of the front line. Often the risk of being killed or wounded in such situations is high for the whole team and the results minimal. Perhaps it is more commonly the case that reporters, with less indulgence in heroics, become involved directly in war events not in the main places, but at secondary sites. But such reports and stories concerning the more peripheral aspects of the war are not appreciated as much by chief editors. They do not fit into the current concept of war 'news drama'.

Experienced war reporters such as Martin Bell from the BBC have a precise idea of an optimal distance from the front line; of being close enough to hear or see something but not so close as to risk being killed or wounded. There is, then, an optimal 'war reporting zone', one in which the BBC for example, was able to obtain spectacular images – 'house-to-house fighting' between Muslims and Croats in central Bosnia – by hiring a soldier from one of the local Croatian troops as a cameraman. Of course the BBC knew that this also might lead to Croatian propaganda, but this was the only way for them to get any images of the actual fighting. Without such 'action' footage, the alternative would be to concentrate on the results of the war: the sadness, the plight of refugees, the burnt and destroyed villages and so on; a much less dramatic and desirable option.

There were other difficulties reporters experienced in their efforts to report the events of the war. The Muslim-dominated 'Third Corps' of the Bosnian army, with its headquarters at Zenica, did not allow international reporters to film on the other side of the front. In this, the Bosnian army was following one of the few laws of warfare that survived in the chaos of the Balkans. This law allows the international press to report on the front line of the *weakest party*. The most obvious example of the enactment of this legality was the behaviour of the Croatians in Hercegovina. As long as the Serbs attacked Mostar, foreign journalists were warmly welcomed. When Croatians started to shoot at the eastern part of the town, foreign journalists were put under 'house' arrest 'for their own protection', and prevented from doing their job.

The Bosnian Serbs were especially inventive in finding ways of bullying and bureaucratically harassing foreign journalists. Almost weekly they changed the place and timespan for the process of 'clearing' journalists. In the winter of 1993, when journalists wanted to pass through areas in Sarajevo controlled by the Serbs, they were obliged to go to the Hotel Bistrica in the skiing area of Jahorina, 1700m above sea-level to get accreditation and even then this was only valid for one week. The Bosnian Serbs also turned certain checkpoints into *de facto* international borders. If a reporter forgot to declare how much money she or he was carrying into the 'country', then the Bosnian Serbs would confiscate it on the grounds that a legal border had been crossed without money being declared.

Reporters had difficulty obtaining information about what was 'really' going on at the front or out in the countryside. Such information as there was always came from 'dubious' sources, and hence it was up to the reporter to decide how much credence should be placed on the reports of amateur short-wave radio operators and other so-called eye-witnesses. It is important to understand the magnitude of this problem. In Bosnia especially, the gap between the reality of the war and the 'reality of the reporters' was so wide that events in the north of the country, such as 'ethnic cleansing', took place without TV cameras ever being able to get any pictures.

For a small television station like the ORF, there is another aspect that is important when choosing stories. International agencies, such as WTN or Reuters TV, offer all broadcasting stations a constant supply of images of events worldwide (including, of course, of Bosnia). For reporters covering the Bosnian conflict this means that they are often receiving less imaged information than the public and that their editorial staff receives these same reported images far faster than they do themselves. This creates a situation where the only way of differentiating reports is to present stories that are away from the mainstream, i.e., stories that are more personal, more human and more exclusive. When, for example, a reporter stands in front of the camera, it is not for vanity's sake but rather because the reporter's editorial staff knows that this provides evidence that one of its teams, however small, is actually there.

Some Striking Blunders and Difficulties

With hindsight, the role of the media in the Balkan conflict has not been very positive. Austrian reporting, for example, was very anti-Serbian: a whole ethnic group was stigmatised as war criminals. When similar Croatian crimes became known, journalists were much more careful with their presentation. Even the more neutral Anglo-Saxon newspapers and television stations were not always successful in presenting aspects of the war entirely without kitsch and exaggeration. Such shortcomings were justified by claims that the Bosnian conflict was so confusing that it had to be presented simply for the sake of the viewers.

An obvious example of the media's over-simplification of such 'confusion' occurred when the defenders of Sarajevo suddenly mutated into Muslims, while in fact all three ethnic groups co-existed within the defending army; indeed, the commander of Sarajevo was for some time a Bosnian Serb. The international press, to make matters simple, took on board the thesis developed by the Serbs, and then accepted by the Croatians, that there were three nations fighting against each other. In so doing, it accepted that every nation was claiming its own 'territory'. A further consequence was that the world forgot that the Bosnian government was the only one arguing for the mutual co-existence of all three ethnic groups. The world also forgot that the concept 'Bosnian' was a geographical term struggling for its own survival.

On the other hand the media was vociferous in its complaints about the scandal of 'ethnic cleansing'. Yet journalists did not talk so eagerly about 'ethnic *language* cleansing'. Another example of the 'confusion' of reportage was the choice of the term 'concentration camps' in Bosnia in a conscious association with the history of the Holocaust. While the Serbs should not be exempted from their war crimes, it is important to recognise that the Serbian camps were not the systematic death camps of the Nazis. Such inflammatory use of the historically fixed term 'concentration camp' can lead to the 'minimalisation' and 'trivialisation' of Nazi guilt and the Holocaust. It is interesting to note that Simon Wiesenthal, a figure known to the world for his active search for Nazi war criminals, protested against the use of the word 'concentration camps' for the Serbian camps in Bosnia.

Winston Churchill once said that history in the Balkans pressed so heavily on its shoulders that it is almost impossible to live under its weight. The war in Croatia and the fighting in Bosnia appear to be a repetition of past historical events and all the warring factions have used history as an excuse for their involvement. History and the present seem to melt together in a chaotic 'stew', thickened by reporting that likes to herald the return of the Thirty Years War to civilised and enlightened Europe. It will have to be determined later whether shortcomings in the reporting of the war in Bosnia developed out of the specific atmospheric conditions in the Balkans, or whether they are a general characteristic of war reporting *per se*. The experience of the

Gulf War leads to the assumption that the latter explanation will more likely prove the right one.

Personal Remarks concerning My Reporting

From the very beginning I have never seen myself as a 'war reporter', but as a 'social reporter' working in an area where there is 'war'. Maybe one of the reasons for perceiving myself in this way is that I started my 'war' reporting only after first undertaking work as an ORF reporter for the Austrian initiative 'Nachbar in Not' ('Neighbours in Need'). During my first visits to Bosnia, when I followed the convoys of vehicles carrying food and supplies to needy areas, I had to learn to concentrate and observe closely so as to get any 'story' available. After a few weeks, I developed a preference for stories dealing with the lives of the people in the war and the numerous absurdities that are connected with this exceptional situation.

It has been especially important for me to show the richness and diversity of life in the war and to try to get away from the clichés that have developed in current reporting. To my mind, reporters should keep their distance and should not include accounts of their own circumstances and experiences of the war, which tend to be problematic. I have often been accused of understatement, that 'war' appears to be in some way absent from my reports. Yet, the same editors who have made this criticism have otherwise been enthusiastic about my documentary reports.

In my opinion reports on the war should follow the same basic criteria as all other reporting: solid research, meticulous checking and rechecking of facts, and careful editing. In this way there would not be such a big gap between the reality and reported situation as there now seems to be. The most 'honest' reports are for me those that show the lives of the population unvarnished, with all its contradictions and absurdities. I have always disliked reports that show a black-and-white picture of the warring factions; the events of the war have shown that all parties have been guilty of criminal acts.

An Analysis of Klaus Hipfl's Documentary Discourse of the Bosnian Conflict: From Close Reading to Reception (Brigitte Hipfl, jan jagadzinsk)

Introduction: General Background

Over the past three years Klaus Hipfl has been presenting documentary evidence of the 'human face' of the war in Bosnia for the ORF through short reports (between one and four minutes long) and several *Auslandsreports* spanning ten minutes or more. Through these brief encapsulations he has tried to capture the drama of war that is often overlooked and ignored, dismissed as too banal to be of any interest to the viewing public.

There have been over thirty of these reports from which we have chosen two samples that reflect his intention to show a diversity of life not normally covered by the major news reporters. Our selections were specifically chosen to provide strongly contrasting reports: the first, 'Kinderpolizisten' (Children's police squad), was chosen to raise the gender issues that are embedded in every war situation. Here, the issue of masculine desire is especially relevant. In her article 'Phantasmen des Krieges: Patriarchat und Mutterland – Heimat und Rassismus ('Phantasms of the war: patriachy and motherland – native soil and racism'; 1993), Renata Salecl, a Slovenian sociologist of law, has brilliantly demonstrated the psychoanalytic role that the purity of a 'homeland', free from the stain and dirt of difference, has played in the Serbian imagination in securing its 'motherland'. Here, as Kristeva (1976) has argued, revolutionary socio-political forces have been rechannelled into fascistic structures by the authoritarian figure of the law-giver and father, in which the mother's body is imaginatively defended against invaders, often in the most violent ways.

Our second sample, 'Zentralbosnien – Kroatische und moslemische Familien' (Central Bosnia – Croatian and Muslim families), was chosen to provide a contrast to the utter futility of war depicted in the other report. Where there is devastation there is also the hope of renewal and redemption; the human spirit refuses to give up hope. This time it is maternal desire which plays a vital part in keeping this dream alive. The first broadcast demonstrates how war reproduces itself, while the second provides hope for a future peace. Although these are only two facets of the diversity Klaus's reporting has presented, they are representative of his objective of pointing up the ironies and absurdities brought about by the exceptional situation of war.

To analyse the reception of these broadcasts, we have interviewed one Croatian, one Bosnian Muslim and five Austrians for their reactions to these news reports. We acknowledge the difficulties in this: many refugees do not have the linguistic capacity to understand the reports and we had no opportunity to work with a translator who might facilitate our task. We nevertheless feel that this small selection offers some insights as to how these reports might be interpreted. The over-representation of Austrians among the interviewees was deliberate in that we were keen to get a glimpse of what might be the current attitude of Austrians to the Balkan conflict. After three years of what appears to be a 'never-ending' and unsolvable conflict, many Austrians have begun to disregard news reports. Historically, there have been close, though ambivalent, ties between the Balkan countries and Austria. This has had both positive and negative consequences in the current conflict. On the one hand, it has meant that Austria has led the way in providing food, support and accommodation for refugees, while, on the other, it has produced a strong Austrian bias against the Serbs. We were interested in how these aspects might emerge in the responses of our interviewees.

Klaus Hipfl's Documentary Discourse of Representation

The discourses Klaus Hipfl offers his viewers in these two stories may be categorised as belonging to the 'interactive mode of representation' (Nichols 1991). As he notes in his personal statement, his goal is to present the human face of the war 'unvarnished' and as 'honestly' as possible, with all inherent contradictions manifest. Ideally, the story should phenomenologically 'speak for itself'.

It should be said from the outset that the discourse of the war documentary probably comes close to its claim to the 'real'. There is a favouring of consciousness, of intention and of programmatic aims. Desire seems banished; the unconscious, delirious, fantastic and ecstatic elements of narrative often appear to be missing. The expectancy of war documentary remains coloured by a soberness brought on by lived experience inscribed by suffering, victimisation and terror – whether these character-istics are sensationally dramatised or subtly understated (Renov 1993). Klaus offers viewers the latter alternative, in which the evidence of 'war' is paradoxically missing.

Examining his rhetoric – the means by which he attempts to convey his outlook persuasively to his viewers, it is obvious that the pragmatics of his discourse is that of a morally and ethically engaged reporter who allows a 'witnessing' to take place. Klaus's 'truth claims' are formed through the journalistic principle of 'balanced reporting' and a general sense of 'unbiased' or 'fair' treatment of his subjects. This is especially evident in these two reports where both sides of the issue are presented. The 'truth claims' are based on the *emotional appeal* to an audience's disposition towards parental concern for the understanding of their own children in the first case, and empathy through the loss of home and belongings in the second. In short, the ultimate appeal is made to justice and human decency. The 'proof' of his 'truth claims' is persuasively conveyed by providing the factual evidence for their demonstration. In the first report, as we shall see, boys are shown in the acts of make-believe fighting, patrolling, displaying their weaponry and obeying orders. In the second, the crew physically relocates itself from one border to the next, and then back again, to demonstrate the evidence of their story.

Unquestionably, Klaus's ethical integrity comes across despite the fact that it is his voice which is dominant. As his rhetoric courts the viewer into believing the persuasive story that his crew has constructed, Klaus's personal style reveals him as its author. He embodies the voice of calm reason, a convincing style that offers his viewers the benefit of a concerned, but always dispassionate, analysis. Like the understated aspects of the war in his documentaries, Klaus embodies, through his commentary, and through the very themes he chooses, subtle questioning of justice. Again, true to his non-interventionalist style, his voice is not one that rages with platitudes of injustice, inhumanity, barbarism or madness; rather, as he himself claims, he recognises that atrocities have been committed by all sides. During the past three years he has managed to maintain a consistent ethical integrity, which has given him credibility as a 'fair' reporter with the editorial staff at the ORF. However, the continuity that exists between his own intentional rhetorics and the filmic event does not exempt him from his own contradictions or from the 'excess' that escapes every documented story, and we shall have occasion to point out examples of each within these two reports.

The production process, and in particular the role of translation and editing is of especial importance. Klaus's interviews are an interaction between himself and the 'eyewitness' social actors whose problems and concerns are being questioned; however, there is a language barrier that has to be overcome. What is not evident in the reports is the role of the translator who is made absent. Occasionally you can hear or see her, but she is not identified as being the translator as such. In other words, the mediated presence between Klaus and the social actors is made virtually invisible. Should the translator appear in any identifiable or interventionist way, it would take away from the credibility of the reporter, delaying the transference of what appears to be an unmediated 'authentic' moment.

The unbroken continuity of the narrative that appears to be taking place in 'real time' is also guaranteed by the production procedure. Reports are edited by the team after the filmic event, and hence it is the voice of the reporter that dominates the newscast, although the voices of the participants can also be heard, thereby adding to the documentary 'realism'. Again, only on occasion is the translator heard, and even then her voice is unobtrusive. Most of the participants are filmed in close-up or mid-shots in order to heighten the intimacy of the presentation. Their identity and background are usually not provided. Most conspicuously absent from the first report is any mention of ethnicity. As Klaus mentions above, the categorisation of the various ethnic groups is exactly what the Bosnian government doesn't want. When possible, it seems that he consciously avoids categorising his social participants as being Croatian, Muslim or Serb.

By allowing his voice-over to dominate, Klaus lays the emphasis clearly on addressing his viewers, rather than on speaking to the social actors. Scenes of his interaction with the participants are rare. However, his camera mitigates much of this direct address to the audience by presenting viewers with a close-up human gaze which establishes a rapport between the camera and the subject. The balance works well since the constructed narrative draws the viewer into the story, with Klaus's voice supplementing the viewer's focus, rather than disrupting it. An ethic of responsibility is further in evidence as the camera underpins the attempt to draw the audience into an empathy with the interviewees by presenting them in their own social contexts and with their own expressive emotions.

Given this background we shall now attempt a close reading of the two reports including that which is unsaid, which is tacit or which is 'excessive' to the frame itself. These two reports were broadcast as part of the late-evening news show, the first on 9 September 1992 (length 2 min 25 sec) and the second on 14 March 1994 (length 2 min 55 sec).

Describing the Reports and Their 'Excesses'
'Kinderpolizisten'
'Kinderpolizisten' is a 'happenstance' story which emerged when the news crew was looking to do a story on a private school. It is perhaps illustrative of the sensitivity the crew had to the seemingly banal and 'ordinary' events that are normally overlooked and ignored as insignificant to an understanding of the psychological aspects that have emerged during the Balkan conflict. When the team arrived at the address given to them by their producer, they came across a group of children who had organised themselves into a 'police squad' with the help of the middle-aged man in charge of defending a district in Sarajevo. These children had been issued with special badges saying that they were officially allowed to police two or three streets in their capacity as 'police' or 'soldiers'. They were especially asked to patrol and prevent the breaking of windows of their school, which was apparently one of the few existing buildings with windows still intact. In accordance with Klaus's own comment about the absence of 'war' from his broadcasts, the graffiti on the walls where the children play is as close as we come to seeing any sort of destruction.

As is made evident by the narrative, the organisation of the boys' 'police squad' remarkably and starkly reproduces the hierarchy of the war, and recreates masculine desire for the excitement and anxiety it brings. The boys can 'act out' the fantasy of war, perhaps as a coping mechanism to ensure the security that they lack within it. There is a self-designated leader, whose status is attested by the weapons he has collected (an army knife and a gun with no shells, both given to him by a soldier) and by the oversized pair of khaki army trousers he sports. His entire ensemble signifies and assures his status among the rest of the children who appear to range in age from nine to fourteen years old, a time where pubescent ideas of heroism emerge and gender formation is important. The camera focuses in and isolates the knife and the gun. There is a split-second shot of two boys in which their fascination with these objects is clearly obvious. There are the phallic symbols they themselves desire, but do not possess.

The opening shot presents its viewers with Klaus nestled in among the 'squad', holding one hand onto the microphone, the other on the shoulder of one of the boys. The presence of a news reporter adds to their status and confirms that what they are doing is worthy enough to be investigated. These children are used to film crews as the Kosevo Klinik is nearby where over thirty television crews have already conducted reports.[1] This is the last time we actually see Klaus, as his disembodied voice takes control of the narrative. After a demonstration of the duties the boys are engaged in, they are shown patrolling the streets; meeting at a designated spot where they report and exchange information on what they have seen and done; actively engaging in acts of self-defence, fighting one another in typical karate style.

There is a remarkable scene where the camera and commentary confirm this hierarchical structure. We see the camera sweep past a row of children, almost as if it were 'inspecting' the troops. The commentary mentions that the children have lined themselves up of their own volition. The leader is then filmed from behind, addressing his 'troops', giving them orders with his German shepherd dog at his side. His khaki trousers are strongly suggestive of those worn by Nazi officers that flared at the level of the thigh. This camera shot syntagmatically displaces the camera's previous glance, which places the subject position taken by the leader as that of the viewer. A frontal view of the squad is shown in the background reiterating the obedient line of boys in front of him. The boys are then shown fighting. The effect of this juxtaposition echoes the obvious fascistic tendencies that are operating at the level of desire. The leader has unequivocally related previously that he would like to kill a 'Chetnik' (Serb) with his pistol.

There are two adults in the narrative who present opposing opinions about the 'play' of these children. First a woman is interviewed who unequivocally states, in an excited voice, that the 'police squad' is a re-enactment of the war. She further implies that these children have nothing to do, as there are no daily chores that they must perform. 'Most of the children spend their time in their basements [cellars]', she says.[2] Her *disavowal* of the children's adultlike status and her expressed concern is forcefully overturned in the subsequent scenes. Over a split-second shot of two boys, one holding his ground in a soldier-like stance, feet spread apart, hands behind his back, like a guard at attention, Klaus Hipfl's voice-over states that perhaps these children have seen too much of the war. There is a cut to an interview with the *one* girl among all the boys who expresses her desire for Chetnik (Serb) children to suffer the same way she has over the loss of her dead friends. The interview with a girl, who 'acts' like a boy, is a further signifier that the children have experienced the suffering of war. This is quickly followed by a third displacement: boys are shown excessively petting the leader's pet dog, confirming the *one* moment in the narrative where 'unadulterated' childhood is presented in hyperbolic fashion. Klaus's voice-over contradicts what is seen, questioning the mistreatment of children by the leader of the district's defence (a male in his mid-fifties). Then a close-up shot of the leader of the district's defence is presented, and he is given an opportunity to justify his action. He mentions that this was an innocent decision on his part, to harness the children's play within the specific circumstances of war, giving them simple tasks which they could carry out. The last displacement is a confirmatory and concluding one which reaffirms that the story is a metonym for the war in Bosnia. Against the scene of several boys fighting, Klaus's voice-over says that many children really believe that they have to fight and that they too might become heroes in their city. The camera zooms in on a rather innocent-looking boy and freeze-frames his face for an instant as the report ends.

Our close reading of this first report suggests that the effect of this narrative is to confirm that fascistic fantasies of war are being re-enacted through the formation of children's 'police squads'. Their enemy is clearly delineated; the phantasms of their desire for retribution clearly expressed. Their flights of fantasy to be city heroes, furthered by father figures like the district defence leader, echo the heroism of the 'Juka army' composed of Sarajevo's criminal elements. The narrative shows the loss of childlike innocence and *hints* at the ethical question: 'Is this right?' by leaving the audience, in the end, an intimate image of the angelic face of a boy's innocence. These children are growing up far too quickly and far too soon, in a world not of their choosing. The woman's voice of the concerned mother/teacher/parent is virtually muffled in this narrative, for there is yet another side to these children's lives that is not represented; the one that hides in the 'basement' which they must repress if they are to survive the war psychologically.

To conclude then, the report is predominantly told from a male perspective with the added irony that the one institution designed to preserve and protect 'childhood' – the school – now has an inverse relationship with their lives. Rather than the school protecting them, they are to protect it. No doubt this was the desired intention of the district's defence leader: to somehow maintain that connection, but to turn it around as loyalty and duty to the city, and of course ultimately to the Bosnian state itself.

'Zentralbosnien – Kroatische und moslemische Familien'

The second report explores the relationship between two displaced families, each of whom the discourse of the war has turned into designated 'enemies': Croatians and Muslims. The theme explored here is the meaning of 'home'. It is a somewhat 'unusual' story, in which a displaced Croatian family's former home now lies in Muslim-controlled territory, only a short distance from their current home in Croatian-occupied territory which was previously occupied by a Muslim family. In other words, an ironical and seemingly absurd situation is presented to the television viewers. The images in the report are replete with the evidence of destruction – empty shelled houses, ruins, the debris left by fleeing Muslim refugees.

The narrative presents viewers with the consequences of 'ethnic cleansing' and the enormous price the civil population pays: the loss of personal memories, belongings and homes. Throughout the report, the total neglect of the environment by the new 'squatters' is self-evident; both Muslims and Croatians have been forced to occupy land they are neither attached to, nor care for. For them, it is very much a 'temporary' situation, a denial and a disavowal that they may never return 'home' again.

The report seeks to explore the desire for 'eventual return' and it is this desire which binds the two families together; the knowledge and insight of each family that the same winds of fate have left them in a similar set of circumstances. This mutual empathetic understanding has mitigated their hate and increased their tolerance for one another, but it has not put out the fires of their desire to return to where they 'belong'. Human decency and strong family ties rise above the duty of ethnic hate. The singularity of suffering and pain of loss unites both families. In contradistinction to the first report, which was a powerful exposition of male desire, we are here presented with its opposite – the desire of the mother, to protect her family and to return to the soil that raised her. The fathers of both families are absent.[3] The strength of this report is that Klaus and the crew are able to bridge the borders that separate the families through their privileged access to both territories. While maintaining a non-interventionist policy, he is able to further the dialogue between them, to promote an intercultural understanding or, at the very least, present the mutual basis of their victimisation for his viewers. However, as in the previous report, there are contradictions in the narrative structure.

The desire for 'eventual return' is presented predominantly from the perspective of the Croatian family. After the initial context of the town's devastation has been established, the Croatian mother is interviewed and asked how she feels about living in a former Muslim home, about having been driven out by the very forces of the people whose house she now occupies. In an almost apologetic manner she answers that she was saving her family in any way she could. There is then an interesting turn of events as the viewpoint of the mother is displaced by that of the son who leads the television crew to the top of a hill, the front line of the Croatian territory from which his former village can be surveyed. Sporting binoculars, the son describes his home, especially noting that he is happy that it is still standing and hasn't been burnt. It is the son who casts the covetous eye back on the former home, not the mother. The son acts as the representative of the missing father. One can only assume that the desire for re-occupation is kept alive from this look-out point. The son and other members of the family can always 'long' for their former house through the binoculars. They are curious about who, if anyone, is living there, and what sort of shape their house is in.

Their curiosity is answered by Klaus and the crew in the next scene in which they are shown them driving along the road into the former Croatian village where, some nine months previously, Croatian refugees had fled, leaving remnants of their belongings scattered along the roadside. A girl opens the door of the (now) Muslim-occupied house in a gesture of invitation to the crew and to us, the television viewers, and we are led inside into a hall littered with rubbish and planks of wood. The early welcome puts the viewer at ease, and almost immediately the camera focuses on a close-up of a child, a girl maybe five years old, staring at us with wide sorrowful eyes; her mother's hand cups her face under her chin in a gesture of protection and embrace. To an Austrian audience that has grown accustomed to seeing such faces before from the orphanages in Romania, there is an immediate feeling of sympathy and sorrow. The little girl clings to her mother's side – she is somewhat shy and startled. The very next cut reinforces the viewer's empathy for the plight of the family. A young girl of about nine or ten, looking rather mournful, is shown dressed in her ethnic costume – a red headscarf and colourful embroidered dress. During these fleeting images Klaus's voice-over tells us that this family has been driven out of Banja Luka by the Serbs. The images and the commentary are a perfect blend of contextual editing to establish a maternal scene that solicits our sympathetic attention. No men or boys have been presented.

There is an immediate cut to a mid-shot of the mother, who is also wearing a headscarf and looking rather drawn and tired. She is asked what she would do if the Croatian family were to come back? She answers that the Croatian (she uses the masculine singular) should come back after they themselves have been sent somewhere else. Her hope is for each to return to their former home: if that were possible, she would be happy. Klaus's voice mitigates the hope of this possibility, taking note that the Serbian 'cleansing' had been done so thoroughly that many Muslims will have to find a new place to live. This is said in the context of three static shots. The first shows a pot full of a mushy, heavy substance. The second is of a room full of children, some of them adolescents, all sitting *still* in the dimmed halflight. Their movement is almost negligible. It is the first time that we have seen any boys. The scene is one that conveys gloom and quietude, resignation almost, despite the little bit of coloured ethnic rug on the floor, which, no doubt, is one of the few artifacts the family brought with them from their former home. Finally there is a shot of the outside of the house, with two children posed in the same frozen way. The effect of the Muslim sequence is to elicit our sorrow and sympathy; the magnitude of the problems seem to far outweigh the desire of the mother to 'return'. The very stillness of the last three scenes makes her travelling back 'unthinkable' for us, the

43

viewers.

Such is not the case for the crew, who return to the 'other side', and view the video footage of the Muslim family with the Croatian family. There is an irony here: the footage is played back for the benefit of the Croatian family, to promote under-standing between them. Yet, we, the viewers appear to take part in their watching voyeuristically. There is an uncomfortable objectification of the Muslim family that seems to take place as the distance of what we have just seen is again doubled through another television set. The build-up of sympathy is quickly deflated. Especially disturbing is the realisation that what was presented for our viewing a minute ago is only a small part of the footage that had been taken. There were, for example, other equally sympathetic scenes between the mother and daughter. Access to the whole film has been denied to us, its viewers, and this 'fact' is experienced vividly here.

Close-ups of the reactions of the son and the mother are shown as they watch the video footage. Strong reactions appear on their faces, especially the son's. He mentions the *physical* destruction of the house, that there are no more window frames and the doors are off their hinges. However, it is the mother who relates to the Muslim family's fate, especially to the presentation of the mother and child. Klaus asks her what she thinks of their situation? The Croatian mother explains their situation as being identical to hers. The Muslim mother had to look for a house to live in, in order to save her children. It was the Serbs who drove this Muslim family out in the first place, and although it was Muslim forces that had driven out the Croatians, this particular family had nothing to do with it. By rationalising the blame on to the Serbs as a common enemy, and by dissociating and differentiating this Muslim family from other Muslims, the Croatian mother is able to place family above ethnic hatred, a remarkably generous concession given the circumstances.

Here, however, another contradiction sets in. Just as the hope of the Muslim mother was overshadowed by the stillness of the last images and commentary, it appears to us that the Croatian mother's voice is similarly overshadowed. The voice-over leaves us, the viewers, with a similar scene of recuperation. Two completely gutted houses are shown. Klaus's voice-over tells us that over 10,000 such gutted buildings exist all over central Bosnia, and that it will take decades before the ethnic hatred finally dissipates. The final images are of a man walking along a street gesturing to the camera a sign of greeting, perhaps recognition. Within the context of the report, it might just as easily be interpreted as an ironic gesture; as if to say 'that's enough – enough destruction for now'.

This second report issues an ethical plea based on maternal understanding that transcends ethnicities, that goes 'beyond' the seeming impossibility of a peaceful restoration. The mother's discourse presents a breach in the paternal law. It ignores the demands of borders, pure ethnicity and a separation of memory from the homes they have left. These two mothers, rather than aiding and abetting their sons to reproduce the fascism of war (as in the first report), are demonstrating that their voices can share the sorrow and suffering that is born in the eyes of their children. In some sense Klaus's report has both aided and mitigated the strength of their desire for a 'return' to peaceful coexistence.

Results of the Interviews

Background: Post-Modern Identities

The third section of this paper analyses a series of interviews carried out with a Bosnian Muslim and a Croatian, both of whom have been living in Klagenfurt for three years, as well as with five Austrians. All interviewees belonged to our circle of acquaintances, and agreement to participate came after the project had been described and discussed with them. At the time of writing we were unable to locate a Serb in order to achieve 'typological completeness'. This gaping omission should, however, be taken in the context of post-modern notions of identity formation; it might also be ironically perceived as the metaphorical silencing of the 'aggressor's voice'.

Although the Bosnian conflict has been identified as a civil 'ethnic conflict', this characterisation of a nationalism based on ethnic grounds alone is a creation of the Serbs. In a city like Sarajevo there was peaceful coexistence between Muslims, Croats and Serbs. The discourse of the war has created an artificial Muslim 'motherland' which had never previously existed in their imaginary field. Nationalist Serbs have forced the Croatians to redefine their former national identity, and to create new nationals myths, which means perceiving themselves in new ways and not connecting their identity to their former homelands. The phantasm attached to this territory is systematically being destroyed.[4]

Indeed, the Muslim Yugoslavs were the only ones who took the idea of the transnationality of the Yugoslav Federation seriously. They believed in brotherhood and in unity. The Yugoslav socialist policy had specifically tried to remove identity based on ethnicity from its organisation. Muslims who defined themselves around religious and patriarchal principles had no difficulties living within the confines of this ideal. When Muslim towns were first bombed, they still maintained this position. Even then they did not attribute any ethnic connotations to the aggressors' motivation, calling them 'criminals' or 'hooligans'. It was only much later that they were labelled as 'Chetniks' or 'Serbian nationalists'. Serbian nationalists tried to undermine Muslim identity by destroying their mosques and raping Muslim women in order to break their religious and sexual identity. In no uncertain terms, rape meant a symbolic death for the women. It struck at the core of the Muslim sense of being. It is said that if an enemy burns down their house, a man will later return and build it up once again. However, should his wife be raped he will never return. By destroying Muslim sexual and religious identity, the war forced Muslims to create a new imaginary 'motherland' so that their soldiers would join in the fight to secure it.

Post-modernity, therefore, presents a situation in which some factions, for example Serbs, Irish nationalists, Québecois and various indigenous peoples such as the First Nations of North America, are turning to an ethnic national orthodoxy as a way of reaffirming their identity, while other factions are re-creating, redefining, and challenging their once established sense of self, and still others live with the hybrid mixture of 'class', 'race', 'nationality', 'family', 'colour', 'religion' and so on which results from the diaspora of post-colonialism.

Reaction of the Bosnian Muslim and Croatian[5]

Dževad's Background

Dževad is a 24-year-old Muslim from Bosnia. He was born in Germany where his father worked for ten years but lived for sixteen years in a Bosnian town and finished his high-school education there. He and his family moved to Klagenfurt, Austria, before the conflict began. Dževad is a student who has made a successful living for himself in sport. He considers himself to be in a privileged position compared to other Bosnians. His wider family – grandparents and cousins – still live in the same Bosnian town where he grew up, and he is still in contact with them using a mobile telephone. At the end of the interview he offered thanks to Austria for its support of Bosnia – both for the goods and supplies, as well as the political support by the Foreign Minister, Alois Mock. 'Austria has always been on "our" side,' he said. The interview with Dževad was throughout charged with emotion.

At the very beginning Dževad stressed that he had special knowledge and information about the situation in Bosnia because of his contact with a number of sources: relatives he is still in touch with; letters he receives from people living there; and a personal friend who is a journalist in Sarajevo. Dževad's friends also drive down regularly to areas in Bosnia, carrying relief supplies. In brief, Dževad is a self-assured young man who claims to be well informed, so much so, that he believes the information he has to offer about the Bosnian situation is far superior to that offered in the Austrian media. The latter is not a useful information source for him, because he feels that it focuses too much on certain situations, particularly on the crisis in Sarajevo, while ignoring reports of what is happening elsewhere. He had already seen the second report about the two families on ORF. In his words, 'he knows what war means'.

After watching the first report Dževad said, 'I can understand that because I am someone from "down there". Because I am better informed, I know. I have watched that in a different way.' He went on to mention that if he weren't a regular viewer who had such a strong background knowledge, he could neither understand nor accept what was being shown. For him, the reaction of the children is evidence that this is a terrible situation. He showed both empathy and sadness and felt that neither these children, nor the Muslims, deserved what was happening to them. Children were the group most affected by the war; they have experienced so much conflict that they will never forget the images and feelings it has thrown up for the rest of their lives.

During the interview Dževad described what it means to live in a war situation. In the letters he receives, people express their despair and absence of hope. No one says that it is getting any better. Even if there were peace, there would be no life. Dževad mentioned that when the war began no one was brave enough to leave their home. Yet, as the war continued, people began to accept their fate, and got on with their lives. The only thing that people didn't like was the stillness, the quiet on the roads; because they had to listen to protect themselves against falling bombs.

During the interview Dževad used the term 'we' and 'us' to differentiate his identity from the Croats and Serbs. He was quite forceful and explicit in his insistence and use in referring to himself using the the Muslim group identity. The first time the word 'us' came up was when three ethnic groups were mentioned together. He then went on to make strong differentiations: 'When somebody says that the Muslims, Croats, Serbs are equally guilty, then I ask these people to look at the Serbian towns. Are they surrounded by military troops? Have *we* put our weapons on top of mountains? Do *we* shoot down on Serbian children and Serbian towns? ... The UN made a mistake because they have not given *us* weapons. *We* don't need other soldiers. Nobody should die for Bosnia. They should give the weapons to *us* and let *us* compare ourselves to those who have attacked us. *We* haven't been prepared for the war. *We* haven't planned it. ... *We* have been forced into the war. But now *we* have to do that.' Dževad clearly sees himself belonging to a collective group. He believes that it is the politicians who are the guilty ones for not taking responsibility.

For Dževad, the boys in the report were Muslims. Mihad, the leader of the boys, is a Muslim name.[6] He thought that there might well be Croatian boys there as well. About the school he said: 'Probably the school still has some meaning because it reminds the children of "normal life" and so the children try to maintain it.'

The second report was perceived by Dževad as being very positive. It showed how people were forced to do something that was not of their own choosing, i.e., they had to move into a house from which they knew that someone had been displaced. This report showed the fate of other Bosnians, no matter whether they were Muslim, Croat, or Serb. The report confirmed for Dževad that people were not responsible, nor guilty for such displacements. There were many families in similar situations. The greatest problem for Dževad was, where should they go back to? Over a million people have been driven out of their homes. Who would ever invest money, he asked, or live in the ruins of these destroyed houses? The saddest thing for him was the plight of those who have remained throughout the duration of the war. They will want to move when it is over because there is no life there, only hatred.

When asked about his comments concerning the two mothers, Dževad thought that nobody would talk about hatred in front of the camera; they were probably honest, but in the back of their minds there will always be ethnic division. Dževad related this to his own family; he knows how they think. 'Of course, everyone is for their own nationality.' According to Dževad, there are no Bosnians living in a foreign country who are not financially supporting their families, their relatives, or the Bosnian army. Dževad even supplied the specific amounts, either 500, 600, or 1000 DM. 'Everyone tries to give as much as they can.' It was clear from our conversation that Dževad felt guilty about living in such a privileged position compared to his fellow Bosnians.

Marko's Background
Marko has been living in Austria for three years. He is a student from Croatia but identifies himself as an Istrian. He refuses to accept 'ethnic classifications' and until three years ago never differentiated between the three ethnic nationalities. He knew he was from Yugoslavia, Croatia. When he had to report to the recruiting officer for his mandatory enlistment in the army he had to state his citizenship and nationality, to which he answered Yugoslav on both counts. He doesn't identify with Croatians and has many friends from Bosnia, Croatia and Serbia. Marko says: 'Four of us are sitting in a restaurant here in Klagenfurt. One of us comes from Bosnia, his mother is Serb and his father is Croat. Another is from Croatia. His mother is Croatian and his father is a Serb. And all four of us are sitting together drinking beer. Wonderful, isn't it? But it could just as easily happen that each of us is on different sides of the front line shooting at the other. I think this says it all.'

The report on the children left Marko 'without words'. He never would have believed that there could be something like a children's police. 'They don't look like "children",' he remarked. The knife reminded him of the knife he had in the army. The children have learned how to fight and hit one another. It was both unbelievable and 'understandable', given the context of the children's everyday lives. Marko was never called a Croatian as a child in Yugoslavia, but now the first thing these children have to learn is 'I am "whatever"'. Although terrible, it was once again 'understandable' that such an environment could produce hatred in these children. Marko, during his time in the army, took part in the war for only ten days and was stationed on the Slovenian–Austrian border where the war had begun. 'Even within the space of those ten days, it was enough to send you crazy.' Marko related this experience to that of the children who had been living with this situation for over three years. 'How will these children, once they survive the war, be "normal" or "human" people?' he asked. Marko believed that they were likely to become 'war-machines'. Having lost their families, their own sense of humanity has been drained away.

For Marko there were elements reminiscent of a 'Hollywood style' in this report. 'When the reporter talks about the knife, you see the close-up of the knife, and then when he talks about the pistol, all of a sudden the pistol comes into the picture.'

Marko felt the report about the families was 'wonderful' and 'super' for two reasons. First, it showed the paradoxes of the war: where Croatians lived before there were now Muslims and vice versa. Secondly, it showed the 'normal' people did not want either the war or the differences imposed through ethnicity. They didn't care if they were Croats or Muslims. They just wanted peace and usually the media didn't convey that. Marko made a differentiation between war reporting which was and which was not 'human'; this report was 'human'. He found the reaction of the women 'wonderful'. In spite of losing everything there was no hatred only hope. For Marko, these women represented the 'continuity' of humanity in spite of war.

Although Marko does not watch television but skips through newspapers, he stresses that he understands the situation. As he said, 'It may be arrogant, but these reports may be for those who do not know the situation.' Marko has visited refugees in camps and hence feels well informed. He believes that the main function of the media in Croatia is to feed the people with news every two weeks so that they can hope that something will change. When nothing happens, then these media broadcasts are repeated again. Consequently, Croatians are becoming totally dependent on and fixated by the news. They either watch the news or the soap opera *Santa Barbara*. The war in Croatia for Marko has been a 'perfect media war'.

Summary Statement and Commentary
The two interviewees offer a marked contrast in their ideas about self-identity, confirming some of our opening remarks about identity formation during the Balkan crisis. Dževad obviously relates to the Muslim plight sometimes in strongly religious and sometimes in 'national' terms, while Marko refuses to be ethnically defined. Another marked contrast is their reactions to the reports: Dževad reacted emotionally: he is impassioned about the war, he feels guilty about not doing enough to help. Marko, on the other hand, is a self-proclaimed pacifist, who distances himself from the conflict by intellectualising the ways in which the media is structuring the situation. He also recognises the former socialist ideal of Yugoslavia. He too is impassioned but on the grounds of an all-encompassing sense of 'humanity'. He has no 'guilt' feelings about not participating in a conflict which destroys a people's sense of 'decency' and 'goodness'. His pacifism provides a base for his physical non-involvement. Both participants found the children's situation terrible, but 'understandable' given the context of war. However, there is a differentiation of approach in the second report. Dževad did not believe that humanitarian empathy between the mothers was not truly possible, and that ethnic hatred still remains a powerful force 'in the back of their minds'. Marko felt just the opposite; the women represented a ray of hope for the survival of 'humanity'.

The Reactions of the Austrians
Christof

Christof is 54 years old and is an accountant. He was obviously touched by the two reports as spontaneous responses were often distinctly heard throughout the viewing. He had never seen either of the reports before. In general, he doesn't watch much television at all, and commented that there had been so much news reporting of the war that he felt over-saturated by it. He has arrived at a point where he simply ignores most of it; it has become so much background noise. 'It's tragic, on the one hand,' he says, 'because it's so close. It wouldn't be so tragic if it was far away.'

Christof could readily understand the first report and that under the given circumstances, war would be acted out by these children: from mimicking war to war becoming a reality for them is how he described the sequence. He understood their play as a form of 'revenge'. In relating the report to his own experiences, Christof recalled that he himself used make-believe weapons as a child from sticks and other bits of wood. The difference here was that these children had 'real weapons'. He questions the judgment of the adults (soldiers) who have given such weapons to children. He believed such a report was good for children in Austria, so that they could see what the situation was for children in Sarajevo. The usual 'horror' pictures of the war were no longer causing any reaction, but seeing children arm themselves was much more likely to affect viewers.

In the second report Christof saw both families as victims. He articulated his confusion concerning the reasons why private houses have been destroyed. Indeed most of his conversation centred around the loss of the house. He commented on the son who was 'looking through binoculars at the house where he's supposed to live', and talked incessantly about the impossibility of rebuilding anything: 'The country is so poor. How will they make it? I don't think they will be able to manage! Everything is destroyed. Even if they want to rebuild this by themselves, they have nothing to build with. To build a house costs money. They are left with nothing. Where should they even start? Many men have been killed, and you cannot expect the women to rebuild the houses.' He saw hope for these two families because of the attitude of the women. It might be possible for these two families to live together, but he didn't see any hope for the country.

Anna

Anna is 23 years old and an administrative secretary. She does not follow the Bosnian conflict anymore, as she did in the beginning. She is still shocked and sympathises with the people, but it is a situation that she has become used to. As she says, 'There are the appeals but when you hear that only 50 per cent of the goods arrive at their destinations, you ask yourself why should you support it at all. Maybe it is an alibi to yourself. The conflict is close, but so far away. There is no danger that you could be affected yourself.' For Anna, these reports are interesting in an interview situation because they force her to concentrate on them; at home she has to deal with her own problems, and it is impossible to deal with the crisis all of the time; it would be too burdening. On the Saturday before the interview, Anna mentions that there was a Sarajevo demonstration which prompted her to make a decision: either take part in it or enjoy the weekend. She chose the weekend.

She was shocked by the child-police report. She had heard about individual children imitating soldiers, but had never expected to see them organised into group formations. The serious faces of the children showed no laughter; they were as

49

disciplined as seasoned troops. The shock was all the greater because at the beginning of the report the journalist appeared to support what the children were doing, and she was dismayed by seeing how racism and prejudice develop in children, and that they were somehow already 'inside' the child, and difficult to get rid of. The children had already learned to think in terms of an 'enemy' and could 'kill' because the 'other' had a different name.

In general, Anna believed that boys like to play with weapons to make them feel stronger, and therefore that part of it was a game and part of it was serious: 'They are taking their roles seriously. They really think that they can help defend their city.'

For Anna the second report explores the question of personal fate. It offers more of a feminist position because in this case mothers were interviewed. She saw it as positive because it gave viewers the idea that in the future people could live together peacefully, and showed that, despite what had been destroyed, there was hope and mutual understanding. Nationalism counted for little under such circumstances.

Birgit

Birgit is a 27-year-old woman graduate currently out of work. In the early stages of the war she had been interested in the reports about the Balkan situation but when she returned from a year's study abroad, the situation no longer moved her. She feels inured to the televised scenes of the dying: 'Whether 3 or 300, what's the difference?' she says. 'A time comes when you cut the war out of your life because it has reached saturation-point.' However, she thinks that these human-interest reports could still have some effect on viewers, despite the fact that the war remains confusing.

The child-police report was a terrifying experience for her because of the way adults were mis-using the children. It immediately reminded her of the Hitler Youth; perhaps it was not so well organised but the children had more tasks to do because of the specific war situation. Birgit understood how this situation could occur when children have nothing to do, and that the formation of 'bands' was natural enough, as she knew from her own experience. The use of 'real' knives was what she found most disturbing. In her view this report could touch viewers because it was so different from the regular reportage of war horrors.

In the second report, Birgit connected the stories of the mothers with a general sense of humanity and a level of emotionality which was in direct opposition to politics. The empathy of the women contrasted starkly with the silence of 'stubborn' politicians, with the implication that men could settle their affairs neither willingly nor peacefully. The parallel situations of the two mothers far outweighed the differences of religion and nationality. Both had seen war in all its cruelty. Birgit was convinced that these two mothers could live together peacefully in the same house. Birgit was further convinced that women could find a way towards peace from the crisis of war.

Hans

Hans is 38 years old and a video producer. He watches all the news about Bosnia and utilises both a conspiracy theory and a media theory to help him explain the inadequacy of the current media coverage of the war. In his view the media should provide pictures of the Bosnian conflict showing all the suffering, pain and terror, in order to keep people watching. As Hans notes, only he and his father continue to watch the news; the women have stopped. Hans wants to force people back to their TVs to take notice of the war again. His position is well intentioned but voyeuristic:

'You really have to show the worst. That's what affects people.' Because he sees the media as very powerful, he believes it can influence people so strongly that their outrage can force politicians to do something. His media theory is therefore underpinned by an ethical dimension as well as by a conspiracy theory. It is his belief that someone in the ORF has reduced the amount of time given to these reports and that this was negotiated with the Germans.

Hans was not touched at all by the first report which he thought contrived and posed. He believed the boys acted and reacted in front of the camera according to requests made to them by the crew. He also felt that the reality of the situation was probably 'worse' than had been presented and that children were being used for all sorts of other atrocities, something actually played down in their report. For him it was not graphic enough; it did not show enough of the real atrocities perpetrated against children. Hans is convinced that children are also collecting 'dead bodies' and referred to the Third Reich where children had been used for 'everything'. He found it tragic to see children being socialised for hatred. According to Hans, even the woman interviewed was playing the situation down. The report should have shown more of the 'real' suffering, with bombs exploding, injured people, children running for help after an explosion. If he were the cameraperson, he would film the 'real' suffering – the raped women and the dead bodies – to get across the fact that 'this is really awful', that these are 'pigs' committing such atrocities. In his view situations like this one are known about anyway. Boys like to play at war and in a situation like Sarajevo they have the real life opportunity to do so. Unfortunately, Hans says, 'when you give a real pistol to a boy, he is very happy.'

The second report Hans saw as much better; it exposed 'real' suffering; there was the sound of gunfire and the visible destruction wrought on the houses. He focused particularly on the role of the house: 'If you can imagine that you have moved out of a house, and then see it on television, with no windows, and it doesn't belong to you anymore. This would be something that would affect the viewers.' Hans mentioned a Bosnian worker, now living in Carinthia, Austria, who began to cry while showing him photos of his wonderful house which had been destroyed. Hans said he himself would probably go crazy if something like that were to happen to him. He doesn't understand why they (those in the report) are so calm. 'Are they so dulled by the situation that they don't care any more?' he wondered.

Hans felt that one serious problem with the report was that it positioned the Muslims on an equal footing with the Serbs, the aggressors. Viewers could get the impression that Muslims were no better than the Serbs; that they are displacing Croats and moving into their houses. This report didn't show that the Serbs were the principal guilty party. He even saw the report as being potentially propaganda material for the Serbs to show that Muslims are committing the same atrocities. He suggests that the report should have included a graphic, or a text, that clarified the Muslim position. He was fascinated by the statement that Muslims were willing to give back their houses, because it seemed such a contradiction. Perhaps one out of ten would make such a gesture.

Elizabeth

Elizabeth is 75 years old, a serious consumer of television, and particularly of information programmes. She calls herself a news freak but she had not seen these two reports. When asked about her age, she said 'Maybe you shouldn't write that down because it may not seem credible.' Elizabeth is proud of her intellectual ability and proud that she has a rich cultural background. She highlights her personal relationship to former Yugoslavia. Everything she relates in this respect has a disturbing whiff of colonialism about it. The country was loved for its hospitality. She mentioned her delight and joy when meeting people who were happy to greet Austrians and remember 'the great Austrian empire'. She refers to touching experiences with simple, naive common people. She has a dear friend in Sarajevo, whose ethnic nationality is unknown to her since it was never an issue. She has no knowledge of what has happened to him. Elizabeth cannot comprehend the current cruelty. The subtext of her conversation suggests that if the Austrian empire were still intact, such atrocities wouldn't happen. She sees no solution for the situation. The only possible outcome, cruel as it sounds, is that they should fight among themselves until one national ethnicity wins.

Elizabeth referred to the first report generally as the 'child problem'. Not once did she point out or mention the fate of a specific child, in marked contrast to her talk about her concern for her own grandchildren, who she hopes will enjoy a full life. For Elizabeth it is an 'us' and 'them' situation. She claims that the difference in religion is a 'natural border' between ethnicities, making life together impossible there. The hatred has been internalised, whereas before inter-ethnic marriages and friendships were possible. She did not find this a useful report; it did not serve peace. She supported this by saying that there are often reports that show children who have been mutilated and wounded. Seeing children using knives and weapons just increases hatred. Children should be protected from such situations. The children are therefore the victims in this case. She saw an association with National Socialism; the situation repeats the phenomenon of the Hitler Youth, but is even more tragic. Her references to Nazism came rather late in the conversation, almost as if she had to build up to it. Elizabeth spoke about news reports that made her feel sorry and tearful. But her emotionality seemed connected to a nostalgia for what 'belonged' to Austria before; such a tragic ending was inevitable after the break-up of the empire.

Elizabeth liked the report on the two families, but could not believe in what the women were saying. She believed that they could never be so generous. It is 'human nature' to put your own family first. The 'man' who was looking through the binoculars at 'his' house reminded her of a situation that took place when the border was put up between Austria and Czechoslovakia and people became separated from their homes because of it. Ultimately, she believes that people cannot live together in Bosnia anymore.

Summary Statement

Our summary is tentative and should be read with the usual precautions that any ethnographic enquiry requires. In general, our interview reflected a widely felt mood in Austria that the Balkan conflict is no longer of primary viewing interest. In 1994, news concerning the European Union and the World Cup dominated, and the issue was placed firmly in the background.

At the start of the Balkan conflict, a great deal of publicity was generated by the Austrian 'Nachbar in Not' initiative, and it was widely believed that help could and should be given. However, as the war progressed, and no easy and obvious solution emerged, Austrians lost interest. Although 'Nachbar in Not' is still in operation, it has proved difficult to maintain the initial high level of concern. Life has returned to 'normal'. The Adriatic seacoast of former Yugoslavia has always been perceived as a 'summer playground' for Austrian tourists, a tradition inherited from the days of the Austrian empire. After the disruption caused by the war, tourism has returned to

Slovenia and parts of Croatia. While the conflict is geographically close, after three years many Austrians no longer think they will be affected. They do not expect further escalation. Although there has been a flood of refugees into the country, this 'flood' has been contained by changes in the law, making it more difficult for foreigners to remain for any length of time in the country. We see the loss of the ability to 'mourn' for the pain and suffering of others as the real tragedy in this situation. Although we do not agree with the means Hans suggests to revive the concern, we share his ethical concern, also addressed by Klaus Hipfl, who offers a solution in direct contrast to Hans's own. Many of our participants agreed that the extraordinariness of the 'ordinary' situations he presents might still prove effective in keeping the sense of 'mourning' alive.

The interviews generally showed an absence of the thematisation of identity. Only Dževad and Hans, when ethnic nationality was mentioned, pointed to the Serbs as the 'true' aggressors in the conflict. This desire to identify who is to blame, simplifying the complexity of the conflict, is in direct opposition to Klaus's intention in these reports. Only Hans insisted on the need to identify an aggressor, in order to mobilise the audience against a named aggressor. In this way, he believed, the current Austrian complacency could be undermined. Unfortunately, this solution is too simple even though in general Austrians perceive the nationalist Serbs as the definitive aggressors and are sympathetic to Muslim and Croatian interests.

In relation to the first report all the Austrian participants believed that all boys liked to play with weapons. Overstepping this 'natural' play happens when 'real' weapons are substituted for fake ones, and when children are 'used' to promote hatred. The need to protect children's innocence was agreed upon by all participants. Children especially represent the future hope and development of the country. Without the potential for renewal, an end to the war seems inconceivable, as the situations in Ireland and Israel have testified. All participants, therefore, were strongly affected by the story but in different ways. Hans even felt that the story was not explicit enough in showing how children are being exploited. He, Birgit and Elizabeth all referred to National Socialism and the Hitler Youth as a reference to what was seen.

The division by gender of interpretations in the second report was almost a matter of cliché. The male participants placed more value on property rights and the destruction of the land than did the women. Elizabeth was the exception, perhaps because her age and her conservativism places her within patriarchal ideology. She, along with Christof, noted the 'man' watching 'his' house through binoculars; a strong implication of the centrality of male ownership of property that is consistent with her patriarchal worldview. The other women placed more emphasis on the relationship between the mothers' belief that they offered a way forward to peaceful cohabitation. Here we have a separation between ideas of property and a sense of home. The former is coded as masculine and 'outside', a reiteration of the need to own specific territory within predetermined borders. The latter is coded as feminine, as 'inside', where children, the family and the hearth take significatory precedence. While Birgit, Marko and Anna saw this as a sign of hope, both Dževad and Elizabeth could not quite credit the women's account.

Conclusion

The situation of media reception is as complex as the Bosnian conflict itself. Our close reading of Klaus Hipfl's two reports shows that his desire to present the human face of the Bosnian conflict also contains contradictory elements. A reading such as

Hans's clearly shows that the human face of the war is exactly what should not be shown; rather, he suggests, the viewers should be presented with more cruelty. It is time to rekindle their anger, not their compassion. For others, especially Marko, Anna and Birgit, Klaus's humanist and rationalist intentionality is precisely what they do want to see – the possibility that a peaceful settlement can be reached and that 'goodness' prevails. For Dževad, ethnic identification is so strong that the reports provide an acknowledgment of the absurdity and pain of war, but ultimately the ethnic hatred has been internalised too deeply to make a difference.

On a personal note, the brother-and-sister relationship in this account has been particularly interesting. Klaus's entire family has watched his reports with the utmost interest, sometimes praising his insights, at other times disagreeing with his presentation. Nevertheless, there has always been a close involvement with and support for his work. The analysis of the reports was undertaken by the third member of the research team to help facilitate a more balanced view. For Brigitte Hipfl, her involvement with her brother's work once again reflects the contradictions and complexities of the Bosnian situation. Both have an impassioned interest for understanding other cultures; both have participated in aid initiatives to Romania, yet both have different sensibilities to the Balkan crisis. Brigitte feels that she could never work as an ORF reporter in the Bosnian crisis. She would too easily be caught up in the emotionality of the stories, unable to provide a 'fair' or 'balanced' perspective. In contrast, Klaus feels that he must be directly involved with the people in order to provide the kind of coverage that would enable his viewers to care. This mutual project has been an attempt to talk and explore with each other these concerns, mediated through a third party.

Notes

1. Background information supplied by Klaus Hipfl.
2. The woman was a teacher from the school, although this information is not given to the viewers. Apparently she had voiced her dissatisfaction with the biased reporting that was going on, and consequently was included in the narrative to give her side of the story. Later, in a chance meeting with the crew in the city, she mentioned that she had seen the report on a local television show which broadcast foreign news and expressed her satisfaction with the report (personal communication with Klaus Hipfl).
3. Information about the fathers was supplied to us later. The Croatian father was in a Croatian enclave in Muslim-occupied territory 'nearby', while the father of the Muslim family is simply 'missing'. It may be that he was killed in action, arrested or has simply deserted (either his family or the Bosnian army).
4. Paraphrased from Renata Salecl (1993), pp. 9–10.
5. Throughout, names have been changed and identifying details avoided.
6. Throughout our report the term 'Muslim' has been used specifically in keeping with the term that is most often identified in news reports themselves. Dževad did not once mention the term 'Islam' but he did refer to himself as a Muslim. Any associations with Islamic fundamentalism were certainly not talked about.

References

Kristeva, Julia (1976) 'Signifying Practice and the Mode of Production', *Edinburgh Review*, no. 1.
Nichols, Bill (1991) *Representing Reality*, Bloomington and Indiana: Indiana University Press.
Renov, Michael (1993) 'Introduction: The Truth about Non-Fiction', in Michael Renov (ed.) *Theorizing Documentary*, New York and London: Routledge, pp. 1–12.
Salecl, Renata (1993) 'Phantasmen des Krieges: Patriarchat und Mutterland – Heimat und Rassismus', *Lettre International*, no. 21, pp. 8–11.

Fifteen Days of Live Broadcasting from Sarajevo

ANTONIA TORCHI

This paper takes the form of a case study: fifteen days of live coverage from Sarajevo under siege (January–February 1994) by Italia 1, one of the Berlusconi-owned channels in Italy. The main areas which it brings into focus are:

– conflict, war reporting and news management;
– conceptualising and representing identities, particularly from a 'marginal' perspective.

A third possible area – implied in the comprehensive discourse, but only partially tackled – concerns the search for a different model of war broadcasting by a commercial television network.

The methodology adopted consisted mostly of content and textual analyses of video-recorded programmes and of interviews with participants (the journalists Sabina Fedeli, Tony Capuozzo and Mimmo Lombezzi, and the Head of Italia's News and Current Affairs Department, Paolo Liguori). Interviews were also conducted with a panel of Italia 1 viewers in Milan (March 1994).

The 'War against Silence' Campaign

In January–February 1994 Paolo Liguori, head of the News and Current Affairs Department in the commercial TV network Italia 1 (Fininvest group), led a provocative campaign, called 'Guerra al silenzio' – a war against the silence which he considered surrounded the war in Bosnia, in which the main television studio was moved from Milan to Sarajevo for fifteen days. He went there with three journalists (two men, one woman) and a crew of three (two Slav-Italians, one originally from Serbia) who work mainly for Tele-Koper and sometimes for Fininvest. The technical staff were recruited from among the technicians employed by Sarajevo Television. The studio from which the Italian news bulletin was broadcast was located in the local television building, in a part of the city where the media are concentrated and where the effects of the war are very apparent. The sense of precariousness and desolation struck the Italian viewers' imagination from the very first bulletin and the setting gave them a sense of participation not usually experienced in external war reporting. This sense of participation was increased by the fact that all news items, even those about Italian events, radiated from the Sarajevo studio.

55

Studio Aperto (Open Studio)

The news bulletin on Italia 1 is *Studio Aperto* (Open Studio). It seeks to be a space open to the world and to citizens' demands; a controversial space, which as the most recent of the national news bulletins, is still in search of an identity as part of a commercial, youth-oriented channel. It regularly takes up a strong stance with regard to contemporary issues and frequently wages awareness campaigns. The Sarajevo campaign was intended as a criticism of the Italian government and its Foreign Office, and in particular former Foreign Minister Andreatta, for their lack of concern towards the Bosnian slaughter. The same charge was made against the EC and NATO, whose lack of concern was seen as even more dangerous, linked as it was with an arms embargo that disadvantages the Muslims more than it does the Serbs.

The defence of the Muslims' rights is common to all Italian television channels. It is an attitude which has neither historic nor religious roots (Guidi 1993: 13) but which can perhaps be attributed to political reasons, in terms of Italy's concern for the Mediterranean region in general, and in recent economic interests in Bosnia-Hercegovina just before the civil war. However, this attitude above all reflects wider public opinion, in its strongly humanitarian concern for the weakest group, the losers and the persecuted.

Sarajevo as a Distorting Mirror

If, as just mentioned, news from Bosnia mostly assumes the Muslim point of view, the decision to broadcast from Sarajevo was intended in some ways to represent a partial break with this dominant trend. Thus, one reporter went to interview the Serb sharp-shooters in the mountains surrounding the city, just before the marketplace massacre. This was not, however, a welcome move: there was a strong reaction in favour of a more tentative approach to such less mainstream viewpoints, and the most successful coverage, therefore, concerned the multi-ethnic nature of the city. But this view of Sarajevo, as a 'multi-ethnic crossroads', hardly emerges in the broadcasts. The recurrent image is rather that of a 'bridge between Europe and the Middle East (Islam)'. If a bridge links, it also signals the gap between its two ends: here 'we' are; there are the 'others'. And thus the bridge metaphor can easily degenerate into the image of 'the last European outpost', as shown in a programme about the 1984 Olympic Games, where the opposition between 1984 (the happy past) and 1994 (the unhappy present) portrays the loss of the 'European dimension' as if it were the worst of fates.

An affluent society then, a miserable society now: the European dimension seems to coincide with the commercial ideal. The clichés, models and values expressed here are in the same abstract logic of the imagined community and solidarity of supranational identification (Robins 1992: 11; Robins and Torchi 1993: 159). An example of this vision in the *Open Studio* campaign was the portrayal of war corruption; denunciatory camera shots of the trade in drugs and the illegal selling of goods sent through humanitarian aid seem bland when seen in the light of the complex composite society of present-day Sarajevo where a barter economy has evolved of necessity. One of the last visual impressions from Sarajevo – at the end of the fifteen days – showed the latest-model BMW, standing out white and spotless against the ruins. The car acts as an abstract sign of both global consumption and global corruption, marking the contrast between surplus and poverty in a Europe without frontiers and without identities.

Good Neighbours

It must be noted, however, that to describe a mosaic-like city as Sarajevo requires knowledge and experience that only a long-term presence could give. War reporters are used to travelling around the world like postal parcels and generally the sensationalism and shock value of their reports are substitutes for serious research. In the 'War against Silence' the participating journalists tried to portray the fragmented reality, adopting either a sentimental approach or the standpoint of the 'good neighbour' (see below): both approaches made an impression on Italian audiences but met with resistance from Sarajevo viewers. It switched between 'war reporting' and 'Televisione di servizio' (a sort of public-access television hosted by a famous TV personality; between a 'pornography of the dying' (quoted in Robins 1994: 10) and the Good Samaritan.

The sentimental approach was adopted when sketching the multi-ethnic character of Sarajevo, using the daily dramas of a broken civilisation: latterday Romeos and Juliets from different ethnic backgrounds; the story of three old friends, one Croatian, one Serb, one Muslim, killed together in the defence of their city and buried side by side, a symbol for their fellow-citizens; children's hospitals, where young patients, with eyes beyond their years, tell their war experiences while sharing beds with erstwhile 'enemies'.

As these small daily stories are privileged, and broadcast at the same time in both Italy and Sarajevo, a kind of dialogue begins to develop, between interviewers and interviewees, guests and hosts, between 'good neighbours'. The Italian TV team enjoys the concert of a family of musicians and shares a humble meal with them; a journalist interviews a young sportsman who, because of the bombs outside, is training himself for the next Olympic Games inside his own flat; another journalist talks with people leaning out of windows while their children play in the snow. There is a mutual exchange of favours: if one Sunday the Italians visit the musicians and are entertained in their home, the next Sunday they will, for example, invite a few citizens to their temporary studio, where by satellite they can finally see and talk to their sons and daughters – refugees in Florence for two years. A further gesture is the welcome given to Italia 1 by the city authorities in front of the studio cameras on the first day of broadcasting, and later an interview with the president of the Bosnian Republic.

A Difficult Dialogue

The difficulties met when confronting the 'other' are particularly acute in the case of a national-populist commercial television channel which, by its nature, aims at flattening and homogenising experiences and lifestyles, particularly those that diverge from the 'norm'. The confrontation between two distant realities (even if not in geographic terms) shows the limits of commercial broadcasting. These limits have been inherited from public television, whose portrayal of society represented (and still in many ways continues to represent) a national compromise. At its inception, Italian State Television (RAI) ironed out regional differences and dialects to present a unified vision of the nation in which republicanism, concern for the family, the Catholic faith and the Roman accent were dominant. All other regional accents were mainly confined to fictional or comic characters. The situation has obviously changed between the 60s and 90s, but RAI's national-populist ideology has been partly followed by the more recent commercial television stations whose principal aim is achieving the highest audience ratings.

The interview with the Bosnian president is a salient example of this tendency in which what was already a difficult dialogue increasingly became two monologues divided by nationality. Immediately before the interview, Paolo Liguori had been concentrating on the recent killing of three RAI journalists in Mostar and was discussing the issue extensively with colleagues in Milan and Trieste (where the three journalists came from). As a result, he kept the Bosnian president waiting, and when, finally, he turned to him, his first, somewhat abrupt, question was to ask the president's opinion on the international community's attitude towards the Bosnian tragedy. The president's answer was a lesson in politeness but, for this reason, was another monologue: he first offered his condolences to the families of the murdered journalists and then went on to connect these particular deaths with that of the many journalists killed in the war and finally with the terrible slaughter in Bosnia in general. It was a straightforward answer, gently expressed, that at the same time drew attention to the Italian's ethnocentric viewpoint.

The difficulty of the interview, the absence of true dialogue, reflects two different ideas about democracy. For the Italian television team this connotes a frank and clear approach to 'inconvenient' topics on the small screen. This is rank-and-file democracy, as seen, for example, in the strong criticism of the Italian foreign minister including an attempt to contact him by telephone on-air. The Bosnian idea of democracy appeared to be much more respectful of hierarchy and formal priorities. For the Bosnians, perhaps because democracy is a recent habit, it still needs clear formal rules; it takes care of 'appearances' (dress, gestures, exchange of courtesies, politeness) in a way that might appear a bit out of fashion, at least from the perspective of an Italian audience used by now to interviews where bad manners and name-calling dominate.

The Resistance of the Normal

The camera frequently displays resistance through normality. This offers an audio-visual truth that is impossible to ignore. The female journalist in the team, Sabina Fedeli, whose reports mainly considered the micro-phenomena of a society changing because of the war, saw 'resistance of the normal' as the most appropriate description of the city's atmosphere; she was moved by the mix of bravery, recklessness, ordinary behaviour and craving for normality expressed by Sarajevo's citizens. She thought that this could be used as the key to a better understanding of the Bosnian tragedy by her Italian audience; it seems to have worked. Her reports avoided the rhetorical and pitiless images that have become quite common in other war reporters' work; moreover, they dealt with the 'marginal' stories, with those aspects that are easily labelled 'trifling'. For instance, she describes the fashions that Sarajevo's women have been inventing under war conditions: scarecrow hairdos and imaginative use of recycled clothing. She also noted the changes that women's bodies have undergone in the course of the war: their increasingly voluminous dresses, worn to disguise weight loss, were far more eloquent of food shortages than many other descriptions.

A Sympathetic Eye, a Respectful Ear

Another of the team's decisions, this time also practised by other Italian reporters, was to avoid direct presentation of the horrors of the war and siege. Instead, these were conveyed through witnesses' recollections; people's despairing eyes and frightening words gave a new dignity to the small screen. Perhaps television is really more of an audio than a visual medium, because of the way it is used by the audience or because of its physical limitations (see Robins 1994: 12, quoting Regis Dubray, who contends that its miniaturisation works against the power of the images).

It seems that a better knowledge of the undifferentiated reality flowing on the television screen, and a rescue of 'the idea' from the indifferent 'image-idea' (Robins, 1994: ibid.) – in this case dealing with war and slaughter – can be achieved by professionals with a sympathetic eye and a respectful ear. For example, in the *Open Studio* case there was the decision not to give on-the-spot coverage to the market place mortar attack (even though the crew had taken lots of pictures) but to describe its aftermath through survivors' statements; there were, too, the touching interviews with children who have been daily facing death and who were asked to describe their fears (of which the most common was death by starvation).

The power of the use of personal witness is in part due, in this live situation, to the fact that the use of dubbing and subtitling was not an option and testimonials therefore kept their original audio-visual strength. This was a new experience for an Italian audience used to an excessive use of dubbing and voice-over which, in many cases, distorts the primary meaning of interviews and reports. The *Open Studio* experience therefore represented an insight into a world previously remote in terms of real knowledge of its political and social problems. It has shown that it is possible to recognise, if not to know, 'others', to respect them, their language, their habits, their hopes, their fears and their feelings.

References

Guidi, M. (1993) *La sconfitta dei media*, Bologna: Baskerville.
Robins, K. (1992) *Unimaginable Community: Tribal Culture and European Medea*, Newcastle: CURDS.
Robins, K. (1994) *Forces of Consumption: From the Symbolic to the Psychotic*, Newcastle: CURDS.
Robins, K., and Torchi, A. (eds) (1993) *Geographia dei media*. Bologna: Baskerville.

PART TWO
Political Influence

Television and National/Public Memory

SANDRA BAŠIĆ-HRVATIN

Just before the Second World War, a very popular scientific work *Karakterologija Jugoslovena* ('Characterology of the Yugoslavs') was published in Belgrade. In more than one thousand pages the author tried to define the national/ethnic/racial characteristics that made up the Yugoslav 'national entity'. In the chapter 'Political Spirit of the Yugoslavs' he considers the distinctive modes of political culture in each of the constitutive 'nations':

> In Serbia, all political development was aimed at allowing statesmen to dominate political life. A completely opposite process is discernable in those Yugoslav territories under Habsburg rule. There, under the restrictions created by the various provincial borders, governments and 'autonomous' regions, a particular kind of politics and politician emerged: the nationalist agitator, the leader, the teacher, the Moses who would lead his nation out of the slavery of disunity, the conspirator, the revolutionary and the assassin. In Serbia – even when there were nationalist tribunes or coups – politics meant primarily strengthening and enlarging the state; while in Austria it primarily meant the destruction of other states. ... The Croatian milieu seems especially to nurture the messiah, the prophet; Croatia's slogan, 'Only Salvation', reminds us of the spirit of Catholicism. It creates a psychosis of intolerance, the fierce morality of the sect, of the believer, the absolute devotion of the follower. ... Hatred of the opponents of one's idea proves one's love for that idea. The degree of hatred reveals the degree of one's love for one's nation, one's patriotism, of which the march and the demonstration are the highest expression. (Dvornikovic 1939: 890–91)

To prove the existence of the Yugoslavs (*People*-as-One) as a model of national entity, the author had to search for pure particularities (One-*Nation*-among-Others). Those particularities (different cultures, religions, languages, customs ...) are the real basis for identification with a nation – 'our Nation'. So, the whole construction of People-as-One missed the key referential point – national identification. To be a member of the Yugoslav national community was to be a member of the nation before anything else.

At the foundation of totalitarianism lies the representation of the People-as-One. In the so-called socialist world, there can be no other division than that between the people and its enemies: a division between inside and outside, no internal division ... the constitution of the People-as-One requires the incessant production of enemies. It is not only necessary to convert, at the level of phantasy, real adversaries of the regime or real opponents into the figures of the evil Other: it is also necessary to invent them. (Lefort, 1986: 297–8)

The whole national memory[1] and national identification in the socialist state was subordinated to public memory and identification with the non-nation state.[2] In post-socialist states that constitute themselves as nation-states, national identity becomes the strongest point of reference for personal identification. National identity becomes an open symbolic space which replaces the destroyed framework of social identification. This new framework helps to reorganise social life and simultaneously it functions as a substitution for an uncertain reality. Once lost, national identity becomes a starting point for the reconstruction of the outer world. To be able to understand a structural transformation in the public/national memory we must answer some basic questions: why is national identity *the* cause which makes the constitution of a social organisation as a *pure* symbolic community impossible? Why are nationalistic political projects based on ideological obsession such threats to nation and national security? And what kind of fantasy structure supports this identification?[3]

Media have played an important role in the process of reproduction and reinforcement of nationalist and ethnocentric discourse in former Yugoslavia. In considering the role of television in shaping a national/public memory, we find three important levels:

1. *Televisual perception of nation* plays an important role in everyday life as a model of individual 'understanding' of nation. National community recognises itself by the 'inscription' of nationalistic discourse in language. On the one hand, nationalistic discourse in media determines public speech (there is a list of linguistically competent institutions and personalities which are allowed to speak 'in the name of nation'); and on the other it 'deterritorialises' public memory through popular consciousness.

2. *Nationalisation of the public sphere* is a process of abolishing and overpowering the autonomy of the public and its subordination exclusively to a national dimension. Media systems are centralised. Information about important events is distributed according to the principle of political–national loyalty. Disloyal (members of other nations or political opponents) become *aneu logou*, like the slaves and foreigners in the polis democracy, losing their right to speak or to communicate. National television plays an important role in forming the field of public discussion in the definition of important themes, and providing interpretations in the frameworks and arguments for political debate.

The media play a decisive part in selecting what the public perceives as relevant because, by virtue of being the most effective modulator of public attention, they have the function of establishing and distributing what may well be called 'attention values' ... their ability to impose a topic on public attention is the result of an infinite number of repetitions, whose total effect is to consolidate communicative similarities and to iron out dissonances. (Zolo, 1992: 160)

3. Media are one of the factors that produce conflicts, because they publicly 'institutionalise' the principle of the *exclusion of the Other*. This media strategy is

based on the presentation of the Other as an aggregate of all kinds of internal/external oppositions. For the nationalistic discourse the Other is a referential point for the homogenisation of 'own nation'.

National Discourse and Everyday Life

In a nationalistic environment media function as a specific way of realising national fantasy, reshaping perception and understanding of everyday life. Salecl (1993: 148) writes: 'Nationalism is the ideological way in which individuals experience everyday problems, how they place blame on somebody else. It builds its power through the creation of specific fantasies about threats to the nation – it represents itself as protector of "what is in us more than ourselves", the protector of us, as a part of a nation.' In the case of new nation states on the territory of former Yugoslavia, ethnonationalism builds its ideological domination on the slogan 'one nation, one state, one religion' and on the popular perception of ethnic community based on 'common roots' and 'blood and soul' ideology. Accordingly, all ethnonational political projects demand that all members of a national entity 'live within the borders of a single state'.[4] At the heart of every ethnonationalistic discourse stands the belief in one's own nation as transcendental principle – nation set above individual, society, State – nation as 'God's mission on Earth' It evokes a pre-modern juncture between State and Church and sets out national exclusivism (exclusion of the Other) as a precondition for national unification.[5]

I noted earlier that the nation is symbolically inscribed into the discourse of everyday life. We can also distinguish between different types of subjects which speak in the name of nation.[6] A 'generalised discourse' is important in the crisis situation when the political discourse shifts from everyday issues of economic and political means and ends, towards a more general level concerned with norms and values. Because of its privileged position in relation to other discursive formations (insofar as 'generalised discourse' positions itself on the highest ethical principles) and because it speaks in the name of the institution (nation=state), any political action is justified to protect basic values. The subject of institutional discourse usurps the position of statement in the name of the *whole* nation.[7]

The problemisation of concrete state politics automatically becomes a problemisation of general/universal principles: Freedom (of the Nation), Independence (of the Nation) ... Institutional discourse defends its privileged position, presenting itself as a subject of national security: loyalty to the institution (nation=state) becomes proof of patriotism, national pride, honour ...

A process of 'refeudalisation' (Habermas 1991) takes place in the public sphere. The classical liberal distinction between state and society, which takes the preservation of the autonomy of a public sphere as a basic principle of any democratic society, is abolished. Instead of a 'reasoning public' we have a 'nationalistic public' and different types of 'moral majorities'. This political vacuum is filled with many different and at first sight mutually exclusive elements: liberalism (market economy and capitalism with a 'friendly face'), aristocratic elitism (e.g. the re-introduction of the old Croatian nobility in Croatia and an obsession with members of the Habsburg dynasty in popular magazines), provincialism and folk tradition, a return to old patriarchal values (families with a lot of children nurtured by devoted mothers), peasant society (with its strong moral order), xenophobia, anti-Semitism, and so on. Historically, populism has not emerged spontaneously during relatively 'normal' times but always developed as a response to concrete threats to existing communities, lifestyles or other established relations. In this dichotomy between traditional community and global society – populism defines itself as a protector of the 'warm and close' community opposed to a 'cold and distant society' (Luke 1991: 72). Populism is characterised by hostility to the status quo, anti-intellectualism, and a clear image of those who permanently threaten our values and our way of life. This ideological heterogeneity is represented politically in the populist movement of the right in Croatia and populist movement of the left in Serbia.

Who is the 'Other'?

> All images of the enemy are based on specific fantasies . . . all nationalism, national identification with the nation (our kind) is based on the fantasy of the enemy, an alien who has insinuated himself into our society and constantly threatens us with habits, discourse, and rituals that are not of 'our kind'. No matter what this other 'does', he threatens us with his existence. (Salecl 1992: 52)

The media produces two prevailing fantasies: a fantasy of 'our Nation' represented as idyllic *Volksgemeinschaft* (which preserves traditional family values, language, culture) and images of the Other which threaten that fantasy. Through television, this phantasmic image is transferred to the popular psyche, recast in the language of everyday life. In other words, in televisual narration, pictures of our world are disturbed by pictures about enemies.[8]

The question of national identity is related to the process of media typification of the Other. Analysis of Yugoslavian newspaper articles from before the Second World War about the stigmatisation of Jews shows that we have inherited a whole repertoire of stereotypes that have been simply transplanted to 'new' enemies. We could say that enemy images are projected from past to present memory using different narration styles. In the past, construction of the image of the enemy was based on two questions: 'How can we recognise an enemy (who is incorporated in our community and can deceive us)?' and 'How can we protect ourselves (or our Nation)?' Today, the media produce popular 'commercials' about enemies.

Zygmunt Bauman in his essay *Strangers: The Social Construction of Universality* shows how the Jews are Europe's prototypical strangers: 'In the context of nations and nationalism, they were the only reminder of the relativity of nationhood and of the other limits of nationalism. They were the very danger against which nations had to constitute themselves. They were the ultimate incongruity – a non-national nation' (Bauman 1988).

Paradoxically, while the enemy is constructed using the typical anti-Semitic portrait of the Jew, Serbs identify themselves with another part of the Jewish image – that of 'the suffering nation' – which belongs to Second World War memories. With this in mind, we can understand why Franjo Tudjman's attendance of the local opening night of Spielberg's *Schindler's List* was the top story that day for Croatian television.

National Memory

After a radical breakdown of the former social order, new nationalistic governments prioritise the (re)organisation of social biography as a model for harmonising personal biographies and memories. Experiences from the Second World War are transmitted through oral narration, stories and tales, popular songs and films, producing a complete symbolic structure based on images of 'great' events, suffering, martyrdom and love for the leader (father) and homeland (mother).[10] On a symbolic level this process is a violent preservation of the linear public memory for future generations. Oral narration is based on a kind of calendrical liturgy, through which the experiences of past events are repeatedly celebrated. Rituals try to visualise fundamental values important for the reproduction of symbolic community. Public memory started from the 'Great Revolution' (1941–5).

The new nation-states started with changes to the public memory (new flags, new national anthems, new uniforms, new street names, etc.) as a way of establishing a new model of representation (or symbolic exchange) between state and citizens. If the former regime marked public memory with 'civil' rituals connected with the Communist Party, new states positioned their collective memory into distant history (fourteenth-century Serbia and the Battle of Kosovo; a nine-century Croatia and the first Croatian king). In both cases public/national memory was colonised with stereotypical pictures produced by those in power.

Now we have a process of double cancellation of an imaginary historical continuity. Reconstructions, changes in symbolic meanings of actual events (even words), demands for repeated co-ordination between personal stories and new 'official' histories.[11]

Television Memory

Analysis of Croatian and Serbian television and their role in the shaping of national/public memory is very difficult because both start from a 'closed' symbolic way of presentation, comprehensible only to members of the community who share a common national 'background knowledge'. Ellis (1992: 5) comments on this theme: 'Broadcast TV is the private life of a nation-state, defining the intimate and inconsequential sense of everyday life, forgotten quickly and incomprehensible for anyone who is outside its scope.'

Television when state owned and state controlled has an exclusive monopoly on 'public speech' and in defining dominant speaking styles. At the same time, the media try to be a substitute for the missing dialogue between state public sphere and private lives dominated almost exclusively by 'linguistically competent' media agents.

The process of codification of the public/national memory passes through different conceptions (and internalisations) of nation:
– *the canonical nation*, represented through national culture. For new nation-states, culture is an important way to hold on to national feelings and to maintain national history. This continuity of history functions to legitimate present national life.
– *the ritual nation*, the production of styles used as a way to spectacularise politics.
– *the popular nation*, the way in which the canonical nation is inscribed into the discourse of everyday life and how national identity becomes a part of popular culture.

Television: Canonical Culture Versus Popular Culture

The director of Croatian Television (CTV) said in one interview that television represents 'the cathedral of the Croatian national spirit'. Celebrating the anniversary of broadcasting in Croatia, Croatian television broadcast a promotion in which it said that 'we are the people who professionally shape your boredom'. These two statements define the relationship between the canonical (first channel) and popular culture (second channel). Canonical culture refers to national identification; it represents those things which make this culture specific and different from others. On the other side popular culture functions as an element of a global, universal world – as a proof that 'our' culture is settled between others. Canonical culture is pedagogical – its aim is to remind the public every day that the nation is a form of plebiscite. Cultural populism is evident in the revival of undefined folk culture: music with extremely nationalistic lyrics or overexposed national sentiments, myths, old forgotten customs, publicity for religious practices, learning about places ... On Croatian television there is a whole list of programmes made for 'the life of the nation': *Good Morning Croatia, Croatia: Land and People, Greetings from the Homeland, Study Croatia, Croatian Language, Croatian Literature, Croatia in the World* ... On Serbian television the most popular programmes are quiz games whose subject is national history, and programmes featuring popular folk music.

Dominant ways in which the television constructs national/public memory in Croatia and Serbia are:

1. *The simplification of events*, by which all information about events relating to the 'Homeland War' are represented partially. The interpretative model is dominated by national interest.

2. *Documentaries which introduce 'new' social values*, of which the most typical are documentaries that portray 'ideal' families i.e. those with lots of children and which emphasise traditional Christian lifestyles and maintain old national customs. Also typical are documentaries about refugees, usually stories about home told by a mother surrounded by her small children or her older relatives. These stories have a particularly emotional influence on public memory: they are a constant reminder of 'What they have done to us'. On the level of symbolic reproduction of the Nation the expatriates (official politics make a distinction between refugees and expatriates) have lost their 'home-heart': 'We will always remember' or 'We would never forget'.

On Serbian television there are two kinds of stories: those which are related to the situation in occupied/liberated areas in Croatia (Krajina) and Bosnia–Hercegovina, where the dominant explanation of events is 'life is going on, we will survive in spite of sanctions', and those about 'historical friends of Serbia' (Greece, Russia). Such stories are usually narrated either through a discourse of everyday life (e.g. great achievements in industrial production), or:

3. *Stories related to our/their military forces*, in which guilt is placed on the other side and the enemy identified with evil.[12] For easier identification enemy images are always stereotyped in a binary opposition (the 'sacred/profane dichotomy'). What is evident also is the naming of the enemy: there are historical enemies, enemies 'reborn' from the Second World War (Chetniks, Ustasha), enemies of civilisation (barbarians), enemy as pure evil (outlaws, criminals, butchers, animals). Our own military forces on the other hand are represented aesthetically. It could be said that the processes of demonisation/aesthetisation in the war are important for two kinds of memories: those of things done to 'us' and a rather different recollection of those things (however similar) done by 'us' to 'others' (Judt, 1992: 89). In other words, there are no images of 'suffering' on the other side. It is always a case of *our* civilians and *their* soldiers. According to the 'instructions on reporting from the war zones' distributed by the CTV Board of Directors in 1991, 'pictures of blown-up, badly wounded or shot Croatian soldiers are not to be shown, nor should statements made by the wounded be broadcast'; similarly, 'crying and lamentations by the population are not to be aired'. The technical term 'ethnic cleansing' means thousands and thousands of refugees, dead civilians ... A phrase, 'we effectively neutralised the enemies military forces', is often used in TV reports about the military situation on the battlefield. Pictures of neutralisation include burnt-out houses and devastated

landscapes, which suggests the real meaning of the neutralisation of the enemy forces is something more – it is the neutralisation of the core of national identity of the 'other': its churches, its cultural and historical monuments, its cemeteries and so on.

4. *Linguistic purism*, which as a way of differentiation is important for national identity. If we speak the same or similar language it means that we share the same or similar community memories. Therefore to differentiate between us and them as two separate communities we have to differentiate our languages.

5. *Religious interpretation of national destiny and the role of religion in civil life*, both of which are often closely tied to populist national projects. There are particular kinds of story devoted to the religious 'life' of the nation, in which religion is the closest tie connecting our present life to that of past and as the strongest and the most intimate way in which we protect our national identity.

6. *Popularisation of national culture*: as we said before, canonical culture is in its essence pedagogical and comprehensible through different symbolic interpretations. To be able to understand national culture we need shared common memories, language and customs. On one side there is canonical culture as 'high' culture, important for the representation of the nation, and on the other, the popular national culture of everyday life, e.g. the inflation of popular songs that give moving accounts of history.

Conclusion

The media plays an important role in the processes of unification and homogenisation of personal memories with collective and national memories. Public memory is colonised with a national mythology, focused by images of the enemy and popular (populist) definitions of reality. Public memory is publicly lived through commemorations and rituals as a way of collective day-to-day legitimation. Television becomes the most important source for information and for cultural consumption. Public memory is assimilated with national memory, even when the methods of their formation and framing are different. It tries to preserve the system's legitimation, and is shared by all members of the political entity including citizens who are not members of the dominant nation. In the territory of public memory it is possible to negotiate between different options of politics. In the former Yugoslavia, with the exception of Serbia, public memory is permeated with anti-communism. The old communist rituals are replaced by new public rituals which are connected with the new ruling elites of the right. National memory has become *the* structural point which dominates perceptions of past, present and future. The exclusivisity of national memory means that if you are a member of our national community you can understand our past and you can sacrifice the present in the name of the national future.

Notes
1. I am making a distinction in this essay between two types of group memory from which individuals draw their identity. *National* memory is structured alongside what I call 'Grand History' – important events that shape the biography of the nation. *Public* memory, on the other hand, is a part of the political education imposed by ruling groups. In the case of Serbia and Croatia there is a fusion between national and public memory (see Connerton 1989: 21–3).
2. According to Smith (1990: 179) the concept of identity includes 'subjective feelings and

valuations of any population which possesses common experience and one or most shared cultural characteristic (usually customs, language or religion). These feelings and values refer to three components of their shared experience: 1. a sense of continuity between the experiences of succeeding generations of the unit population; 2. shared memories of specific events and personages which have been turning points of a collective history and 3. a sense of common destiny on the past of the collectivity sharing those experiences.'

3. Alain Grosrichard in his analysis of the Orient and despotism emphasised that the only way for understanding 'despotism as an incomprehensible (from the Western point of view) way of domination and subordination' is through a specific set of 'imaginary'. This self-image is created for the external world. The phantasmatic frame exists actually as an empty space which is alternately 'filled in' and 'emptied' with different interpretations and images.

'Imaginary' is the concept which enables us to reflect not just a reality of political relationships between a despot and the people but the concept of despotism as a phantasm. '... if the despotic East is the Other which we see, it is also the Other which looks at us [*qui nous regarde*] in all meanings of this word' (Grosrichard 1985: 30).

In our analysis we would like to compare two sets of images about nation: one which is made for internal use ('We-images') and is shared by members of the same national community, and another one – the set of images from outside – perceptions of our nation from the point of view of a stranger, an outsider. In the case of former Yugoslavia these two 'types' (which are mainly produced through the media) are used as an important interpretative matrix in understanding 'We-They' relations.

4. Serbia has based its political project of Greater Serbia on the demand that 'all Serbs must live (and want to live) in the same state'. This political project is very close to the *Nationalitätsprinzip* ('One Nation, one State') popular in German political thought of the 19th century. This demand is confirmed by the statement that 'Serbia is where Serbian graves are' which shifts the entire process of national identification to the symbolic level. It was because of this that Serbian authorities removed the bones of King Lazar (who died six hundred years ago) from Belgrade to Kosovo as a symbolic confirmation (with political implications) that Kosovo is and has always been the cradle of the Serbian nation. On the other side, the Croatian government uses the older/ traditional project of national unification based on common religion: 'One God, One Land, One Nation'. In this project religion, culture and language are the most important elements of national identity and the only way in which the Croatian nation 'survived' through the centuries.

5. The old Croatian salute 'God and Croats' which is today used by the extreme right-wing Croatian political party is based on this transcendental principle. Also, in everyday language the synonym for Homeland is 'Our beautiful', which is in fact the first verse of the Croatian national anthem.

6. Foucault understood the rules of shaping a hegemonic discourse as a mechanism of exclusion which repeatedly defines the 'other'. In the present instance we have a situation in which there is no communication between those 'outside' and those 'inside' – there is no common language and no shared meanings (aggressor, war, etc.).

7. 'The elementary operation of democracy is the evacuation of the locus of power: every pretender to this place is by definition a "pathological usurper" ... and the crucial point is that 'nationalism' as a specifically modern, post-Kantian phenomenon designates the moment when the Nation, the national Thing, usurps, fills out the empty place of the Thing opened by Kantian formalism, by his reduction of every "pathological" content' (Žižek 1992: 32).

8. Idyllic *Volksgemeinschaft* is represented through individual stories: it is always someone who is telling us a story, visually incorporated into a familiar landscape, with long shots, bright colours and with lots of detail. On the other side the enemy is stylistically prepared for public consumption as a visual presentation of pure evil.

9. Croatian Television broadcast two very symptomatic 'enemy spots' in prime time: one was concerned with Serbs and was titled 'They Are War Criminals' (black-and-white pictures of Yugoslav army generals) and a second one about Muslims during the fighting in Bosnia and Hercegovina: 'What Have They Done To Us!' (footage of burned Croatian villages in Bosnia set against footage of 'idyllic' life in Muslim refugee camps in Croatia).

10. On the linguistic level there is a difference between the notion '*očevina*' (*otac* = father) and '*djedovina*' (*djed* = grandfather) and the idea of *Domovina* (Homeland). The first concept is based on the principle of patrimonial community, a male property inherited through generations (Fatherland), and a second one which is connected with intimate (female) community: hearth, fireside, domestic circle, home. Nationalistic discourse mobilises these two feelings of nation on different levels.

11. In the special issue of *Telos* devoted to German unification Habermas put a question about German identity ('DM Burghers') which is based on traditional – national dimension. 'Auschwitz

70

can and should remind the Germans, no matter in which state territories they may find themselves that they cannot count on the continuities of their history. Because of that horrible break in continuity the Germans have given up the possibility of constituting their identity on something other than universalist principles of state citizenship. ... Post traditional identity loses its substantial, its unproblematic character, it exists only in the method of the public, discursive battle around the interpretation of a constitutional patriotism (*Verfassungspatriotismus*) made concrete under particular circumstances' (Habermas, 1991: 98).

12. For Spillman and Spillman (1991: 171–2) the 'syndrome of the enemy image' includes seven elements: distrust, placing the guilt on the enemy, negative anticipation, identification with evil, zero-sum thinking, de-individualisation and refusal to empathise.

References

Bauman, Zygmunt (1988) 'Strangers: The Social Construction of Universality and Particularity', in *Telos*, no. 78 (Winter), pp. 7–42.

Connerton, Paul (1989) *How Societies Remember*, Cambridge: Cambridge University Press.

Deleuze, Gilles and Guattari, Felix (1980) *Mille plateaux: Capitalisme et schizophrenie*, Paris: Les Editions de Minuit.

Dvornikovic, Vladimir (1939) *Karakterologija Jugoslovena*, Belgrade: Kosmos.

Ellis, John (1992; first edition 1982) *Visible Fictions*, London: Routledge.

Grosrichard, Alain (1985) *Structure du sérail: La Fonction du despotisme asiatique dans l 'Occident classique.*

Habermas, Jurgen (1991) 'Yet Again: German Identity – A Unified Nation of Angry DM-Burghers?', *New German Critique*, no. 52 (Winter) pp. 84–102.

Judt, Tony (1992) 'The Past Is Another Country: Myth and Memory in Postwar Europe', *Daedalus*, Fall, pp. 83–118.

Lefort, Claude (1986) *The Political Forms of Modern Society: Bureaucracy, Democracy, Totalitarianism*, Cambridge: Polity Press.

Lotringer, Sylvere (1992) 'Stroj za ubijanje: Fotografija in smrt', *Likovne besede*, no. 21/22, pp. 84–6.

Luke, Tim (1991) 'Community and Ecology', *Telos*, no. 88, pp. 69–80.

Salecl, Renata (1992) 'Nationalism, Anti-Semitism, and Anti-Feminism in Eastern Europe', *New German Critique*, no. 57, Fall, pp. 51–65.

Salecl, Renata (1993) *Zakaj ubogamo oblast? Nadzorovanje, Ideologija in Ideološke Fantazme*, Ljubljana: Državna Založba Slovenije.

Smith, Anthony (1990) 'Towards a Global Culture?', *Theory, Culture & Society* vol. 7, nos. 2–3, pp. 171–193.

Spillman, Kurt and Spillman, Kati (1991) 'On Enemy Images and Conflict Escalation', *International Social Science Journal*, no. 123, pp. 57–77.

Žižek, Slavoj (1992) 'Eastern European Liberalism and its Discontents', *New German Critique*, no. 57, Fall, pp. 25–49.

Zolo, Danilo (1992) *Democracy and Complexity: A Realist Approach*. University Park: Pennsylvania State University Press.

Controlling National Attitudes

War and Peace in Croatian TV News[1]

HRVOJE TURKOVIĆ

Introduction

Articulating the problem

With the onset of the war between Croatia and Yugoslavia there were clear changes in the news discourse of *HRT* (Hrvatska Radio Televizija – the only nationwide, state-controlled network in Croatia). Within these changes, two traits stand out: the predominance of war-related reports, and the adoption of an overtly propagandistic stance. The first is consistent with what happens in news coverage the world over when a national, particularly war-related, crisis occurs. The second, the propagandistic stance, can be understood, however, as *the* distinctive feature of the *war discourse*, the one that determines all other features.

Propaganda is typically understood as a pre-eminently *manipulative* phenomenon. In the first place, it is considered to be a *top–down process*: an 'action', plan or strategy, initiated and controlled by the political elite of the state, carried out by the TV institution and its executives and aimed at the target social group, which in wartime is tantamount to the entire population. Second, it is assumed that the audience will be thus guided to adopt a particular stance regardless of their own interests and will; that, in short, they will be *manipulated* by the propaganda discourse. Third, the propaganda deliberately abandons the *impartiality* of news presentation, favouring a *partisan* approach. Finally, there is an assumption that the planned propaganda strategy of the power elite is the exclusive source for all the distinctive discourses in the war news coverage.

Such assumptions, however, need not be accepted. Despite criticism of some uses of propaganda in HRT news programmes, 'insiders' (the audience members and the citizens of Croatia) have shared an implicit conviction that 'our own' propagandistic stance, faced with that of the enemy (e.g. the Banja Luka TV programme broadcast from the Serbian Krajina which can be seen in Zagreb) is in fact a 'natural', 'necessary', and 'normal' one. Such a conviction implies that the overt propaganda of the HRT war news is not just a wilful act of the governing elite, but also a kind of professional and civic obligation, a fulfilment of a deep-felt need of citizens living in a country at war. It might be said, therefore, that the function of such propagandistic news is not just to manipulate the masses, but also to satisfy their needs. The conviction implies further that 'our own' propaganda, although of a partisan nature, generally represents a 'just' expression of the state of affairs and is therefore basically 'the truth about Croatia'. 'Our' propaganda is therefore not adequately described if judged only by its possible infringement of some particular truths, or by its deviant selectivity with regards to facts: there is a 'higher', more 'general' truth at issue.

Of course, such a set of convictions might itself be interpreted as a product of propaganda, as an 'interiorisation' of its 'ideology', as a result of an identification of 'ideology' with 'reality'. However, such an interpretation would be inadequate. The overt propagandistic aspects of the wartime news programmes were felt *immediately* and defined as the 'necessary' consequence of the internal war situation. There were disagreements only about the final 'make-up' of particular HRT propaganda (what and what not to submit to a propagandistic articulation; the kind of propagandistic 'language' to be used, and so on). Therefore, the acceptance of propaganda as a 'natural feature of the news programme discourse' cannot be ascribed to propagandistic indoctrination itself, but should rather be taken as a consequence of the same 'forces' that have pushed the presentation of the news into the overt propagandistic rhetoric.

What are these 'forces'? This paper assumes that the 'organising force' behind the war news can be detected through an analysis of the patterns of discourse deployed in the daily TV news output. It therefore undertakes a basic feature analysis of the news, and then interprets this in a wider perspective, in order to determine the 'force' that produced it.

The Background to the Samples

Two instances of the prime-time news programme broadcast by Croatian Radio Television (HRT) are analysed here – one broadcast in 'peacetime', the other during the war. Both went out at 7.30 pm.[2]

The wartime sample (WS) was transmitted on 18 November 1991. Its duration was 29 minutes and 19 seconds. At that time, fighting was underway across most of Croatia, with the Socialist Yugoslav People's Army (JNA) and the Serbian troops attacking on a broad front. They were opposed by the forces of the Croatian police and the newly established National Guard, which consisted mainly of volunteers. Most of the main cities in Croatian territory within reach of the neighbouring republics of Serbia and Bosnia–Hercegovina (e.g. Osijek, Nova Gradiška, Slavonska Požega, Sisak, Karlovac, Gospić, Dubrovnik, Split, Šibenik, Zadar) were being shelled and rocketed and were under constant air attack. The previous day – 17 November – the Croatian town of Vukovar had fallen into the hands of the Yugoslav and Serbian forces, having been under heavy siege for several months. In many other towns, garrisons of the (JNA) were under siege from the Croatian police, National Guard and civil guard volunteers. Some of the JNA garrisons were shelling the towns they were located in, while others were negotiating. JNA and Serbian troops were only 30km from Zagreb, the Croatian capital. Zagreb had also experienced air raids and had been under direct air and rocket attack on several occasions. Although a self-proclaimed independent state, Croatia at that time had not yet been recognised by other countries, or by the UN, as an independent, sovereign state.

The comparative peacetime sample (PS) was transmitted on 17 November 1993. It lasted 38 minutes and 17 seconds. The surrounding circumstances were as follows: almost one-third of the Croatian territory was out of Croatian government control and in the hands of Serbs (the so-called Republic of Serb Krajina, RSK). UNPROFOR were patrolling both the separation lines between the Croatian government-controlled territory and the Krajina territory and inside the UNPAs (United Nations Protected Areas). They also controlled the so-called 'pink zones', areas held neither by the RSK nor by the Croatian government. Skirmishes were still occurring along some separation lines, between the Croatian army and the Krajina forces. Some Croatian towns (e.g. Zadar, Šibenik, Županja) were still being shelled by the RSK forces. While Croatian-controlled areas were basically at peace, there were still the unresolved issues of the 'occupied zones' (as the Krajina territory was officially designated by the Croatian side), the influx of refugees from both Serb-controlled areas of Croatia and Bosnia and Hercegovina, and the very limited economic and political acceptance shown Croatia by the international community. While the main conflict in Bosnia and Hercegovina was between the Bosnian Serbs on one side and Bosnian Muslims and the Bosnian Croats, on the other, there were also serious conflicts between the Bosnian Croats and the Bosnian Muslims. The Croatian state was involved in the conflict on the side of the Bosnian Croats.

Discourse Characteristics

The ambiguity of the PS (peacetime sample)

For any longtime viewer of the HRT prime-time news, there is a strong ambiguity about PS. Compared with WS, there has obviously been an attempt to give the impression of it not being a 'wartime programme' but rather a 'peacetime programme'. At the same time it does not want to be taken as ordinary, standard news coverage: it is made clear that a long-term 'political crisis' is underway and that the programme is actually a 'crisis programme', although within the limits of an essentially peaceful situation. In spite of the non-war programme agenda, there are numerous tell-tale signs that even in Croatia there are events that signal the maintenance of the war situation. Moreover, the war in Bosnia and Hercegovina is considered to be almost an 'internal' war, even though it is taking place in the territory of another sovereign country. I will analyse some of the programme's indicators of this ambiguity later.

'Wartime programme' indicators of WS

What are the basic overt differences between a wartime and peacetime programme? In WS there are several obvious characteristics:

a) It is entirely dedicated to war-related news. Even the international news part of the programme is explicitly presented as a review of reactions to the war situation in Croatia, and in particular to the 'imminent' fall of Vukovar ('imminent' because the fact that Vukovar had already fallen is not explicitly stated in the programme).

b) Although the WS consists of an accumulation of 'atomic' news items – a standard discourse feature of news (see Ahmavaara et al 1974: 165–6) – there is a strong thematic unity of the descriptive kind, with all individual items of news portrayed as aspects or parts of the overall situation. The thematic unity of a particular series of news items is underscored by introductory remarks made by the news presenter, who is also the acting editor ('Let us see what is happening on the Croatian battlefields' or 'Let us hear reports of the world's reactions to the situation in Croatia'). While the prototype news discourse is thematically heterogeneous, the wartime news discourse tends towards homogeneity.

c) There is no visible attempt to establish even the appearance of an impartial approach to war-related events: the reports are decisively and overtly biased; they give only 'our side' of the story.

d) The enemy is always described using attributes or names with strongly negative connotations ('Chetniks', 'Serbian terrorists', 'occupiers', 'the aggressor's forces', etc.). In PS there is no fixed standard designation of the enemy.

e) There is a marked reduction in the number of images used in support of verbal expositions: stills or freeze frames are used abundantly as the background for telephone and off-screen reports. Some news blocks (for example in the headline, or contents, block) are in WS delivered by the 'talking head' of the presenter without illustration, while in PS there is visual presentation of events accompanied by the announcer's voice-over. In terms of imagery, there is in WS both a reduced diversity and an impoverishment of quality, when compared to PS (e.g. PS has 361 shots over a timespan of 38.17 minutes, and the WS has 173 shots over its 29.19 minutes duration).

f) The programme is explicitly marked out as 'non-standard' by the slogan '*Za slobodu*' ('For freedom') which always appears behind the presenter during his delivery.

'Peacetime programme' indicators of PS

The PS shows obvious differences:

a) There is a better balance between news items related to the war and those unrelated. There is more news about other countries and their concerns and about economic problems in Croatia not directly connected with the war situation. There is a stronger emphasis on the 'civil' aspects of internal life in Croatia.

b) Even when the war in Bosnia and Hercegovina is dealt with, there is at least one survey that attempts to give an impartial view of the situation.

c) News items about restive areas of Croatia (e.g. those bordering on UNPA zones) are placed low in the running-order and are not announced in the introductory overview.

d) Although there are news items in which the opposite side is presented in a negative light (e.g. the situation in Vukovar and reports from the battlefields in Bosnia and Hercegovina), there is a higher proportion of neutral or unmarked designations of the conflicting parties than in the wartime programme. Serbs are called 'Serbs', Muslims, 'Muslims'; the armies involved in the conflict are mostly given their official names: HVO – (Bosnian) Croatian Defence Council; MOS – Muslim Liberation Forces.

e) The construction of the PS discourse is predominantly heterogeneous, as is usual in the peacetime news. The presenter's introductory comments do not try to link the news items but mostly prepare the audience for changes in topic. There is a diversity of news and of supporting images, and a greater proportion of pictorial coverage with accompanying off-screen voice-over. There is very limited use of stills.

'Crisis-bound programme' indicators of PS

There are, however, indicators showing that the programme is 'crisis bound':

a) A proportionally larger set of news items relating to the conflicts in the former Yugoslavia is placed at the very beginning of the programme, immediately after the introductory sequence. These are thematically unified as reports on the search for a solution to the crisis of the breakdown of Socialist Yugoslavia: the status of Croatia; the status of UNPA zones; the involvement of Croatia in the Bosnian conflict. Examples include: the declaration of the Presidential Council; the activities of the Minister of the Exterior; and the parliamentary delegation to the European Parliament in Strasbourg.

b) The section on the conflicts in former Yugoslavia also shows a more cohesive internal discourse than does the rest of the programme, with the exception of the field report on the war in Bosnia and Hercegovina. In addition to the mediating 'links' made by the presenter, many of the crisis-related factors are repeatedly mentioned in several items (e.g. the Croatian peace proposal, the French and German peace proposals, the Minister of Foreign Affairs, UN Secretary General Boutros Boutros-Ghali, etc.)

c) Even in the reporting of civil problems, there is a tacit understanding that these problems are somehow crisis related: refugee protests, economic problems due to the lack of foreign loans, the presence of humanitarian aid.

Wartime programme indicators in PS

Although there is an obvious effort to suppress the possible interpretation that Croatia is still at war, either in its own territories or in Bosnia and Hercegovina, there are many tell-tale signs, symptomatic of the wartime programme, that imply the contrary:

a) There are still reports that remind us that the war in Croatia is not yet completely over; for example, the report on new refugees from the Serbian-held zone (under UNPA jurisdiction) in the Zadar region.

b) In this same report, the internal part of Croatia (the Zadar hinterland) is still designated as the 'bojišnica' – Croat for 'battlefield'. The UNPA zones are consistently treated as 'unsolved problems', with the assumption that their unresolved status is a consequence, and therefore a latent generator, of war.

c) Although there is an impartially styled overview of the war in Bosnia suggestive of its 'foreign affair' status, the additional 'field report' has a strong partiality: Bosnian Croats are implicitly treated as 'our side', and Bosnian Muslims as 'enemies'. This partiality manifests itself in the following features:

i) Bosnian Muslims are referred to in negative terms (e.g. 'Muslim snipers looking for inattentive victims', 'the Muslim crime', 'horrible Muslim crimes'), while Bosnian Croats are described in a way that implies their status as victim.

ii) Only Bosnian-Croat civilians and army people are shown and interviewed, mostly as witnesses.

iii) Some consequences of the sniper fire on Bosnian Croats are shown directly (e.g. blood on the asphalt). While the slaughter of some Bosnian-Croat priests is not pictorially documented, it is given relatively extensive verbal attention.

iv) Only Bosnian Muslims are reported 'to have attacked' Croats, thereby implying that they are the aggressors. If a Croatian victory or advance is mentioned, it is described as a 'counter-attack', thereby implying it is the result of a defensive action.

v) There is a multilayered embedding structure to the Bosnian field report: the presenter announces one field reporter; the first announces a second, the second announces a third, and then back to the first reporter and again to the main presenter, strengthening the perception of coherence in the whole report, and presenting it as an interconnected argument about the 'wickedness' of the Bosnian Muslims.

vi) The account of the fall of Vukovar incites a return to the rhetoric of war and reminds the public that the war situation is not yet over.

Hidden propagandistic aspects of PS

The wartime atmosphere is also supported by other, hidden, propagandistic features of the PS.

a) Both the declaration of the Presidential Council of Defence and National Security, and the speech of the Minister of Foreign Affairs, as well as the reported speech of the Prime Minister strongly state the success of official government policy both in foreign affairs and in the economy. Such reports, entirely without reservation or comment, assume complete confidence in the 'positive' value of what 'our party' is doing.

b) Even when more gloomy, unresolved problems are addressed, such as the non-existence of Croatian tourist resorts in British holiday brochures, the problems with domestic heating in Zagreb, or the refugee protests, the impression of the government's lack of success is 'corrected' by the up-beat conclusion of the PS presenter-editor, or by optimistic statements from government representatives.

c) In an 'impartial' report about the establishment of the War Crimes Tribunal in The Hague, and in the report on the Bosnian situation, the new federal state of Serbia and Montenegro is not designated by its official name (Savezna Republika Jugoslavija – Federal Republic of Yugoslavia) but by a derogatory substitute ('Združena Srpsko Crnogorska Država' – 'Associated Serbian–Montenegrin State'; or just 'Združena Država' – 'Associated State').

Interpretation

The norm change

The transition both from WS to PS and, within PS, from peacetime to wartime indicators and back again is characterised by changes in the construction of the discourse, within the context of a *changed norm of news delivery*.

The basic norm which governs the peacetime news programme – *the* norm of *impartiality* – is not just 'loosened' in the case of the wartime news programme, and so permitting some degree of propagandistic manipulation, but is changed altogether into its opposite, the *norm of partiality*, that is partiality to 'our cause'. In the case of the HRT news programme, this means partiality to the Croatian side – to the Croatian 'cause', the Croatian nation, to ethnic Croatians, to the Croatian mother-land. Specifications of 'our side' and the 'enemy side' vary in the identification, range and emphasis of referents, but during the war and any war-threatening situation the distinction between 'us' and the 'enemy' is promoted to the level of a norm, and is merged within the norm of partiality.

The 'impartiality' of any news programme is, of course, open to doubt. As Zaller (1992: 13) puts it '. . . it is never "just information", because it is unavoidably selective and unavoidably enmeshed in stereotypical frames of reference that highlight only a portion of what is going on' (cf. Schlesinger 1978: 163–204; McQuail 1987: 30–2). But such criticisms do not count out the presence of an impartiality norm that affects news practice. Norms serve as behaviour regulators in particular sets of situations but their application as it relates to actual behaviour is complex and often opaque. For example, the question may arise as to which norm is applicable in a particular situation; which norm should take precedence if norms come into conflict; whether the chosen norm is really adequate at all.

In view of all these difficulties, what is commonly asked for is that the participants in a situation to which a particular norm is applicable publicly acknowledge their acceptance of that norm, by manifesting certain patterns of behaviour and by using certain stereotyped signals associated with compliance. The 'validity' of a particular norm, therefore, does not simply depend on its 'just application', but on the stereotyped 'signalling pattern' that indicates that it is in play. There is a legitimate *distinction in genre* between news governed by the impartiality norm and that governed by the opposing norm of partisanship. Such a distinction implies standardised procedures ('routines')[3] and genre discursive 'signals'. Thus, for example, in impartial news, factual statements will prevail; there will be a clear distinction made between factual statement and evaluative comment; designation and naming of parties will be stylistically unmarked; where opinion is involved, a variety will be presented.

Analysis of the partiality norm

The norm of impartiality as applied to news programmes has been, in general, adequately analysed in existing literature on the media. The presence of the partiality norm has, however, not even been noted, let alone analysed.

I will attempt to point out some components of the partiality norm as signalled in both WS and PS. These components might be termed 'sub-norms' that help to signal the presence of the *general partiality norm*:

a) *The norm of unconditional conformism.* All public acts (including the news and its articulation) have to conform to the officially stated national 'goals', 'needs' and 'interests' as well as to specific 'orders' and 'requests' that are publicly formulated to be 'of national interest'. This norm justifies the introduction of all kinds of censorship, both governmental and self-censorship, and the blocking of dissenting voices' access to the public media. The presence of this norm is principally signalled by the use of stereotyped designations and words with strong evaluative connotations. These include the use of the newly created elements of speech in Croatian such as '*glede*' and '*u svezi*' – archaic-sounding synonyms for 'in regard to', 'in connection with' – as well as labelling of the enemy.

b) *The norm of success.* In this norm, which might also be understood as the 'norm of optimism', no one has the right to voice doubt publicly about the eventual success of national policy, for example, President Franjo Tudjman's military policy in Croatia and Bosnia and Hercegovina. The national policy is the only one possible in the given circumstances, and its fundamental successfulness must be reiterated. This explains the 'success syndrome' which permeates public discourse, from the speeches of President Tudjman to interviews with military commanders, from official statements on the economy by Prime Minister Valentić to the comments of the editor-presenter in the PS, which often 'correct' the pessimistic implications of a given report.

c) *Norm of righteousness.* Anything 'our side' is doing is morally right and justifiable. Atrocities caused by 'our side' are not mentioned, or, if mentioned, have to be set against some incomparably greater atrocity committed by the 'enemy'. Any ethically 'wrong' act by our side is contingent, a one-off, something completely untypical of the general behaviour of 'our side'. This norm permeates reports from the battlefield where the Croatian forces are involved. The application of the norm of righteousness can therefore be an indicator of which party in ongoing battles is considered to be on 'our side' in Bosnian and Hercegovina.

d) *The norm of the enemy's inhumanity.* This is the counterpart to the norm of righteousness: anything the 'enemy side' is doing is essentially wrong and unjustifiable. But it is not just simple 'wrongness'; the enemy must be characterised as fundamentally non-human, below 'the lowest possible level of humanity', or as something 'outside humanity', 'opposed to civilisation'. Only in such a way can 'we' explain how it can be that they are against 'us', and why they are as destructive as they are reported to be.

The application of this norm can be recognised in the obligatory ascription of all known massacres (even those that are unconfirmed) to the enemy side. Although normally avoided, the visual presentation of massacred bodies are permitted as evidence of the 'viciousness of the enemy', as in, for example, the report on the fall of Vukovar. But, the presence of this sub-norm can also be seen in the careful avoidance of presenting information that might suggest the enemy side is 'human' or 'normal', is as civilised as we are. There is a systematic absence of pictures and information about everyday life inside Serbia and in Serbian Krajina. If such scenes are presented, they tend to deepen the impression of the 'troubled', 'subhuman', 'bizarre' or 'unethical' life led there.

e) *The norm of national centredness.* The presentation of the domestic agenda is always paramount in prime-time news programmes everywhere. During a war situation it is, moreover, considered almost 'indecent' to deal with the problems of other nations when there is such internal pressure. This norm, however, implies something more: the refusal to relativise 'our situation', which would otherwise be the necessary consequence of drawing attention to events in other countries. If too many of the problems of the outside world are brought in, there would be a danger that our problems would appear to be no more important than those of others. Therefore, 'the world' is permitted to enter the wartime news programme only insofar as it is concerned with 'our situation' and 'our problems'.

There is a latent, and often expressed, generalised xenophobia at times of war, and in the presentation of war news. Such xenophobia can even become a sub-norm of the norm of national centredness.

f) *The norm of aggressiveness.* In wartime, there is an implicit requirement that unrelenting aggressiveness be displayed not only towards the enemy but also to anything that transgresses the sub-norms of partiality. Such transgressions are considered as a 'contribution to the enemy cause', and the transgressor as an 'enemy of the nation', as a 'traitor'. All peace movements during the war – as the intentional transgressors of the norm of aggressiveness – are automatically seen in this light.

In the prime-time news programme this norm is manifested in the form of obligatory support for military advances of 'our side' on the battlefront and support for its occupation of enemy territory. Examples include the occupation of Muslim villages and Bosnian-Croat regions of Bosnia and the regaining of Serb-occupied territory at Maslenica, as well as wholehearted celebration of all military 'victories'. The interviewing of people on the streets ('the voice of the people') who demand aggressive military action, who argue against post-war cohabitation ('suživot') with former Serbian neighbours and who insist that those with 'blood on their hands' be brought to trial, is another manifestation of this norm.

Attitudinal social homogeneity as wartime requirement.
Since the impartiality norm seems to be the 'prototype norm' for the news, the partiality norm takes the dominant position only in very special situations such as revolution, extreme social and political conflict, under repressive regimes and in war. (Here it is interesting to compare Schlesinger's analysis (1978: 205–43) of the partial abandonment of the impartiality norm by the BBC in its treatment of Northern Ireland.)

As I pointed out in my introduction, the 'takeover' of the news by the partiality norm may be, and usually is, very rapid, with the crisis imminent, and is an 'internal affair'. These general conditions are 'accepted' by the media 'manipulators' but not produced by them.

The partiality norm, as described above, in fact contributes towards the homogenisation of public attitude. And although this homogenisation is very useful for the governing elite, and they will do what they can to aid and control its process, the process itself seems to be caused by the crisis, and not by the propaganda manipulation alone.

Montagu (1976: 259–82) states that violence in war situations is not due to the 'natural aggressiveness' of men but rather to a specific social conformism that is induced in army recruits. It seems, however, that this conformism is required not only of recruits but of the populace in general. War, as a general threat to the order of everyday societal life, challenges the existing routines of social conformism and simultaneously contributes to their revision in the desire to restore a crisis-resistant social order. The partisan attitude, which aims to strengthen the endangered social integration and to create a new homogeneous consensus against the enemy, is fundamental to this. Meanwhile, many of the norms that usually regulate social intercourse and private life appear to be suspended.

The media, acutely sensitive to societal tendencies and supportive of the main social order, are quick to respond to these forces and eager to contribute to them. The change in the governing norm of the news is the consequence of media compliance with the citizens' need to restore a 'world order'.

Notes

1. This paper is based on work done for the 'Media and War' project at the Austrian Study Centre for Peace and Conflict Resolution, Stadt Schlaining, Austria. The project is partially subsidised by a grant from the Humanitarian Foundation Soros, Zagreb.
2. The HRT prime-time news was chosen because HRT is the only nationwide network, nominally under the jurisdiction of the Croatian Parliament (Hrvatski Sabor) but generally considered to be subject to the powerful influence of the government and the governing political party (HDZ). The 7.30 pm bulletin was chosen because it has the biggest viewing audience, and is widely considered to give the most significant representation of 'official opinion'.
3. For an analysis of such 'professional routines' in news governed by the impartiality norm see Schlesinger 1978.

References

Ahmavaara Y., Nordenstreng, K., and Peltola, P. (1974) 'Informational News Criteria', in K. Nordenstreng (ed.), *Informational Mass Communication*, Helsinki: Tammi Publications.
McQuail, Denis (1987, 2nd edn) *Mass Communication Theory: An Introduction*, London: Sage Publications.
Montagu, Ashley (1976) *The Nature of Human Aggression*, Oxford: Oxford University Press.
Schlesinger, Philip (1978) *Putting 'Reality' Together: BBC News*, London: Constable.
Zaller, John R. (1992) *The Nature and Origins of Mass Opinion*, New York: Cambridge University Press.

Real-time TV Coverage from War

Does it Make or Break Government Policy?*

NIK GOWING

As Diplomatic Editor for Channel Four News, I monitored day in and day out, and as best I could, the proliferation of ethnic and regional conflicts the world over. This proliferation is matched by that of lightweight technologies – portable video cameras such as the Hi-8 and fly-away satellite dishes – which let us cover an increasing number of these conflicts. Watching the matrix of incoming video on the monitors in our newsroom – twenty or thirty channels – I sometimes think of all this conflict coverage as so much 'supermarket war video'. There is far more real-time war than we have ever seen before.

Editorially, we can pick and choose – just like walking down shelves of breakfast cereal. One day Nagorno Karabakh. The next day Tajikistan, or perhaps Georgia or Afghanistan, then a bit of Angola, Liberia or Yemen and perhaps Algeria if we are lucky. All of it streams relentlessly into our news machines. Much of it is never transmitted, at least not in Britain or Europe. And usually – like every good supermarket – a lot of the goods these days are cut price, especially if shot and reported by enterprise freelances and independents with those Hi-8s. But the main principle is: no pictures, then no serious coverage of a conflict. In television, a dot on a graphic is not enough to report a conflict, a massacre or a humanitarian catastrophe.

The conventional wisdom – the assumption – of many in the media, the military and government is that real-time television coverage of the horrors of Bosnia or Somalia or Rwanda not only creates a demand that 'something must be done', but also drives the making of foreign policy. The assumption is of an *automatic* cause-and-effect relationship. Televised horror in Bosnia: instant policy response in Whitehall or Washington. In this essay I will detail some important challenges to that belief. The relation is not what it seems.

This cause-and-effect relationship is an issue which has intrigued and troubled me since the Gulf War. It troubles policy-makers too. They curse the horrors I and my colleagues put on television. In the Gulf, governments could control and choreograph TV coverage of a war over which they had ultimate control, and thus coerce the public to back their war aims. They were helped in this by the desert terrain and the Saudi reporting restrictions.

* This paper was delivered at the *Turbulent Europe* Conference, 19 July 1994.

In his excellent book on censorship during the Gulf War, *Second Front*, Rick MacArthur, publisher of *Harper's Magazine*, described what he called 'a stunning loss of prerogative' by the media. Since then things have changed. In many ways journalists have distinguished themselves in Bosnia, even though coverage has been far from complete and much of the horror away from Sarajevo – as in Mostar – was never reported – certainly not on a regular basis. In just three years, I believe we have entered a new phase of civil and ethnic armed conflict. Government rules to control us – as contained in the so-called Green Book in Britain – are virtually meaningless.

In Bosnia or Somalia governments cannot censor. They cannot dictate what we shoot, report and transmit on our satellite dishes in places like Bosnia. But one senior military officer in Bosnia has detailed to me what he called a 'gentle form of news management' where, by their own choice, TV teams worked and lived close to UNPROFOR troops. In its own way this skewed and controlled coverage. More broadly, however, it seems that the overall inability to control TV crews and journalists in Bosnia may have become a pivotal fact in convincing governments *not* to become involved in conflicts – unless, that is, the military/UN operational objective can be achieved within a matter of days, before public support, exposed to the powerful images of TV coverage, begins to wane.

In 1994 I was invited by the Shorenstein Barone Center on the Press, Politics and Public Policy in the Kennedy School at Harvard University to undertake a more detailed and structured analysis of this new roller-coaster relationship. It is a relationship where both 'we' – the TV news organisations – and 'them' – the government machines – are on a sharp new learning curve. It goes to the heart of governance. The more I have researched and dug into it, the more I realised that most people in government and the TV news business make glib, unsubstantiated assumptions that are wrong.

With the support of my employers, ITN, I stepped back from daily journalism to unpick this relationship; the thick of the daily grind is not the best place to analyse it. There, one accepts conventional wisdom without question. What follows here are the headlines of a considered, closely argued analysis based on more than one hundred interviews with diplomatic and military insiders.

My purpose is not to defend government policies. Neither is it to take sides in what are often highly emotive armed conflicts. Nor is it to make moral judgments on which side is right and which wrong. Nonetheless, emotion and partiality cloud analysis. This is a progress report – not yet a definitive conclusion. My analysis is not a closed book. I want to advance the debate and encourage new perspectives.

We work in what Martin Bell has christened the 'Decade of the Dish'. Real-time television images virtually live from a battlefield satellite dish in Sarajevo, or the British UN base at Vitez, have highlighted some conflicts and put them on the diplomatic radar screen. In Bosnia, the dishes made Sarajevo into a visible symbol of Serb aggression, accessible to the outside world. But because of the dangers, there was no satellite dish to transmit what UN officials call the even more evil horrors of the Croat siege of Mostar.

Until relatively recently, there was no satellite dish near the heart of the Rwandan horrors – simply because of the dangers and physical difficulty of getting there. But that important limitation was an important reason why the world was never shamed into mobilising during those first dreadful days and weeks. They heard about the horrors, and saw them intermittently on TV. But not night after night, relentlessly, Sarajevo style. The same goes for many other regional conflicts: no satellite dishes equals little TV coverage – certainly no real-time coverage, that is, live or virtually-live pictures, with very little time delay between an incident being recorded on videotape and being transmitted.

In the early months of the Bosnian war, in particular, such real-time images provided valuable raw information and corroboration of badly resourced intelligence assessments, which had at times compromised the safety of reporters and camera-men. Hence my temptation to harness Erasmus's saying from the 16th century: 'In the country of the blind the one-eyed man – the television camera – is king.' No one – certainly not me – can challenge the power of that single eye to provide enduring images and horrific impressions that no words in a diplomatic cable or military signal can ever convey. Indeed, whenever I approached ministers, policy-makers, officials or military officers and told them of my attempt to unravel the precise impact of real-time television on their work, without exception their reactions were amusingly predictable. First came a knowing smirk, then a grin, finally the raised eyebrows and a chuckle.

The information and nuisance value of TV images was clear to diplomats, who, as one reflected, 'are used to working methodically, slowly, systematically and reflec-tively'. Real-time TV pictures compress response times in a crisis. They put pressure on choice and priorities in crisis management. They skew responses. They shape the policy agenda but do not dictate responses. They highlight policy dilemmas but do not resolve them.

So – and this is the heart of my findings – TV's unquestioned ability to provide a contemporaneous, piecemeal, video ticker-tape service – a tip-sheet of raw, real-time images virtually instantly – must not be confused – as it usually is – with a power to drive policy-making. By and large it does not, even though we on the television news side might hope it does – especially if the blood, the shredded limbs, the tortured faces and the misery of war are there in front of us. And even though the policy-makers talk despairingly of the new power and role of TV news.

Lawrence Freedman, Professor of War Studies at King's College London, has written of 'the basic failure [of governments] to watch passively as the Yugoslav crisis brewed'. In other words, television did not have an active impact on policy-making. In retrospect, the graphic TV images merely highlighted the West's impotence and failure to find enough of a diplomatic consensus to prevent or pre-empt war. It was the missed opportunity. Governments worked to apply diplomatic bandages while the warring parties deceived them.

In a marvellous example of diplomatic understatement, I heard Alvaro De Soto, UN Assistant Secretary-General, put it like this: 'Bosnia was not a diplomat's dream,' he said. 'It was like diving into an empty swimming pool.' On this steep learning curve, ministers, diplomats and the military have learned by and large to resist the power of TV pictures with a steely determination. As in Bosnia, their fundamental long-term strategy was to engage in low-risk, low-cost, minimalist policies which gave the impression of a full engagement when the political will was anything but that. As one British official put it to me echoing the words of many others: '[In Bosnia] TV almost derailed policy on several occasions, but the spine held. It had to. The secret was to respond to limit the damage, and be seen to react without undermining the specific [policy] focus.'

Washington is little different. Charles Kupchan, former Director of the European Affairs desk on Clinton's National Security Council, struck much the same note: 'Television does not have much day-to-day impact,' said Kupchan. 'As a source of information for the National Security Council [television] is not that important. Gross pictures of suffering [in Bosnia] were not going to force intervention because the policy-makers have decided these fights are not worth picking.'

When I was seeking out reactions to my research, another senior British official was all too clear: 'There is nothing worse than not getting it right. I still think we got it just about right in Bosnia.' In other words, television informed, but it did not pressure.

Over Bosnia and Somalia, I believe, there was what I would call a carefully crafted policy of ambiguity over true political intentions, even though the British Foreign Secretary Douglas Hurd made it clear on many occasions – though these remarks were not widely reported – that 'What we are doing in Bosnia is not abdication, but sense.' Official statements expressed outrage and a determination to bring the war to an end 'by all means'. Sound-bites and declarations of horror or condemnation were usually misread in TV and newspaper reporting as signals of a hardening of policy – which they were not. They were what one official described to me as often 'pseudo-decisions for pseudo-action'. As a senior US administration figure put it: 'Reacting can be anything from a UN resolution to sending a press spokesman out.' Hence the reluctant, hesitant commitment to humanitarian aid and 'safe areas'. But such measures could only be called palliatives or alibis. They were not policies to force an end to war.

Indeed, as the persistent anguishing over the presence of UN forces in Bosnia underlined, the deployment of forces for humanitarian operations for a long time made it virtually impossible to carry out a more decisive policy designed to end the fighting. Senior Red Cross officials resentfully told me the palliatives were forced upon politicians by TV coverage, but usually the actions 'were not the most appropriate' and could not be made to work. In Bosnia, the UN aid convoys saved an unquantifiable number of lives and created humanitarian ghettoes. But many now argue – including some in the UN – that the aid in response to television pictures merely distorted the war and therefore probably prolonged it.

It is a doctrinal debate now consuming parts of both government and military as they prepare themselves for whatever preventative or pre-emptive actions might be demanded in future conflicts. There is also a growing political belief – little stated in public – that even diplomatic intervention in virtually every case has little chance of ending a war as long as the belligerents are determined to keep waging it – or certainly until the fighting reaches what Clausewitz called the 'culminating point'. Hence the international indifference and total absence of commitment on Rwanda (apart from humanitarian support), as the Overseas Development Administration in the UK, and non-governmental organisations like the Red Cross, will bitterly tell you.

Inherent in the cause-and-effect relationship between TV images and foreign policy are sharply defined limits – just like the limits of the ultimate ability of ministers and diplomats to end a war like Rwanda or Yemen. In future, real-time television coverage of the proliferation of regional conflicts will create emotions, but ultimately make no difference to the fundamental calculations in foreign-policy making. No journalist should delude himself by believing otherwise, however ghastly the horrors he witnesses and reports on. It is likely that *something* will be done: a procession of statements of concern or condemnation; perhaps expressions of outrage; probably a modest humanitarian commitment like Britain's fifty trucks for Rwanda; but not much else.

Some working in TV news coverage bridle at my suggestion. They say: 'What about Srebrenica? or the Ahmići massacre? Or the Sarajevo market massacre? Or the dead US ranger being dragged through the streets of Mogadishu?' Surely these were examples of how television forced changes in policy? In some of those cases – and in others besides – they are right. In Srebrenica, for example, the cause and effect is clear. But the Sarajevo market bomb on 5 February which killed sixty-eight Bosnians is an example of an *apparent* impact of TV images that is not borne out by the facts. It was the massacre itself, not the TV images, that catalysed a diplomatic process that had been underway for several weeks.

I contend that a handful of examples where governments were caught on the hop by events and TV coverage do not in themselves constitute a paradigm of automaticity between TV images and foreign policy-making. As Kofi Annan, the UN Under Secretary-General, who has been at the heart of all political conflicts over peacekeeping operations, expressed it to me: 'When governments have a clear policy, they have anticipated a situation and they know what they want to do and where they want to go, then television has little impact. In fact they ride it.'

There is therefore an important distinction to be made between the *tactical* impact of TV – its localised, immediate impact – and its medium-to-long-term *strategic* impact on overall government policy-making. I will give examples of this difference below, but what is clear is that the relationship between TV and government policy-making is fickle and unpredictable and still evolving. Its precise influence continues to be disputed both by journalist colleagues and at the highest levels of government.

A key problem in the conventional wisdom is that very few ministers or officials in Europe ever have the time or inclination to watch TV news. If they do, it is because an incident has been brought to their attention by an anguished member of their family or staff, or by a driver. The British Ambassador to Washington, Sir Robin Renwick, once told me: 'There is a fair determination to resist and limit the power of television.' Then he recalled pressure on Bosnia from his own teenage daughter at home and he added, 'But we are susceptible and we hate horrors too.'

In Washington, of course, there are the administration officials who are CNN junkies, but not as many as is conventionally assumed. And again they tend to use the incoming video as useful raw ticker-tape information, not as defining information to be acted on without delay. Time and time again I heard from sources that when they see television coverage, often they do not trust it – not because it lies, but because it skews impressions. 'Trite and crude' was one frequent description. The commentary lines came in for particular criticism: one of Douglas Hurd's officials described them as usually 'playing too much to the heart, and not enough to the head'. Instead, officials tend to use images as useful raw data – in the latter stages of the Bosnia conflict particularly to corroborate intelligence, but no more.

The complexity of this whole relationship is underlined by the calculations governments make on the political impact of ghastly images. Throughout the Bosnian crisis, ministerial post-bags pressuring for action were 'shallow' and never overwhelming. One senior source described the claims that 'public opinion wants this' or 'public opinion wants that' as largely 'cant' and 'bogus'. On issues like air strikes, public opinion is regarded as ill informed, over-emotional, uncritical and therefore unreliable. It is cited only when political convenience demands some kind of justification, however dubious. 'An additive to bolster an argument' was how the White House Communications Director described public opinion. I have heard Bill Clinton's Special Policy Adviser, George Stephanopoulos, say that the White House does not conduct opinion polls on foreign policy, a fact confirmed to me by the office of Stan Greenberg, Clinton's private pollster.

There is, however, one way in which TV most certainly does influence government machines. It is by way of what were described to me rather appropriately as 'political sonic ripples'. These ripples are the small elite of newspaper editors, leader writers, Op-Ed columnists and motivated politicians who do monitor real-time television. For them TV coverage is sometimes – but certainly not always – the cue to create political issues no minister can risk ignoring. Again, this is a fickle process. Without exception, ministers and officials who played down the impact of real-time television on themselves pointed to this numerically tiny but politically powerful elite as the group that does influence foreign policy-making based on what it sees on television.

The influence is via Op-Ed columns. Politicians devour them in their morning newspaper cuttings as a shorthand sample of public opinion. Or as one official put it: 'There are no summaries of broadcast news, so there has to be a fuss in the papers first.' The 'fuss' is then picked up by MPs or Congressmen, who also spend little time watching TV coverage. As Marlin Fitzwater, White House Press Secretary to Presidents Reagan and Bush, told me: 'The pressure of television on decision-making is always indirect.'

The random, fickle nature of what generically has become known as the CNN factor – but which could also be called the Superchannel, BBC World Service or Sky factors – was best encapsulated by Rick Inderfurth, deputy to Madeleine Albright, US Ambassador to the UN. As Ambassador Inderfurth told me: 'There are many times when there are horrific images and there is no policy impact. It is very difficult to work out and anticipate how the CNN factor will come into play. It is like waking up with a big bruise, and you don't know where it came from and what hit you.'

Policy Panic

I will now address those big bruises – the moments when TV coverage of war horrors can be said to have had a pivotal effect on policy-making – both tactical and strategic. I have called them moments of *policy panic*, although officials object to that phrase. But they are the instances when events occur unexpectedly, blowing apart a government's ability to maintain its iron will for minimalist engagement.

Kofi Annan, UN Under Secretary-General for Peacekeeping, was probably the most direct on what governments do at such moments. 'When there is a problem, and the policy has not been thought [through], there is a knee-jerk reaction. They have to do something or face a public relations disaster.' There are moments when the relationship is at its most fickle and unpredictable, and when governments get into a policy mess. They end up committing themselves more deeply than they wanted to.

The most vivid recent example is the Serb siege of the Muslim town of Srebrenica that began in March 1993. For many days humanitarian organisations had been reporting the hell of Srebrenica: a small town swamped by refugees desperate for food who had been herded there by Serb forces. None of us could conceive the horror. It was known to humanitarian organisations but the Bosnian Serbs had blocked all efforts to truck in food aid. Then Tony Birtley, after three weeks of trying, smuggled himself in with a Hi-8 camera. He was hit by mortar fire getting the story, and almost lost a leg.

In a response that still haunts me I remember Foreign Office Minister Douglas Hogg telling Radio 4's *Today* programme: 'If you are asking me if we have a policy that will certainly save Srebrenica in a few hours, the answer I regret to say is no.' The Foreign Office dismissed talk of creating a Safe Area to save Srebrenica as a bad precedent to set and a bad principle to adopt. But at the UN, Birtley's images defied such government resistance from the big powers. On the Security Council the majority of non-aligned nations – including several Islamic countries – refused to be bullied by the Permanent Five. While the big nations had an extensive diplomatic and intelligence machine to brief them, the smaller nations relied on Birtley's TV images. Led by the flamboyant President of the Council, the Venezuelan Dr Diego Arria, the non-aligned took on the UN Secretariat – whom they didn't trust – and countries like Britain, which they accused of hoodwinking and deception over Srebrenica. After a bitter and chaotic week at the UN, Arria's determination won through. Late on a Friday night – 16 April 1993 – the non-aligned thwarted the big powers. Without knowing quite what they were doing they forced through a resolution making Srebrenica a Safe Area. General Wahlgren was ordered to draw blue lines on a map around the town and make the Safe Area work, although he did not have the first clue how to do it. As Dr Arria later told me, they were not interested in all the warnings about the Safe Areas becoming Balkan Lesothos. There was a humanitarian disaster on TV. The Security Council had to respond.

The irony is that in the UN operation on the ground the resolution was seen as irrelevant because senior UN officers had already independently negotiated an agreement between the Serbs and Bosnians to freeze the war around Srebrenica. More ironic still was the fact that the Safe Areas developed all the worst character-istics their original opponents had feared. They became rest and recuperation camps and 'divisional supply dumps' for Bosnian forces. While preparing for renewed fighting the Muslim fighters could live off UN food handouts under the UN's protective umbrella and prepare attacks against the Bosnian Serbs. Arguably the biggest disaster was that in defining the boundaries of Safe Areas, the UN froze the military situation on the ground. It thereby recognised Serb territorial gains and complicated peace negotiations, especially the drawing of settlement maps.

The diplomatic resentments run on to this day. 'It is a sheer miracle that we have not had a disaster', one senior UN official confided to me. He added: 'The Safe Area is an irresponsible concept. It is totally unviable and undefendable, with no chance of normal economic activity. It could have gone wrong so easily.' Dr Arria's reflection a year later was also telling. I asked him whether in retrospect he thought both his dependence on TV pictures and the Security Council's defiance of diplomatic advice had been right? 'I did not know that what we were creating was a trap,' he now concludes.

Another of Ambassador Inderfurth's diplomatic 'bruises' occurred a short time later on 22 April 1993. It happened by chance when British UN forces received word of a massacre somewhere up in villages not far from their base at Vitez in central Bosnia. Led by Colonel Bob Stewart, a small party of armoured Warrior vehicles from the Cheshire regiment set off not knowing what they were going to find. With them were a single British-pool TV cameraman and reporters Paul Davies of ITN and Martin Bell from the BBC. The importance of their coverage of what turned out to be the Ahmići massacre was not the emotional impact. The discovery suddenly put on the diplomatic and political map the viciousness of the Croat–Muslim war in central Bosnia which while well known to Western governments was not publicly acknowl-edged.

That fighting had been underway for several months. It received virtually no television coverage – to the annoyance of some UN officials and UNPROFOR officers. Croat forces were blocking roads and torching Muslim villages. 'The Croats were doing what the Serbs were doing', as one officer put it. But Western capitals took no notice. But in the weeks before Ahmići, governments were quietly satisfied. The plight of Sarajevo and the broader ethnic cleansing offensives by Serbs – like the one against Srebrenica – remained the main focus of media attention. But one source told me that four months before Ahmići, the UN military in Bosnia had been deeply concerned about the Croat offensives. They suggested to a meeting of senior British cabinet ministers that the Croats be identified as 'by far the biggest culprits' in the war. That suggestion was 'roundly sat on', said my source. 'It was information they did not want to hear. There was a belief that the Croats were OK and could do no wrong. Our reports on the Croats were being dismissed.'

Diplomatically and journalistically there could only be one black hat – the baddie – the Serbs ... and two white hats – the Croats and the Muslims; an issue which may still seriously skew American coverage in particular. Then came Ahmići at a time when in NATO capitals there seemed to be a head of steam building towards preparing for air strikes. It was a momentum that was sharply undermined when the chairman of NATO's Military Committee, Field Marshal Sir Richard Vincent, blew the West's bluff by openly asking what the politicians wanted him to organise.

Instantly, coverage of Ahmići diluted the public consensus against the Serbs. There was a noticeable intake of breath among politicians who were actively debating at the time the wisdom of air strikes. Suddenly they began to understand the shallowness of their perceptions of a war which did not just involve the Serbs as the main aggressors. There was a second aggressor – the Croats. Why should there not be air strikes against the Croats too? And what about the Muslims too? But the same Ahmići coverage also served Whitehall's policy aims. Privately they welcomed it as useful cover for rejecting air strikes. As one senior Downing Street official told me later: 'Images [like Ahmići] that complicated the Bosnia–Hercegovina story made it easier for us [to reject air strikes].'

Nevertheless, the impact of Ahmići in highlighting the Croat–Muslim war had a relatively short life. It was soon forgotten, and the Serbs quickly regained their position as sole evil party in the war. It also led to a distorted perception of what subsequently developed in central Bosnia. After the Croats were fingered as murderers of Muslims, UN forces witnessed a 'huge land grab' by the mainly Muslim Bosnian government forces throughout the Lašva river valley towards Gornji Vakuf. But, the UN says, the media showed virtually no interest in Muslim atrocities. Their attention had returned to Sarajevo. As one senior UN officer told me: 'While the world was seeing the hard-pressed Muslims in Sarajevo, the [Bosnian] Third Corps was pushing the Croats back relentlessly. In my area the air strikes would have to be against the Muslims, but that was not politically correct.' Another officer told me: 'Central Bosnia was ignored because murder became normal – a daily occurrence. There was a "total normality". As soon as a level of fighting becomes a certain level it is no longer news and therefore not newsworthy.'

So the Ahmići massacre revealed both the profound impact and the consequent inadequacy of TV coverage. The diplomatic agenda against the Serbs briefly stood unmasked. But soon – much to the relief of Western capitals – both the agenda and TV coverage returned to most of their preconceptions. The Ahmići pictures had great emotional impact, but they caused no long-term changes to policy.

The Real Impact of Real Time TV
There are two central themes in my analysis of the relationship between policy-makers and TV coverage. First, only rarely is there a change to overall strategy,

although quite frequently, there is a new twist to local tactics. Secondly, there is policy panic after the unexpected, about which I want to debunk some common misconceptions.

Who can forget the horrors of the Bosnian Serb detention camps at Omarska and Trnopolje revealed by ITN two years ago? It was my challenging of Radovan Karadžič in London, which led to the award-winning reports by Ian Williams and Penny Marshall. Roy Gutman of the New York newspaper *Newsday* had already broken the story. Maggie O'Kane had written a similar story in the *Guardian*. But Ed Vulliamy, Maggie's *Guardian* colleague who accompanied Ian and Penny to witness these scenes, admitted that without ITN's TV pictures his own award-winning front-page story would never have had the enormous impact it did.

The camp story came out of the blue, and it rattled governments. The duty Foreign Minister Lynda Chalker in our studio that night was not only moved; she was politically flustered by it. President Bush was in the White House briefing-room within an hour to condemn the camps and to promise America 'will not rest until the international community has gained access to all detention camps'. This was policy panic.

Senior officials at the time have now confirmed that the US Government had possessed significant details about the camps for at least two months before the ITN revelations. US Deputy Secretary of State Lawrence Eagleburger denies this. But a senior official has said on the record that the highest authorities at the State Department gave instructions 'deliberately not to tell the truth'. A senior official told Congress just before ITN's revelations that there was no 'substantiated information that would confirm the existence of these camps'. The UN knew. So too, to a lesser extent, did the International Committee of the Red Cross, although they were unable to work in Bosnia at the time because of threats against their staff. The UN claimed to have circulated a document to its member governments, and yet no one in the British Foreign Office could remember seeing a copy.

One can sound over-sanctimonious about this. But the fact is that we now know the ITN reports smoked out a most uncomfortable reality that governments and the UN seemed unable to find the political will to tackle. Indeed Washington had suppressed what it knew. As a senior Red Cross official said to me: 'Governments have been compelled through these [ITN] pictures to put the issue of prisoners at the top of the agenda,' before he added rather cynically 'at least for several weeks'. Eventually all the camps were closed – albeit slowly and to a schedule that was at the Serbs' tactical convenience.

But humanitarian organisations say the pressure of television actually furthered the Serb ends. By moving refugees out of the camps and out of Bosnia, TV coverage actually forced virtual international complicity in ethnic cleansing, which was the precise opposite of its stated aims. A policy panic thus produced rapid responses and results which were at odds with Western policy.

As I mentioned earlier, the Croat siege of Mostar barely received any television coverage. The main reason was the immense danger of getting there to cover the plight of the Muslims in the east of the city. The few UN staff who ever reached Mostar described the Croat siege as worse and more evil than the Serb stranglehold on Sarajevo. In November 1993 the BBC's Jeremy Bowen reached the city and produced a brave 45-minute documentary for *Assignment*, with excerpts for news coverage. It was vivid, relentless stuff; a rare and moving television insight into a humanitarian catastrophe that few knew about. Not long afterwards, a tape of Jeremy's programme reached the UNPROFOR base at Kiseljak where, one evening,

UN civilians and officers watched it in the mess. They were both horrified and moved when they realised what was going on not far away from them in their own patch. Between them they agreed that something had to be done – at least an attempt to reach the city. One UN official, Larry Stachewicz, described the mood to me after the Mostar film: 'It said we have to get into Mostar. How can we do it?' Eight days after viewing Bowen's tape, Stachewicz led a small UN team into Mostar 'at great risk'. Even the armoured Spanish UN battalion rarely went there because of the dangers. A month later, the team used UN cash and every ounce of initiative to persuade the Croats to allow in a mobile field hospital donated by South Africa – although the fighting made it impossible to make it operational for months afterwards.

'TV spurred us to make a policy, but we could not implement it,' Stachewicz told me. 'TV [coverage of the city] would have changed the whole balance on Mostar. It would have given us [the UN] strong leverage.' Mostar showed how for every horror witnessed by a journalist there could be ten, a hundred, or perhaps even a thousand more. Stachewicz told me how in March this year he drove through a village near Vares where he said he saw large numbers of Muslim men, women and children hanging.

Neither incident – as in an unknown number in Bosnia – was witnessed by a TV camera. Therefore neither created any public revulsion or international political outrage. Humanitarian workers regularly witnessed horrors, but routinely they did not carry cameras. Imagine the international fury if we had seen more of what they saw. Yet the most vital ally for humanitarian operations was television. As Sylvana Foa, spokesperson for the High Commission for Refugees, put it: 'Without TV coverage we are nothing. Our operations and their impact would die without TV.'

But it works both ways: for humanitarian operations, for the UN and even for the warring parties.

The deluge of phone calls to Downing Street after reports on 'Baby Irma' forced John Major to mount a British airlift. Irma's personal plight did more to highlight the misery of Sarajevo than the usual round of more depersonalised stories about the city. It generated offers of 1800 beds worldwide. But many hardened Bosnian media veterans like Martin Bell thought their organisations had 'taken leave of their senses'. There was also deep resentment among UN and Red Cross officials; the priorities of hard-pressed evacuation procedures were being flouted just to satisfy an ephemeral and random pressure created by television.

The resentment generated by television's somewhat random focus, which skews official priorities, is often widely felt. UNPROFOR officers have complained to me that often head offices in London or New York got a view of the situation in Bosnia from television that was highly skewed, often sharply at variance with the reality on the ground. There is also resentment at enterprising TV coverage that suddenly forces UN operations, for example, to change their priorities instantly. The story by Kate Adie, for example, in November 1992 about a mental hospital at Pazaric (near Tarcin, south-west of Sarajevo) put great pressure on Colonel Bob Stewart and the Cheshires to do something to relieve the hospital's plight. At one point the Danish UNHCR representative, Anders Levinson, rushed into the regiment's mess. One of those present described to me what happened. 'Bob Stewart and the officers were having tea. Anders said that Kate Adie had discovered a mental hospital near Tarcin and he had to go to deliver aid and blankets.' The British force commander, Brigadier Andrew Cumming, was there too. He asked Levinson whether he already knew about this hospital and the conditions. Levinson said he had known for some time. 'So why do something now?' the Brigadier asked. 'Because Kate Adie has been there.' According to one officer, the Cheshires 'had to drop everything and do something about it'.

But the hospital mission irritated UNPROFOR and the UNHCR. First, it took British forces into the Spanish area of responsibility. More importantly, it deflected them from their main job of escorting food to warehouses. As one officer put it to me: 'It was a one-day wonder; a pain in the arse. London asked what we were doing up there. We got our fingers rapped. [Planned] UNHCR operations were delayed for forty-eight hours.'

But the impact cuts both ways.

In June 1993, the Croats agreed to give safe passage for a 400-vehicle Bosnian humanitarian convoy into Muslim areas in central Bosnia. It was known as the 'Convoy of Joy'. Near Novi Travnik, however, Croat forces halted the column. UNPROFOR officers quickly worked out that the Croats had given permission for the convoy so they could stop and plunder it unwitnessed in an area under their control. The British troops urged TV crews to join them to cover the Croat ambush. TV coverage achieved precisely what the UN hoped for. It uncovered the Croat deception. UN officers believe international transmission of the ambush shamed the Croat leadership into forcing HVO Vice President Dario Kordić into releasing the trucks. As UNPROFOR's Chief of Staff at the time, Brigadier Vere Hayes, put it to me: 'TV had exactly the effect we hoped it would have. It gave the convoy an insurance policy.'

Conclusion

Looking for the best way to summarise my findings I found it in America's Presidential Decision Directive No. 25, announced in May 1994.

The Directive severely delimits American involvement in future 'Peace Operations'. Announcing PDD 25, US National Security Adviser Anthony Lake said this: 'When I wake up every morning and look at the headlines and the stories and the images on television of these conflicts, I want to work to end every conflict, I want to work to save every child out there, and I know the President does, and I know the American people do. But neither we nor the international community have the resources nor the mandate to do so.'

He speaks for all governments.

The Media as Impartial Observers or Protagonists

Conflict Reporting or Conflict Encouragement in Former Yugoslavia

JOHN BURNS

Among the millions of words written and spoken about the current civil wars in the former Yugoslavia, the predominant themes in the news media have been individual atrocities, the failure of international institutions to prevent conflict, the apportioning of blame both for that failure and for the civil war itself, and suggestions for action to solve the situation.

However, if the wars are able to teach us anything, then the process of conflict reporting (information gathering and interpretation and the role of all the media, both electronic and print) is surely one of the most important that needs analysis. Perhaps what is most significant is that many of those characteristics of journalistic practice criticised in this paper are not unique to the Yugoslav context, but are intensified and highlighted by the emotional hysteria surrounding that subject. If we accept the following criticisms as valid, then the lessons drawn should be applied to the wider field of conflict reporting.[1]

Most serious journalists would claim that they wish to find out the truth about events, interpret and analyse what they see, and disseminate to the wider public the facts as they know them and the conclusions to be drawn. Few would admit to deliberate bias and yet the Yugoslav civil wars – some of the world's most reported conflicts – demonstrate the clearest examples of one-sided reporting, resulting from a pack psychology among journalists,[2] in which it is almost impossible for a commentator to question the received wisdom of those around him or her. Normal good journalistic practice disappears and stories are transmitted without the verification that should be second nature.[3]

The results of such a pack mentality are more far-reaching than the individual journalist may wish to admit. In particular, because the media have concentrated huge resources upon reporting atrocities in former Yugoslavia and have laid blame for those atrocities almost wholly on one side, not differentiating between those of the same 'ethnic' group in different geographical areas, the conduct and formulation of the foreign policies of Western governments and institutions have been pushed in directions that are not necessarily those best suited to a positive outcome. Indeed, on those occasions when policy has shifted significantly, the perceived benefits have been far outweighed by the drawbacks.

UN Secretary-General Boutros Boutros-Ghali complained (ironically to a CNN conference held in Atlanta in May 1993) that, 'Today, the media do not simply report the news. Television has become a part of the events it covers. It has changed the way the world reacts to crisis. ... Public emotion becomes so intense that the United Nations' work is undermined. On television, the problems become simplified and exaggerated.' The British Foreign Secretary Douglas Hurd expressed similar sentiments in the House of Commons during the same period and has continued to do so from time to time ever since.

These few clear thoughts from men directly responsible for the formulation of international reaction reflect fundamental truths about the style and methods of conflict reporting in the Yugoslav context. Almost as soon as a civil war began, first briefly in Slovenia and then over a longer period in Croatia, media, particularly television, began to bombard the Western public with the most gruesome images of man's inhumanity to man without either any properly considered explanation of background or reasons why these atrocities were taking place, or, indeed, verifying whether the attribution of atrocities was correct at all. On several notable occasions the murdered bodies of one side were characterised as 'ethnically' that of their murderers.[4]

The first element in our criticism of the journalists' methods lies, therefore, in their simplification of a complex political scenario.[5] In Yugoslavia of 1991 this was reduced to a plain struggle between the so-called progressive 'Western-looking' democratic states (Croatia, Slovenia) and an ex-Communist, expansionist, 'undemocratic' state of Serbia, seeking to create its dream of a 'Greater Serbia'.[6] Once that basic hypothesis had been postulated, all other facts and events were misinterpreted on the basis of it and subsequently used to prove it. No attention, for example, was paid to the absurdity of labelling one actor, the President of Serbia, 'ex-Communist', while ignoring the fact that many of the senior leaders in Slovenia and Croatia were themselves 'ex-Communists'. The label was meaningless except to denote that the protagonists were career politicians, not recently elevated individuals.

From the earliest days of the conflict, events or concepts that did not fit the established hypothesis were either not properly reported, or ignored. Many examples can be found from 1991 to 1994, but a few sample illustrations will demonstrate the trend.

When the federal government of Yugoslavia, in June 1991, ordered the securing of the international border posts in Slovenia, which was followed by short bloody clashes with the Slovenian Defence Force, no Western commentator questioned the right of the Slovenes to attack the federal army, although this was the army of the federal state of which they were a part and which had been a founder member of the United Nations, and which was still the internationally accepted entity with legal personality.

As civil war erupted in Croatia, the received view of the conflict was heavily based upon reports emanating from Croatian government press conferences and spokesmen, with little first-hand verification.[7] The reasons for this were largely because of the dangers of visiting combat zones, but also due to the reliance upon local interpreters and stringers for information. In addition, few reporters were placed in Belgrade or Serbian territories. Film of corpses and destruction appeared on British and American televisions as evidence almost entirely of Serb military operations. The term 'ethnic cleansing' was rediscovered as the sole occupation of Serbs and no one questioned the evident inconsistencies in this one-sided representation. Hardly any reports spoke of the suspension by the Croatian government of police and judicial authorities in the municipalities that had voted against Franjo Tudjman in 1990, nor the publication of a book listing all Serb family names in western Slavonia, preparatory to the commencement of removing Serb families from villages in the

Slovenska Požega district.[8] These and similar events are not attractive to the photojournalist or television reporter but are crucial to understanding the currents in a developing conflict. Similar omission of contributory factors towards conflict are to be found in the Bosnian scenario, notably the reporting of the fighting in the enclave centred on Srebrenica, ignoring the massacres of Serbian villages around Bratunac,[9] and the push into Goražde, ignoring the military assets housed inside a 'safe area' and the debate that should have been had as to what constituted a 'safe area'.

Little has been said about the claimed right to self-determination of the Serb-inhabited areas of Croatia, in terms parallel to those which had been accorded to Slovenes and to Croats. Nothing significant was reported during 1991–2 of the 251,000 Serb refugees from Croatia housed in Serbia and reported on in detail by the UN Secretary-General in March 1993. Photographs, captions and articles appeared that spoke of the destruction of monuments and churches, but almost none admitted to the identity of a church or monument as Orthodox or Serb. This would be perfectly understandable as propaganda or as the product of a public relations firm on behalf of a party to a war, but it is insupportable as supposedly impartial reporting.

The second major criticism that must be levelled against journalistic practice in the reporting of the Yugoslav conflict is the omission of contrary evidence, or the deliberate underplaying of facts that point away from the preconceived conclusion. The war in Bosnia–Hercegovina provides examples of this.

Perhaps one of the most potent themes that has arisen from the chaos of the Bosnian civil war is that of the abuse of women. As a topic to arouse the fiercest condemnation and moral outrage against the alleged perpetrators, it has unmatched force. However, the case of the alleged systematic rape and abuse of Bosnian Muslim women by Bosnian Serbs provides a salutary lesson in the wrong method of conflict reporting.

The period 1992–3 saw the development of two related charges against the Bosnian Serbs, based upon unproved allegations and supposition: the systematic rape of women and the concept of the 'concentration camp'. Roy Gutman won his share of the 1993 Pulitzer Prize for his reports of camps for prisoners, described as 'concentration camps', evoking the collective memory of the Nazi camps. No evidence has ever been produced nor, indeed, has the claim ever been made, interestingly, that these camps were functioning in the same way as Dachau or Auschwitz, but the nomenclature stuck.[10] Reports in European newspapers show that the nomenclature came from the Ruder and Finn Public Relations firm in New York, working on behalf of the Bosnian government.[11] The most used photograph was that of an emaciated figure, not wearing a shirt, standing at the wire around Omarska camp. Neither Penny Marshall fronting the ITN follow-up coverage of this camp and that in Trnopolje nor Roy Gutman or any other of the three hundred or so journalists drafted in to cover the 'death camp' stories bothered to mention or perhaps find out that the man was not Muslim but Serbian, a certain Slobodan Konjević, arrested and confined for looting, and that he was dramatically emaciated due to tuberculosis, not starvation. This is not an isolated example of photographs of Serbs being used to illustrate a story about the suffering of one of the other groups. Usually this appears in the form of photographs of corpses or refugees on the road who are Serbs, used as illustrative material for reports of the actions by the Serbs against another party.

None of the reports during this period covered the Bosnian Muslim and Bosnian Croat camps, which together held larger numbers of prisoners than those of the

Bosnian Serbs.[12] These were ignored. Indeed, except for a brief period when one news agency acquired film of Bosnian Croats marching Muslims out of Mostar to a camp, there has been almost no coverage of Muslims in Croat camps or Croats in Muslim ones. The previous ethnic cleansing of thousands of Serbs out of Mostar by the Muslims was not mentioned at all. Yet, despite these gaps in the public knowledge, there seem to be few instances of the public questioning what is placed before them.

The tendency to play down inconvenient facts was not temporary. On 16 March 1994 the pre-advertisement break headline for an ITN report by Penny Marshall referred specifically to 'Serbian camps' when the report covered the first arrests for trial on war crimes. Miss Marshall's commentary referred in passing to arrests in various parts of Europe of men 'from all sides', but almost the whole piece centred on a Serb, Tadic, who was accused with crimes at Omarska camp. Again, in the commentary, Miss Marshall acknowledged that the person who identified Tadic was stated to have no direct knowledge of atrocities, but the effect of the piece reinforced the concept of camps being organised solely by one side.

The *New York Times* correspondent John Burns won a share of the Pulitzer Prize for his reports of interviews with the captured Bosnian Serb soldier Borislav Herak. Herak's videotaped confessions of multiple rape, prior to his 'trial' in Sarajevo, confirmed the image of systematic abuse that had been propagated for some weeks beforehand. Neither the published articles by Burns nor the broadcast extracts from the tapes referred to further allegations made by Herak against the former UNPROFOR commander, Lt. General Lewis Mackenzie, accusing him of committing similar atrocities.[13] Apart from the fact that such accusations were apparently absurd enough to undermine the credibility of the witness, not one journalist or editor, either from the television news programmes which were using the video footage, or from the Pullitzer Prize jury, seemed able to wonder whether confession extracted before a camera in these circumstances could remotely be reliable. One could contrast media treatment of the miscarriages of justice in the UK and the associated extracted confessions, or one could contrast the treatment of the confessions on video by the two British RAF pilots shot down over Iraq during 'Desert Storm'. Normal scepticism or rational analysis was not operating during this period.

These episodes showed the media gearing up to evoke the strongest feelings of disgust and moral outrage in public opinion to blame one side as the sole perpetrator of evil. The culmination of the process arose during December 1992–January 1993, with the Edinburgh summit of the European Council reacting to media reports of hundreds of women raped systematically (reports such as those of Maggie O'Kane in the *Guardian*), condemning the abuse of women in this way and setting up a commission of enquiry to look into the facts. Normally sceptical journalists seemed unaware of the illogicality of deciding that an event has taken place and condemning it with great moral force and then afterwards undertaking some basic research to find out whether or not these events were true or not.

In the event, the numbers game became the main preoccupation of newspapers and media pundits during the next few weeks. The figure for victims was established at around 20,000 in the EC's Warburton Report, a figure extrapolated from interviews conducted through interpreters with eight women in five days in Zagreb.[14] The French member of the EC enquiry team resigned because of the publication of such an unreliable estimate,[15] and, in addition to the doubt thrown by professional counsellors on the method of enquiry used in these trauma cases, the reports of the ICRC and the UN's Special Rapporteur, Tadeusz Mazowiecki, showed that the number of proven rapes was still under two hundred, out of all the crimes committed by all parties in the civil war. All else is based on speculation (e.g. *Paris Match*'s 60,000 women raped by Serbs) or hearsay evidence. Such information feeds upon itself, often in circular form, at second, third and even fourth hand and anecdotal perceptions achieve the force of truth.[16] It is for this reason that Professor Frits Kalshoven finally resigned his position as the first Chairman of the UN Commission for the Investigation of War Crimes in former Yugoslavia, since he criticised the wild speculation and unsubstantiated evidence apparently accepted by some in the Commission.[17]

Such political arguments develop from the intense atmosphere in the media which builds up a perception of moral outrage against evil deeds and creates expectations in the public that are not based on a sound knowledge of the facts, but on the excitation of emotion and the impact of immediate forceful images in film and photograph. As the Minister of State at the UK Foreign Office Douglas Hogg observed on one occasion, 'Moral outrage is not a conclusive element in determining policy. It is a relevant factor, but not conclusive.'[18] The cause of the severe problems seen in the credibility of the UN and other institutions lies in the clash between this public perception of events engendered by the media, evoking so-called moral arguments, and the analysis of facts by government agencies and individuals which are based on a much broader view of events than that provided to the public at large.

In fact, the media in general contribute significantly to the weakening of international institutions by a pack mentality that quite deliberately ignores swathes of evidence which would otherwise balance the picture in a conflict scenario. One example from January 1994 illustrates this particularly well. The *Guardian*, in a manner similar to that of several of the British broadsheet daily newspapers, devoted a large front-page photograph and two separate front-page reports to the mortaring of a playground in the suburbs of Sarajevo, which caused death and injury to about ten children. The language of the reports was particularly emotive, comparable to that used in some of the rape case pieces in the same newspaper. The mortaring was attributed to Bosnian Serbs, although no evidence was brought to show this.

Few readers would have realised that an identical mortaring incident took place on the same day in a different city. Only those who persevered to the back page continuation of the front-page articles would have found an unsigned two-inch single column quoting a bare report of the death of six children and the wounding of others in a mortar attack in east Mostar. No rich language here, not even a hard, incisive attribution of guilt for the murders of these children. But here, the dead were Muslims mortared by Croats – an unfashionable combination for the emotional treatment found most frequently in the coverage of fighting involving Serbs. For example, there was never any attempt to feature nightly two-minute slots on the pounding of Mostar, as BBC2 did in the case of the siege of Sarajevo. The physical destruction of Mostar has been described as more complete than anything in Bosnia–Hercegovina or even Vukovar.

Shortly after these incidents, on 5 February 1994, the Sarajevo marketplace explosion took place with around 68 people reported killed. It is interesting that the coverage of this explosion, following on from the kind of reporting cited above, was both extensive and yet strangely sketchy in key areas, particularly with regard to the type of weapon use and the numbers killed and injured.[19] The figure for the dead, a constant 68, was widely reported within six hours of the explosion, yet the figures for an explosion in Johannesburg were fluctuating between 18 on BBC television news and 34 on radio reports, some thirteen hours after that bomb-blast. Of course, the marketplace explosion, unattributable though it was, became the ostensible catalyst for a NATO ultimatum regarding heavy weaponry in and around the city and it is that sequence of events which became the main thread for media reports thereafter. This in itself was a severely distorted line for the media to take, bearing little relationship to the actual long-term political negotiation and discussion which concluded in the withdrawal of the majority Bosnian Serb heavy weapons from Sarajevo and the placing of the remaining Bosnian Serb and Bosnian Muslim heavy weaponry under UN control. The myths are perpetuated even in learned foreign policy journals, since no account is taken of the role of Lord Owen or Thorvald Stoltenberg in the previous three months. However, this was not for want of information on this occasion. Lord Owen explicitly outlined the process to Sir David Frost on BBC television the morning after the explosion.[20]

From the tenor of the above comments it should be clear that, unlike newspaper editorials, or television journalists, governments and institutions should not react to individual events without fully considering the wider intelligence picture and all the implications for a course of action in a given situation. However, by their very nature, democratically accountable politicians have to be seen to take account of public opinion, by whatever means that is expressed. In the Yugoslav context, 'public opinion' is largely based on the message consistently put across in the media. If that message is distorted, as is quite clear from an objective knowledge of the wider picture, then the pressure from public opinion drives the politicians and eventually the institutions towards possibly ill-conceived or wrong actions.

As time passed, the truth of this proposition was to become more apparent. Whereas in 1992 or 1993, a small number of senior political figures and analysts were arguing almost alone against taking certain actions in and concerning Bosnia, for fear that the consequences would be unforseeable, the results would not be those which were desired and the simplistic portrayal of events in the various media was not a sound basis for decision-making, by 1994 all observers could benefit from more sober reflection. Most dramatically, in April 1992, when an agreement on constitutional principles had been reached in Lisbon between all three sides in Bosnia–Hercegovina, it became clear that the United States had encouraged the Bosnian government in ways that led it to withdraw from the agreement.

Once recognition of Croatia and Slovenia had been accepted, it was inevitable that both Bosnia–Hercegovina and Macedonia would seek to take the same road. In Macedonia's case, there were no intractable internal problems; in Bosnia–Hercegovina's case, the reverse was true and it was known in advance that the process of recognition would be a cause of civil war. The media gave little weight to the UN Secretary-General's warnings nor those of Lord Carrington or José Cutilheiro. Indeed, few analyses or books that take as their subject the so-called failures of the Western institutions to 'act decisively' over the problems of former Yugoslavia recognise the responsibility which lies at the door of the electronic media for creating the conditions in which policy errors have been made. Even United States Secretary of State Warren Christopher admitted this in *USA Today* in June 1993 with regard to the precipitate recognition of Croatia followed by that of Bosnia–Hercegovina.

Bosnia–Hercegovina and Croatia are, of course, by no means the only theatres in which the major powers have felt pressured to intervene in continuing civil wars. However, the experience of the US, in particular, has been unhappy, exemplified by its ignominious retreat from Somalia after an unprecedented media circus at the first beach landings by Special Forces some months earlier. The eagerness for intervention in civil wars is slowly receding to the same degree that the role of the media in reporting such conflicts is coming under closer scrutiny. CNN, in particular, has become the focus of some attention because of its power as an immediate source of effective images.[21]

However, the 'CNN curve' alone is not responsible for the failure of institutions to deal successfully with major conflicts around the world. It could be argued that the institutions are no less successful now than they ever were, it is simply that public expectations have been raised far above the practical realities of implementation. If the media continue to allow themselves to sink into the morass of conflicting propaganda without effective quality control for their sources and balance, then they bear a heavy responsibility for subsequent failures. Journalists cannot expect to be received as impartial observers of conflicts, judging events by absolute standards, if they become party to the narrow pack mentality identified above. The harder they press for action, the greater their personal responsibility, for which they may have eventually to account to the peoples about whom they report. It is wholly unremarkable that Mohammed Sacirbey, then Bosnian Ambassador to the UN (later, Foreign Minister), hit out strongly at the UN and Western governments when his expectations were aroused to the same degree as those of the general public by the single-minded calls for particular actions that came from a wide spectrum of the media. It cannot be said that in these circumstances, the media merely report what happens and encourage the public to reach conclusions. The media are protagonists in conflict for as long as they are unable to provide the highest standards of objective and balanced reporting while still presenting themselves as impartial arbiters pressing for action.[22]

Notes

1. The primary source for opinion forming remains editorial and analytical passages in the print media, particularly daily newspapers, although the immediacy of television and, to a lesser extent, radio has a profound effect. See the incisive criticisms of the journalistic theses by Simon Jenkins, *The Times*, 20 April 1994; for example, 'History knows no more dangerous lie than that a Balkan war is in some mystic sense "the world's fault".' Cf. idem, *The Spectator*, 23 April 1994, and most recently, *The Times*, 31 May 1995. For a more cautious critique see James Gow and Lawrence Freedman, 'Intervention in a Fragmentary State: The Case of Yugoslavia', in Nigel Rodley (ed.), *To Loose the Bands of Wickedness* (London: 1992) p. 112.

2. David Binder of *The New York Times* enunciates this tendency most clearly; see Nik Gowing, 'Real-time Television Coverage of Armed Conflicts and Diplomatic Crises: Does it Pressure or Distort Foreign Policy Decisions', Working Paper, The Joan Shorestein Barone Center on the Press, Politics and Public Policy, John F. Kennedy School of Government, Harvard University, Cambridge MA, June 1994, p. 63; and his contribution to this book based on this Paper, in which he quotes a source regarding a UN briefing to a Cabinet Committee, identifying Croats as 'by far the biggest culprits' (p. 88). An unpalatable message for them to hear. See also Misha Glenny in the Vienna magazine *Profil*, 28 February 1994.

3. Roy Gutman, credited with the first media exposure of Bosnian Serb prison camps, is attacked for this; Joan Phillips, *Living Marxism*, May 1993, pp. 12–16. Gutman himself, in an interview for *American Journalism Review*, July 1994, admits that he abandoned strict objectivity in order to pressure governments to act.

4. Sylvia Poggioli, an award-winning journalist, cites examples of this manipulation in 'Scouts without Compasses', (*Niemann Reports*, Fall 1993, p. 3). The cavalier attitude to factual accuracy by gross errors in captioning photographs is well illustrated by an example in *The Christian Science Monitor*, January 1994, depicting Mostar bridge, captioned as destroyed by Bosnian Serbs, although the episode in question was between Bosnian Muslims and Croats.

5. Gowing ('Real-time Television Coverage', p. 62 n. 334) quotes an editorial from *The Daily Telegraph*, 28 April 1994, which at this late stage criticises all media for oversimplifying issues and calls on journalists to be detached. Joan Phillips, in 'Bloody Liberals', *Living Marxism*, September 1993, pp. 10–21, strongly challenges the basis upon which the current media campaign is constructed. See also Rod Thornton, 'A Conflict of Views: The Press and the Soldier in Bosnia', *The South Slav Journal* vol. 15 no. 3–4, 1992, pp. 10–17, esp. p. 11, and Victor Dricks, *The Phoenix Gazette*, 10 March 1994. Cf. *The Christian Science Monitor*; see n. 22 below.

6. The *Frankfurter Allgemeine Zeitung* was prominent in creating this scenario, in particular

through regular commentaries by Johann Rathskeller during summer 1991. Wolfgang Pohrt, in *Konkret*, no. 9, September 1991, analyses German print media in detail. Only later, in 1993 and 1994, did the analagous concepts, with an equal historical background, of Greater Croatia and Greater Albania begin to emerge in the general media.

7. Misha Glenny, in *The Times*, 22 September 1992, recalls that 'the overwhelming majority [of foreign journalists killed] were on their first assignment in Yugoslavia.' Ian Traynor in *The Guardian* sometimes relies for whole stories on one source: 'Croatian government spokesmen' and 'official', 24 July 1991; 'Croatian government spokesmen' and 'officials in Zagreb' and 'Croatian Defence Minister', 26 July 1991. See, in particular, Poggioli, 'Scouts without Compasses', n. 4, pp. 2f., where she describes her experience both in Slovenia and Croatia of the careful guidance and psychological manipulation of foreign journalists.

8. See Dossier no. 2, 15 November–30 December 1991, Serbian Council (a human rights NGO), regarding activities of Croatian authorities of Slavonska Požega ordered on 29 October 1991.

9. Joan Hoey (formerly Joan Phillips), *The Times Educational Supplement*, 18 March 1994. The massacres of Serb civilians around Bratunac were referred to by both generals Morillon and Rose at different times, but the themes were not developed beyond one BBC Breakfast TV report in 1993. Cf. the *Guardian*, 29 December 1992, where a map insert depicts Serb villages in the area, silently contradicting the first paragraph of the text referring to 'a string of predominantly Muslim towns'. For omission of events, cf. Roy Gutman in *Newsday*, 13 December 1992, where he refers to the murder of Serb civilians in Serdari which he had visited in early September. The report was with little effect; and Louise Branson, *The Sunday Times*, 12 July 1992, who provides a rare attempt to investigate even-handedly accounts of atrocities on all sides, four committed by Serbs, five committed on Serbs by others.

10. Phillips, 'Bloody Liberals', n. 3, criticises Gutman's methods in detail.

11. Karl Waldron, *New Statesman and Society*, 31 July 1992, pp. 12f.; Tom O'Sullivan, in 'Truth Is the First Casualty in PR Offensive', *The Independent*, 21 August 1992, shows that Ruder Finn Global Public Affairs worked for the Croatian and Bosnian government accounts. See also Jacques Merlino, *Les Verités yugoslaves ne sont pas toutes bonnes à dire* (Paris: 1992), where he interviews James Harff, Director of Ruder Finn; *The Atlanta Journal*, 28 February 1993; and Alfred Sherman, *Perfidy in the Balkans: The Rape of Yugoslavia* (Athens: Psichogias 1993), p. 130.

12. The most notorious of the Croat camps were those in the Capljina district, at Dretelj and Gabela, housing Muslims expelled from the Mostar area. Bosnian Muslim prisoners were held in severe conditions in the Celebici and Tarcin prisons. A. McGregor, in the *Guardian*, 14 August 1992, reports that the ICRC said that 'all factions in the Bosnia conflict were guilty of inhumanity and brutality in running their detention centres. The organisation had visited 12 camps run by Muslims, Croats and Serbs since July 7th and all violated the 1949 Geneva conventions.'

13. Lewis MacKenzie, *Peacekeeper: The Road to Sarajevo* (Vancouver/Toronto: Douglas McIntyre 1993), pp. 326–7. John F. Burns, in the *Guardian*, 3 December 1992, and Maggie O'Kane, in the *Guardian*, 24 December 1992, accept the statements with regard to 'rape camps' etc. in the same text as reference to MacKenzie without questions, while questioning the veracity of the MacKenzie evidence.

14. Roger Caseby, *The Sunday Times*, 28 August 1993. The extrapolated figures were from Bosnian and Croat sources. Linda Grant, in the *Guardian*, 2 August 1993, states that there is no reliable figure and criticises the tone of reporting on this subject; on 17 February 1993 she acknowledges that the majority of abused women were Muslim, but also that Croat and Serb women were abused.

15. See Phillippe Marcovici, *Le Quotidien de Paris*, 23 November 1993. The UN Commission on Human Rights, 10 February 1993, reported an estimated 2,400 victims, from all 'ethnic' backgrounds, based on 119 documented cases. See also Beatrix Campbell, *The Independent*, 28 April 1993.

16. E.g. M. Trau and M. O'Kane, *The Guardian*, 19 December 1992: 'Reports ... have been confirmed by the *Guardian* in interviews with 20 women ...' Bosnian government figures are regularly quoted in the same newspaper, 14,000 (19 December 1992), 17,000 (24 December 1992, 50,000 from Muslim/Croat sources, 20,000 from EC Warburton Report (20 January 1993). On the background to the formation of the 'rape camp' stories, valuable is Linda Grant, 'Rape Babies: What Do We Know?', *The Independent on Sunday*, 10 January 1993.

17. It is worth noting that American politicians have, on occasion, criticised the British for providing a very small amount of evidence to this Commission, based on the debriefing of refugees in the UK, but the Americans have not appreciated that quality and not quantity of evidence is paramount.

18. Interview, BBC TV April 1993. Cf. Edward Bickham (adviser to Douglas Hurd), in *Spectrum* Autumn 1993, p. 3; Nik Gowing, in this book, 'emotion and partiality cloud analysis'; Misha Glenny, *The Times*, 22 September 1992, 'an emotive response can only exacerbate a political

problem. [Television] cannot explain the reasons behind the conflict.'

19. This Markale market explosion was quickly assessed as a possible Muslim propaganda act, similar to the Vase Miskin bread queue massacre in 1992. For the market explosion see: James Rupert, *The Washington Post*, 9 March 1993, 'UN team said it could not pinpoint the source of the attack …'; and Boris Johnson, *The Sunday Telegraph*, 13 February 1994, who remarks on the editing of the television footage released by CNN and analyses its influence on the whole episode. For evidence of Muslims perpetrating the Vase Miskin explosion see: Leonard Doyle, 'Muslims Slaughter their Own People', *The Independent*, 22 August 1992; and Roger Boyes, *The Times*, 24 August 1992, who quotes the leaked UN report which 'said they [the Muslims] were responsible for a mortar attack on a Sarajevo bread queue, the shelling of a funeral and mortar fire during Mr. Hurd's recent visit …' Cf. MacKenzie, *Peacekeeper*, p. 308, n. 13. Ian Traynor, in the *Guardian*, 23 June 1992, persists with attribution to the Serbs, although he admits, ibid. 29 May 1992, that this 'could not have come at a more uncomfortable time for Belgrade'.

20. See also Simon Jenkins, 'Bombs and Blind Faith', *The Times*, 13 April 1994. Cf. Gowing, *Real-time Television Coverage*, pp. 69–95.

21. Recently, Ben Macintyre, *The Times*, 3 June 1995: 'News arrives on screen virtually unfiltered, more often driven by pictures than analysis …'

22. The daily edition of *The Christian Science Monitor*, 23 May 1995, discusses media influences and the negative effect of the simplification of complex issues. Contrast the views expressed by Lt. General Sir Michael Rose, *RUSI Journal*, June 1995, with the insubstantial propaganda by Noel Malcolm, *The Spectator*, 10 June 1995, pp. 14–18, which attacks in almost equal measure the FCO, MOD, UN and Lt. General Lewis MacKenzie, without consideration of proved counter-argument.

PART THREE
War Studies, Media Studies

The Strategic Imperative for Media Management

JAMES GOW AND JAMES TILSLEY

At the end of the 20th century the ability to manipulate, mobilise and maintain mass media support at both international and domestic levels is a crucial element in the war-winning capacity of a political community. In the former Yugoslavia, mass media was an integral part of each of the combatants' strategies. The Gulf War had already given a pertinent demonstration of the way in which modern mass media could be successfully utilised as an adjunct to combat. The various Yugoslavs were not slow to realise this. As will be shown, they learned lessons from the Gulf and incorporated these in their strategies.

In the Gulf Conflict, mass media instruments were used to communicate messages broadly within the international community, as well as playing an important role within the UN-authorised coalition engaging Iraq. This type of dual-level propaganda with resonance in both internal and external environments was also present in the Yugoslav War. With regard to the Gulf, the purpose of domestic media management was largely to mobilise public support and understanding for the coalition's objectives. It was also to counter fears, played on by the Iraqis that the war would become a bloodbath in which large numbers of coalition soldiers would be killed. This reflects the need for preparation as well as the need for a responsive and flexible media campaign.

These were added to lessons drawn more broadly from modern mass media practices and techniques, especially in Western countries. Lessons involving what may be described as the 'psychological' weaknesses of Western societies were clearly understood and were used at the international level to good effect.[1] The present analysis is concerned to show the ways in which media management was an integral and indispensable element in the military–political campaigns of the combatants in the Yugoslav War of Dissolution.

Preparing for War: The Serbian Story

Lack of adequate preparation, as we shall see, appears to have been one mistake made by the Zagreb authorities during the war in Croatia during 1991 and 1992 (although it was a lesson well learned by 1995). The Serbian side proved itself to be adept at using subtle messages to shape international conceptions of the conflict at crucial moments. This was especially true when the prospect of armed conflict was being debated in the West, in particular conjuring images of new Vietnams, quagmires and military catastrophes.[2] The Serbian side was most effective in preparing and maintaining internal public support for the war, as well as in later de-emphasising the war when it suited Serbian President Slobodan Milošević.[3]

Soon after coming to power in 1987, Milošević tightened political control of the Serbian media. News reports on Radio Television Serbia (RTS) began to set the parameters of a conflict about the future of the Yugoslav federation. The final struggle between the republics and between the republics and the central authorities of the federation began in Belgrade. Milošević had risen to power on a campaign to restore Serbia's authority in the Autonomous Province of Kosovo (one of two such provinces within the federation, both part of Serbia). Indeed, the media had played a central part in his rise.[4] In line with this, the Serbian media increasingly focused on Kosovo, while the authorities began repression of political movements in the province. The focus of this media–political crusade was separatism among the Albanian majority in the province. This sent, as must have been intended, a clear signal to other parts of the federation: watch out for Serbia. However, as much as the message struck fear in other Yugoslavs, it also encouraged them to oppose Serbia.

Fear was an important part of Serbian media campaigns. The fears of Croatian Serbs were an issue. The use by Croatian nationalists of symbols associated with the Ustasha regime which had been responsible for the deaths of more than 300,000 Serbs during the Second World War was meat to the organised Serbian media in the early stages of conflict.[5] Milošević may later have used fears of attack by a US-led international 'Balkan Storm' coalition to control his constituencies of support.[6] Fear also had a key role in motivating Yugoslav People's Army (JNA) personnel during the autumn 1991 Dubrovnik campaign. This campaign largely involved Montenegrin reservists who had been led to believe that Croatian 'fascist' forces were planning to attack Montenegro at Herceg Novi. This was supplemented by reports that the Croats were committing genocide against the Serbs in Croatia.[7] At the same time, the JNA may well have hoped that the capture of Dubrovnik, had it been achieved, would have been a propaganda coup. Fear was essential to the effort to capture the town. JNA experience in Slovenia and elsewhere in Croatia at the beginning of the conflict had shown that conscript-based forces were only effective if motivated by fear or hatred.[8]

Conversely, the JNA's relatively poor performance in Slovenia and Croatia may have been due to propaganda aimed at reducing morale. Certainly, army morale was a major difficulty as the draft was being widely ignored during the second half of 1991,[9] although weak leadership compounded this problem. The dilemma for the JNA in this period was that it could not clearly state what its objectives were to bolster support in Serbia and among Serbs outside Serbia. In terms of modern strategic media management this would have seemed essential. The JNA, however, also had to address an international audience. It could not openly admit that it was prosecuting a war for the borders of a new Yugoslavia to be inhabited by the Serbs because that would invite open condemnation by the international community. International opinion, which was anyway uncertain and divided, had to be left either confused, or persuaded that the JNA was doing no more in Croatia than peace-keeping. In order to prevent any possibility of international armed intervention, Belgrade's military and political leaders had to leave themselves in a weak position in terms of explaining Serbian ambitions in the war.

Whereas the JNA suffered from a necessary inability to explain its war aims, Milošević could avoid being badly damaged by steering media criticism against the generals (thereby facilitating his control of the military). In the domestic sphere, the Serbian regime was more than capable of maintaining its position through propaganda messages. In doing so, it came to be helped to some extent by the imposition of comprehensive sanctions against Serbia and Montenegro for sponsoring the war in Bosnia by the UN Security Council. Sanctions helped in promoting solidarity among the Serbs – they could easily be used to signal that the world was against them. Domestic propaganda remained important for the Serbian leadership throughout the war and its period of international isolation.

The sanctions régime also helped the government to control, or muzzle, opposition media. It did so by creating shortages of newsprint and technology. This ensured that the majority of Serbs outside Belgrade were reliant on state-controlled television for news.[10] This complemented government activities that restrained the open media (which nonetheless continued to operate), such as persecution – including violence, control of employment and, in some cases, ownership as mergers were forced.[11] The Milošević régime was very successful in maintaining domestic support during a war that had a harsh effect on the Serbian economy.

Media–strategic Synergy: The Slovenian Story

Media management was essential to Slovenian strategic purpose.[12] Slovenia had studied the Gulf War as part of an analysis of the world they were seeking to join. Two features which emerged from this analysis were incorporated in preparations for independence. One was the importance of a short campaign with a big impact. Slovenian defence planners formed the belief that if it came to a fight, they would need to be efficient in combat in order to secure a quick and favourable outcome. Indeed, it was judged that their aims could only be realised through a short, sharp campaign in which the 'occupier' was beaten as soon as possible.

The second was that use of information media would be extremely important.[13] To this end, the Ministry of Information organised what was in reality a massive propaganda campaign. The Ministry hired the major cultural and conference centre in the Slovenian capital Ljubljana, the Cankarjev Dom, and established it as a slick, modern media centre on the eve of the declaration of independence. In this way, they were able to present their case to the world, thereby mobilising support in Western countries in particular. The press centre reflected an understanding derived from the Gulf War on the importance of controlling the media and the sense that one of the best ways of doing this was by 'making their lives easy' for them, giving them efficient, regular briefings on the state of events. To this end they also proved adept at manipulating information.

The Slovenian propaganda campaign was, in part, directed towards federal institutions and Belgrade – most importantly, the army. The JNA was at once portrayed as being an army of occupation led by communist Serbian generals and as an army of conscripts who did not want to fight and who were opposed to the operations of which they were a part in Slovenia.[14] This apparent contradiction represented separate messages being sent in different directions. First, there was the intention to impress on outsiders, particularly in the West, that the Belgrade generals were entirely responsible for the conflict and were committing aggression against a sovereign republic. There was also the intention to undermine any sense of rightfulness in the JNA's position by showing that the soldiers themselves were not interested in fighting an unjust aggressive war – which message could also be used to undermine cohesion and morale in JNA units, finding resonance with soldiers who did not understand why they were fighting in Slovenia.[15]

Slovenia was particularly adept at waging a media war. With the advantage of national homogeneity providing a solid underpinning for Ljubljana's independence policy, the authorities identified factors which would determine success in the struggle for international recognition, including use of international news media. As one Serbian analyst observed, the 'Slovenian media campaign was well organised and precisely targeted and soon tilted the sympathy of the international public in its favour.'[16] Western media and public opinion, especially in Germany, largely fell firmly behind the image of the war as a fight for political and economic freedom from a centralist, Bolshevik bureaucracy. The image of the JNA as aggressor was perpetuated. Although there was clearly some sense in which this was true and was to gain in truth later in other places, the actual situation was less clear.

The probability seems to be that Slovenian forces fired first.[17] A Slovenian information ministry chronology does not report any firing before Slovenian Territorial Defence Forces (TO) shot down a helicopter over the capital Ljubljana.[18] This incident was clearly in Ljubljana's interest. Slovenian authorities had warned General Andrija Rašeta, the JNA 5th Military District Commander in Zagreb, not to send helicopters, or they would be shot down. Rašeta called Ljubljana in tears after the incident, unable to believe what had happened.[19] It does not seem unreasonable to suppose both that the Slovenes, having made a threat, had to carry it out to maintain credibility and that the incident was a deliberate part of Slovenia's strategy. If Slovenia's campaign was to work, it needed to provoke an incident. It was certainly fortuitous for Slovenia's cause that the incident occurred in the early evening over the capital Ljubljana where Slovenian TV could promptly provide images of the wreckage to the world, in time to catch early and mid-evening news broadcasts across Europe. With no time for the details to be checked, the image of plucky little Slovenia ably defending itself against the JNA was cast.[20]

As a result of successful media management, or propaganda, the particulars of the conflict in Slovenia were swiftly made irrelevant. Slovenia's case had inherent merit: it was overwhelmingly supported by the population, it was based on strong legal arguments and was being implemented effectively. In this context, all details were integrated in one picture. For example, the Minister for Information Jelko Kacin briefed journalists about the location of a burned-out JNA armoured personnel carrier; the journalists raced off to get pictures of it, assuming that it had been destroyed by anti-armour fire, although it later emerged that the vehicle had been abandoned by its crew and later set ablaze by local youths. Kacin had not lied, but had given the journalists enough information to allow them to jump to conclusions that supported Slovenia's case.[21]

Slovenia's proficient media management campaign was adapted from the General People's Defence doctrine formulated to secure federal Yugoslavia. Yugoslavia's armed forces comprised two elements: the JNA, the regular army intended to be the first echelon of defence; and the territorial defence forces, organised in each of the six republics.[22] It was planned that the JNA would hold off an invading force for forty-eight hours while the territorial forces mobilised. The doctrine assumed that an invasion could not be completely repelled if it had not been deterred. The territorials and remnants of the JNA would fall back into mountainous territory and use guerrilla tactics to harass the enemy. Among other aims, it was supposed that this type of action could be used to show a willingness to resist and to generate international support which would ultimately be necessary, whether military or political, to evict the invader. Slovenia's media campaign waged by the ministry of information was, therefore, an integral part of its strategy. Slovenia had an organised programme to keep Western journalists informed and so feed them their stories.

Victim Strategies: Croatia, Bosnia and the International Arena

Slovenia's successful, fully integrated military and media strategy was in contrast to those of Croatia and Bosnia – at least in the first three years of the Yugoslav War. All three could be characterised as victims. Whereas Slovenia, in addition to political advantages such as an ethnically homogeneous population, had justifiably emphasised achievement and competence in its self-portrayal, Croatia and Bosnia both put considerable stress on the degree in which they were victims and the extent to which their Serbian attackers were brutal and merciless. As was the case with Slovenia, the content of the images projected was based in the reality of the situation: both were weak, subject to attacks of considerable cruelty and in need of international help. Unlike Slovenia, the status of victim was accentuated and weakness even exaggerated as media manipulation became not so much a complement for military engagement as a substitute for it.

A significant weakness in Croatia's position concerned its Serbian minority, which accounted for around 11 per cent of the country's population, half of whom traditionally inhabited rural areas in the Dalmatian hinterland on the borders with Bosnia. During the Second World War, these communities, and similar ones across the border, had been subject to attempted genocide by the Nazi puppet régime of Ante Pavelić's Ustasha, an independent state of Croatia. Serbs in the Krajina region of Croatia now established an autonomous region, while Serbs in eastern Slavonia followed suit, before the two were combined as the 'Republic of Serbian Krajina'. This had happened with support from Serbia, but was also in response to rather tactless use of Croatian national symbols which, in Serb eyes, were associated with the Ustasha period. Along with other measures, such as changing references to the Serbs in the constitution and reorganising the police force to remove communists who happened to be Serbs, this fuelled Serb fears and propaganda. It also harmed Croatia's international image.[23]

Croatia failed adequately to counter the impression in the international community that Zagreb had provoked the Serbs almost as much as it had been attacked. Partly, this was because the Croatian authorities had not prepared the kind of comprehensive strategy which Slovenia put into effect and which was essential to a successful war effort. Although the Hotel Intercontinental in Zagreb acted as a centre for the press, Zagreb did not manage the international media in the way Ljubljana had: whereas the latter had fed journalists stories and organised excursions, the former was less professional in furnishing stories and frequent official statements. As a result, many journalists, looking for a story, went to the front.[24] Many of these found and reported on situations which put Croatia in a compromised position. The Croatian government, although retaining some strong support in a divided international community, lost full control of the international media as a part of its strategy.[25]

Zagreb did attempt to shape international interpretation of the war. For example, it used towns under siege to prod Western attention: Vukovar and Dubrovnik were under siege, but Croatia seemed more interested in using them to gain Western support than in relieving them.[26] Zagreb, rather than committing itself to significant defence of the towns, preferred to make them the focal points of a 'victim strategy'.

Vukovar was utterly destroyed in the 86-day Serbian siege. But the government of President Franjo Tudjman manipulated its position, rather than defending it.[27] Zagreb's relationship with the defenders of Vukovar made its victim strategy clear.[28] If it offered strong resistance, Vukovar would go against the grain of Croatia's strategy. Zagreb seems effectively to have refused to send material support, although

Tudjman claimed that some assistance was sent.[29] For the most part, the authorities claimed that it was impossible to reach the town – even though others offered contradictory evidence.[30] Whereas the 'Wolves of Vukovar' (the label given to the local defenders) openly criticised the Zagreb régime and its strategy, Zagreb was more ambivalent, not offering unequivocal support, but also unable to denounce the defenders of Vukovar because they symbolised the desire to resist that was growing and putting increasing pressure on the Tudjman régime.

The tension between Vukovar and Zagreb was evident when Vukovar eventually fell after a three-month siege. Mile Dedaković, a Serb known by the *nom de guerre* 'Jastreb', military leader in Vukovar, was arrested by the Zagreb authorities. Dedaković was arrested initially for 'desertion', although he claimed that he had been ordered to leave his position by the General Staff; it appears that these charges were dropped and Dedaković was, instead, to take ten days' leave. In the meantime, he was further accused of misappropriation of funds and of being an agent of the federal military counter-intelligence, KOS. This, however, was only after he had demanded at a press conference that the government explain what had happened to the $17 million that the finance ministry had dedicated to the defence of Vukovar. Whatever, the details, the tension between Zagreb and Vukovar's defenders was obvious and the real reason for the government's actions against Dedaković connected with their discomfort. Vukovar's resistance not only embarrassed the Tudjman régime, but undermined the Government's strategy. Croatian President Franjo Tudjman's strategy was for his forces to do as little as possible but defend where necessary to show the world that his country was a victim and needing assistance by, at least, gaining international recognition.

The situation in Bosnia was different to the extent that Bosnia was more obviously an innocent victim: if Croatia was weak, but played the victim to emphasise its position, Bosnia was genuinely a victim. With limited forces initially available to the Bosnian government, some resistance was offered and encouraged. However, the main part of the Bosnian effort seemed to be put into generating international interest and obtaining an international armed intervention. Sarajevo invoked the precedent of the Gulf conflict as an attempt to mobilise an international intervention became part of the Bosnian government's strategy.

The Bosnian government initially had the sympathy and support of the international community because it had made strenuous efforts to co-operate with international efforts to avoid war. The Bosnian leadership went out of its way to co-operate with both European Community and UN mediators, as well as the leadership of the JNA in the Bosnian capital Sarajevo, to work for peace in the republic as it teetered on the edge of violence. Alongside this, Bosnian President Alija Izetbegović and his interior ministry forces co-operated with Col. Gen. Milutin Kukanjac, the JNA Sarajevo 3rd Military District commander, in efforts to disarm paramilitary and to place the weapons of the Bosnian Territorial Defence under army control. A corollary of this was that the Bosnian government, both despite and because of the storm clouds gathering, undertook no preparations for defence of the republic, lest these be mistaken as preparations for belligerence.

The co-operative relationship with EC and UN representatives gave Bosnia's leadership the impression that good behaviour would mean the newly independent republic being offered more international protection than there had been for Croatia.[31] As a result, clear and overt references to the Gulf War were made as the Bosnian government sought to mobilise an international military intervention.

Bosnia's only real chance of containing Serbian forces depended on the actions of the international community, whether this was a matter of lifting the arms embargo on Bosnia and Hercegovina, exerting economic and diplomatic pressure, or the engagement of military forces at one level or another. To this the end, believing that an international media message would be important, the Bosnian government employed the services of an American public relations firm, Ruder-Finn.[32]

Bosnian Foreign Minister Haris Silajdžić tried to get support for an intervention à la Desert Storm at the UN: 'The United Nations can provide the umbrella for such an operation just like the one we had in the Gulf.'[33] Ejup Ganić, Izetbegović's deputy, demanded that, 'Either the UN should pass a resolution to send in intervention troops or they should allow us to get weapons.' Comparing Bosnia with Kuwait, he somewhat bitterly expressed a generally perceived distinction between the two: 'If you are a small country without oil, without strategic resources, the world only sends you messages like "stay brave".'[34] This confirmed a message being read in places other than Bosnia: only where important actors in the international system had particular strategic interests (and local conditions were suitable) was there likely to be an armed intervention on behalf of the international community.

When the UN Security Council voted to allow the use of 'all necessary means' to ensure the delivery of humanitarian aid in Bosnia and Hercegovina, the Bosnian leadership gave it a mixed reception. Although Izetbegović was glad of some international moves to relieve the suffering in his country, he pointed out that his people 'dreamed of a Western intervention', not just humanitarian aid.[35] However, as Col. Gen. Lewis MacKenzie, UN Commanding Officer in Sarajevo, indicated, for the Bosnians, even humanitarian intervention served their purposes. One of the government's advisors had told him: 'Let Bush come with humanitarian aid, take control of the roads, get his troops or his helicopters shot at ... and pretty soon he'll find he's fighting the same war as us.'[36] It would appear therefore that the enfeebled Bosnian government had hope of a greater international commitment.

The hope of provoking an international armed intervention led Bosnian government forces on numerous occasions, according to UNPROFOR, to fire on its own positions and on UN forces.[37] This led to speculation each time a major incident occurred, especially in the Sarajevo area, that government forces were responsible for what was ostensibly a Serbian attack on government forces, or Muslim communities.[38] Two incidents in particular were a focus for attention: the 'bread queue' massacre in May 1992 and the massacre at the Markale market square in Sarajevo in February 1994. Both resulted in official verdicts that responsibility was unclear. In the end, given the greater truth of the war which was the Serbian project to create new borders and ethnic maps, it could be argued that it was not important who had actually fired a particular missile – in cases where the Bosnian government had clearly been responsible for a self-inflicted attack, or one on UN forces, General Philippe Morillon, UNPROFOR Commander in Bosnia, noted that it was understandable for the militarily weaker Bosnian government to try to offset its inferiority with its intelligence, as he probably would himself.[39]

What should be a matter of concern is that the immediate assumption was made that the Bosnian Serbs were responsible in both cases. This may well not have been the case in May 1992, but almost certainly was for the February attack on the marketplace (although the Bosnian government appears to have done much in its attempts to manipulate the incident, which itself raised suspicions[40]), yet both prompted international action – pressure for sanctions in the first case and the serious threat of air strikes in the second. In neither case was the matter clear-cut. In a similar situation, where there was greater equivalence between the sides, the immediate transmission of an image, the making of assumptions and the taking of decisions based on them could lead to major errors. Had the Bosnian government been clearly identified as responsible for the Sarajevo market attack, the threat of air strikes against the Bosnian Serbs would already have been made before assessments could be made and the truth was known: satellite TV transmission would have sent immediate images which prompted immediate decisions. TV immediacy in another, but similar, situation could lead to major mistakes.

Conclusion

The ability to manipulate, mobilise and maintain mass media support at both international and domestic levels played a critical role in the Yugoslav War of Dissolution. Media management was vital to strategy. As brave defenders, or as victims, the various Yugoslavs used the mass media to disseminate images in the international community. Equally, propaganda was essential domestically to prepare to support war. In this respect, in some cases, lessons were drawn broadly from the Gulf Conflict particularly, and from Western media procedures generally.

Serbia was adept in preparing the road to war, while Slovenia was clearly the most sophisticated of the warring Yugoslavs in its comprehensive integration of the media into strategy. In similar, but significantly different ways, both Croatia and Bosnia made incomplete attempts to manipulate the media to amplify a strategic approach based on gaining support for a helpless victim. However, unlike Slovenia, these were not integral elements of proactive armed operations. Media management was an essential strategic feature, with Slovenia's success underlining the importance in post-modern war for an integrated political–military–media policy.

Although a basis in truth was required, including some military success, the omnipresence of modern mass media meant that, rather than actually winning a war on the battlefield, what counted was to be seen and understood to be conducting a successful campaign: marketing was almost more important than winning – as the Serbian side discovered, forcibly occupying much territory, but failing to project the right image, even among the Serbs. The image of military success contributed to and possibly outweighed the substance of military–political success. More than ever before, propaganda has become a vital factor in war.

Notes

1. Marjan Malešić (ed.), *The Role of the Mass Media in the Serbian-Croatian Conflict* (Stockholm: SPF, 1993), p. 11.
2. See Nik Gowing, 'Real-time Television Coverage of Armed Conflicts and Diplomatic Crises: Does It Pressure or Distort Foreign Policy Decisions', Working Paper, The Joan Shorestein Barone Center on the Press, Politics and Public Policy, John F. Kennedy School of Government, Harvard University, Cambridge MA, June 1994, p. 73. See also James Gow, *Yugoslavia and Lessons from the Gulf War*, CNSS, Los Alamos National Laboratory, Center for National Security Studies, 1992. Mimeo
3. See Mark Thompson, *Forging War: The Media in Serbia, Croatia and Bosnia–Hercegovina*, (London: Article XIX, 1994), pp. 51–129 *passim*.
4. See *The Death of Yugoslavia*, Programme 1, Brian Lapping Associates/BBC TV, 1995.
5. The symbols in question, such as the red-and-white checkerboard flag, were technically different from those of the Ustasha and were argued by the Croats to be of older heritage than the Ustasha period. However, whether or not a red-and-white sequence began with red or white was not immediately obvious to fearful observers and provided easy targets for the Serbian media.
6. *Nedjeljna Dalmacija*, 1 July 1993.
7. James Gow, 'Military–Political Affiliations in the Yugoslav Conflict', *RFE/RL Research Report* vol. 1 no. 20. 15 May 1992, p. 20.
8. This was pointed out by Dragan Vasiljković, 'Captain Dragan', the man at one stage charged with

the task of training a new Serbian army (the venture was curtailed) in November 1991. See Gow 'Military–Political Affiliations', p. 23.

9. Ibid., p. 20.
10. Stan Markotich, 'Government Control over Serbia's Media', *RFE/RL Research Report* vol. 3, no. 5, 4 February 1994.
11. The same was also the case with reference to the Zagreb authorities' attitude to the media.
12. The following is adapted from Gow, *Yugoslavia and Lessons*.
13. Jelko Kacin, Minister for Information, Republic of Slovenia, interview with James Gow. Kacin had been Deputy Defence Minister before masterminding the propaganda campaign as Slovenia became independent. In 1994 he became Minister for Defence.
14. This could be seen, for example, in *The Case of Slovenia*, a variable collection of articles by Slovene intellectuals published during the crisis (Ljubljana: Nova Revija, 1991).
15. This was one rather moderate instance of what Predrag Simić has described as 'demonisation' of the opposition, although it is primarily used for domestic purposes in his analysis: 'In all cases, members of ethnic groups were portrayed by the opposing media as devoid of human characteristics, so that violence would not only be allowed but desirable.' Predrag Simić, 'The Former Yugoslavia: Media and Violence', *RFE/RL Research Report* vol. 3 no. 5, 4 February 1994, p. 43.
16. Ibid., p. 44.
17. John Zametica asserts this. Zametica's work has to be treated with caution, as he was an advisor to Bosnian Serb leaders and became official spokesman for the Bosnian Serbs. However, on this point he seems to be right. Zametica, *The Yugoslav Conflict*, Adelphi Paper No. 270, Brassey's for the IISS 1992, p. 13.
18. *War in Slovenia*, Ljubljana: Informacija Slovenije (1991), pp. 56–7.
19. Ironically, the helicopter was carrying bread to JNA troops in barracks, and the pilot, who was killed, was Slovene (*The Death of Yugoslavia*, Programme 2).
20. This period is ably covered in Christopher Bennett's fine account, *Yugoslavia's Bloody Collapse: Causes, Course and Consequences* (London: C. Hurst, 1995), pp. 156–62.
21. Interview with Jelko Kacin.
22. See James Gow, *Legitimacy and the Military: The Yugoslav Crisis* (London: Pinter 1992), pp. 46–8.
23. See J. F. Brown, *Nationalism and Democracy in the Balkans* (Dartmouth: Rand, 1992).
24. See, for example, Paul Harris, *Somebody Else's War: Frontline Reports from the Balkan Wars, 1991–1992* (Stevenage: Spa Books, 1992), esp. pp. 13–45.
25. Malešić, *Mass Media*, pp. 35–6.
26. Simić, 'The Media and Violence', p. 45.
27. Ibid., p. 41.
28. The following is based on Gow, *Yugoslavia and Lessons*.
29. *Death of Yugoslavia*, Programme 3.
30. *Danas*, 28 January 1992, carried an interview with Liljana Toth, wife of one of the town's defence chiefs, in which she derided official claims that supplies could not get through, claiming that it took them a maximum of three-quarters of an hour to get from where the official convoys stopped into Vukovar.
31. This is based on interviews with Haris Silajdžić, Foreign Minister of Bosnia and Hercegovina.
32. Sylvia Poggiolli, 'Scouts without Compasses', *The Niemann Reports*, Fall 1993.
33. Quoted in the *Guardian*, 16 May 1992.
34. Quoted in the *Guardian*, 1 August 1992.
35. *The Guardian*, 12 August 1992.
36. *The Independent*, 13 August 1992.
37. Lt. Gen. Lewis MacKenzie, *A Soldier's Peace*. Transmitted 7 January 1995, BBC 2.
38. See, for example, Peter Brock, 'Dateline Yugoslavia: The Parties and the Press', *Foreign Policy* vol. 93, Winter 1993/4.
39. General Philippe Morillon, *Croire et oser: Chronique de Sarajevo* (Paris: Grasset, 1993), p. 133.
40. For example, many of the wounded ostensibly harmed by the mortar attack who were airlifted out of Sarajevo by the UN had old wounds, suggesting that the government was trying to embroider the truth. Interview with a senior British official.

Television News and the Bosnian Conflict

Distance, Proximity, Impact

ALISON PRESTON

Distance and Proximity

This essay outlines the contrasting narratives that are traceable in television news reporting of the conflict in Bosnia, and begins to investigate some of the assumptions that were made about the impact of the coverage, particularly in the UK. Overall, two co-existent narrative templates can be identified in the coverage, based around the motifs of either distance or proximity. The template of 'distance' can be laid over the subject matter of diplomacy or politics; dispassionate documentation as a reporting style; a target audience of elites; and an emphasis on the complicated or difficult. The narrative template of 'proximity' can be laid over humanitarian issues, which in turn emphasised the geographic and societal closeness of the war. The ordinary individual was highlighted, encouraging empathy and also clarity: the simple imperative of personal suffering.

These narratives were formed to an extent by factors within the newsgathering process: the technological capacity to undertake certain kinds of reports, the logistical imperatives of newsgathering, and the explicit emphasis of the journalists themselves. Newsgathering technology (ever-smaller ENG cameras, portable satellite dishes for sending back images and for telephone contact, and capacity for field editing[1]) increased viewer engagement with the war by enabling journalists and their teams to film clandestinely in places that would otherwise remain unpublicised; through the ability to send material quickly or even live; and through the increase in volume of stories and footage. On the other hand, this expansion of television news outlets also led to an informational remoteness from the conflict. It was difficult for journalists to find new information, because there was pressure for them to remain in one place in order to feed stories and appear live on an increased number of bulletins. The BBC journalist Martin Bell (1995: 209) said of his experience in Bosnia that 'our first admitted failing was that because of the ever-pressing rush of deadlines we didn't get out and about as much as we should have'. The increasing use of news agency footage by broadcasters on the one hand inserted a physical newsgathering distance between the person who shot the images, the person who described them in the accompanying text, and the person who eventually did the voice-over. On the other hand, this very reliance on news agency footage meant that there was a greater need by broadcasters to have a story that was not the same as everyone else's, and so the instance of 'authored reports' increased, connecting viewers to the news item via (domestic) reporters.

Particular issues of logistics also shaped the newsgathering process and consequent reports. Because the theatre of war was highly dangerous, especially in Bosnia where there were few rules of engagement, the need to ensure a reasonable degree of journalist safety meant that there was instead more coverage of refugee situations and the aftermath of attacks. The coverage was often far from the fighting but closer to aspects of suffering. If war footage was obtained, it was often from either military videos or freelancers, so again the chain of newsgathering was lengthened as the reporter verbally commented on a situation his or her production team had not actually witnessed.

There were, then, 'physical' degrees of distance from and proximity to the news event, those of logistics and newsgathering technology. These underwrote the degrees of 'emotional' distance and proximity, found in the reporting style and the subjects covered. Emotional proximity tended to eclipse the other aspects of a narrative in which it was positioned. When reports linked, for example, the round-up of the day's diplomatic meetings with showing the plight of refugees on the road, the former seemed less important. There was an absolute clarity to personal suffering, which dominated any other discourse. It was intensely difficult to report suffering in a way that didn't crowd out other, perhaps qualifying, factors. Showing a balance of suffering on each side only paralysed the issue.

Emphasising emotional proximity is, of course, intensely problematic. If it is done then it can block wider comprehension and enable only the personal to be understood. If it is not done then real lives are reduced to ciphers. It is of note in this context that the Bosnian conflict altered the degree of emotional proximity that many British journalists have hitherto displayed. A number of the British journalists covering Bosnia have said it is the hardest war that they have reported from: the most difficult logistically, the most dangerous, the conflict in which they have become most personally involved.[2] Such journalists have deliberately emphasised the emotional in their reports in order to signal the extent of their commitment, and their belief that detachment, or distance, should not be inserted.[3]

The Impact of Television News

The wish to highlight emotional proximity is intrinsically bound to a wish to proselytise (although most journalists would probably prefer 'inform' or at strongest 'educate'), and thus to a belief that television news has a definable impact. The narratives of emotional distance and proximity are only resonant if there is expectation that either discourse will have an effect on the audience.

The assumption that television news had an impact during the war in Bosnia was common in Britain.[4] There was widespread dissemination, by broadsheet and tabloid press, of the motif that television news had been pivotal in altering government policy towards the conflict.[5] The national press emphasised the role of television news in making certain events during the war particularly resonant, for example the discovery of the existence of Serbian detention camps in July 1992, and the marketplace mortar attack in Sarajevo in February 1994. There were also a number of television programmes about the media coverage of the war. These focused on the partiality – in both its 'partisan' and 'incomplete' meanings – of journalistic reporting; the politics of taste and decency imperatives in television news bulletins; the role of the media in forcing changes to government policy; whether the portrayal of war should have been graphic or euphemistic; the legitimacy of taking individuals as ciphers for the conflict; and the journalist's role as advocator or as documentarist.[6]

It can be argued, then, that there was widespread public awareness of the idea that British television news had an impact on public opinion and possibly government policy over Bosnia. However, there was disagreement, or contradiction, over the characteristics of this impact, as the following evidence from government and the press shows. The television news coverage of Bosnia was characterised as being both too plentiful and not plentiful enough. Reporting was too proximate to events and too distant. It was too polemic and not polemic enough. It resulted in viewers militating for government action and in viewer desensitisation.

For example, the former Armed Services Minister Archie Hamilton talked of the 'saturation coverage' from Bosnia in September 1993[7], at the same time as the Foreign Secretary Douglas Hurd made similar remarks about the selective 'search-light of media coverage' (1993a). Three months later, however, Hurd implied that in fact there needed to be more journalistic awareness-raising: 'As the war struggles on, media coverage has reduced. Earlier this year, amid the blaze of publicity, I argued the importance of not doing or saying things simply because of intense media pressure. We must intensify our efforts this winter to save lives and to search for peace. The tragedy remains a tragedy, even out of the headlines' (1993b).

The television coverage was held to be interventionist through its documentation of humanitarian suffering. Its power was accepted: there were a number of broadsheet press editorials which talked of the ability of television '[to arouse] intense public emotion, perhaps beyond the capacity of politicians to control';[8] 'When television nightly brings the world evidence of atrocities, destruction and suffering in the Balkans, governments cannot stand aside.'[9] The legitimacy of such power, however, was queried by these same newspapers at other points in the war. The arbitrary nature of television coverage was stressed: 'Television lights are simply the contemporary version of the will of the gods. There is no justice or virtue in media coverage, only luck'.[10] There was concern over the power of television news in the absence of government strategy: 'If war is too important to be left to the generals then it is too important by far to be left to the journalists. The uproar caused by the harrowing television coverage of the ethnic cleansing camps in Bosnia prompted the government's original [response] ... without forethought for the political or military consequences.'[11] Thus, the television news coverage was both lauded and criticised for its supposed powers of intervention in the policymaking process.

There are a number of ways in which television news intervenes. The first is that it is *directly* used by policymakers.[12] Protagonists watch each other directly, using television as a form of diplomatic channel: 'Dr Karadžić himself was known to call up the BBC's *Nine O'Clock News*, on air, and demand the right to refute a statement just made' (Bell 1995: 140–1); 'General Mladić is not taking the UN commander's calls, so the threat is delivered by means of a crowded news conference' (Bell 1995: 255). Another direct link between policymakers and television news is the use of journalists as information-gatherers for government. There was an 'absence [in Bosnia], for the first two years of the war, of any British diplomatic presence on the ground' (Bell 1995: 39). Because of this, journalists were used by government as their 'eyes and ears': 'There are no independent witnesses there any more. ... Only the Press are independent witnesses and I grant you we have no government mandate but governments do get to hear of what's happening through us. I know that because people come up and talk to me. Ministers and so on.'[13]

However, the third link that is commonly made, that television news journalism has an impact on 'ordinary' viewers, who aggregate into public opinion and hence influence policymakers, is more problematic. In this model, news viewers are defined as latent public activists. Yet viewers have a variety of relationships to, and uses for, television news: for instance that it is better in the abstract than in actuality, that it provides a sense of solidarity or communality rather than any sense of political control or influence.[14] 'Active' viewing – lobbying, writing letters – is not the only measure of television news legitimacy. Additionally, promotion of the concept of the active citizen does not always explicitly consider its drawbacks. There is potential for damaging incitement as well as positive encouragement. The society- and event-specific nature of the model that promotes viewers as latent activists in political and civic life should not be ignored.

In summary, contrasting narratives of distance and proximity can be traced through the coverage of the war in Britain, and through the understanding or valuation of that coverage. The fact that such contradictory narratives existed is not unusual. What is more rare is the degree to which the contradictions were made explicit and the degree to which the motif of 'complication' dominated discourse about Bosnia. The resonance of the contradictory narratives lies in their power to construct the parameters of understanding about the conflict. What appears on television news is a large part of what most viewers see of an event. After Baudrillard (1991), what was shown on television *was* the Bosnian war for most British audiences. Instead of a unilinear discourse, British viewers received a dual narrative.

The importance of documenting these patterns of discourse resides in their 'implicit normative functionalism',[15] which has begun to be challenged here. Work needs to be done on mapping and questioning the imperatives of television conflict reporting. Is it there as a reflection of reality, and if so, which narrative type is most 'real', empathy or dispassion? Which subject matter is most 'real' – documentation of combat, of diplomacy, of the suffering of civilians – in other words where is the epicentre of the conflict? This then leads to the issue of for whom is conflict reporting produced, for what purposes is it recounted. Is it primarily for elites or for a mass audience? Is the mass audience being asked overall to empathise, to lobby, and/or to understand?

This essay has started to outline the complexities of certain assumptions about the values of distance and dispassion, proximity and empathy. The chapters before this have developed and illustrated these themes. By doing so they reveal that narrative discourses are valued according to society- and event-specific criteria.

Notes

1. See MacGregor 1995.
2. The most literal example of this was the ITN journalist Michael Nicholson, who had reported from Vietnam, the Falklands and the Gulf among other conflicts, temporarily bringing back to Britain to stay with him a child from Bosnia.
3. See, for example, author's interviews with BBC, ITN and Sky News journalists 1991, 1992 and 1995; *News World* conference Berlin: 1995; Centre for Defence Studies and SSEES conference, *Semantics and Security: The Meaning of the Balkans*, September 1994; session 'La realtà riportata' at *Antennacinema* conference, Conegliano, Italy: 28 March 1995; *Tales from Sarajevo*, BBC2, 1993; *War Correspondent: The Troubles We've Seen*, BBC2, 1995.
4. Although the war in Bosnia was not a conflict in which the British were protagonists, it was resonant within the UK because of the deployment of its troops as part of the UN peacekeeping force, and also because the war was taking place on mainland Europe, with periodic historic references both to Nazism and to the policies of appeasement.
5. See also chapters by Gowing and Burns above.
6. The *Bloody Bosnia* season on Channel 4, August 1993; *Journalists at War*, Channel Four, 28 August 1993; *Tales from Sarajevo*, BBC2, 21 January 1993; the *Naked News* season on Channel Four, March 1995; *War Correspondent: The Troubles We've Seen*, BBC2, 2 and 9 September 1995. Although these programmes were not seen by large audiences – for example the two *War*

Correspondent programmes had audiences of around 380,000 – the audience would nonetheless have been composed of a range of social classes and backgrounds (see Patrick Barwise and Andrew Ehrenberg, *Television and its Audience*, London: Sage, 1988).

7. Archie Hamilton quoted in the *Guardian*, 18 September 1993.
8. *Daily Telegraph*, 16 April 1993.
9. *The Times*, 7 September 1992.
10. *Daily Telegraph*, 11 August 1993.
11. *The Times*, 30 December 1992.
12. Of course this use of television as a diplomatic channel is not new. Robin Day interviewed President Nasser of Egypt in 1957, to press comment that 'For the first time on record a national leader ... bypassed all protocol and sent his message into the homes of another state' (Day 1961: 92).
13. Martin Bell on *Tales from Sarajevo*, BBC2, 21 January 1993. Also, discussion during the session 'The Representation of the Balkans in the Media', at *Semantics and Security: The Meaning of the Balkans*, 21–23 September 1994. International conference organised by the Centre for Defence Studies and SSEES.
14. See Jensen 1990, Hagen 1994, and Brough Williams above.
15. See Schudson 1991: 156

References

Baudrillard, Jean (1991) *La Guerre du Golfe n'a pas eu lieu*, éditions galilée.

Bell, Martin (1995) *In Harm's Way*. London: Hamish Hamilton.

Day, Robin (1961) *Television: A Personal Report*. London: Hutchinson.

Hagen, Ingunn (1994) 'The Ambivalences of TV News Viewing'. *European Journal of Communication* vol. 9.

Hopkinson, Nicholas (1993) *The Media and International Affairs after the Cold War*. Norwich: HMSO.

Hopkinson, Nicholas (1995) *The Impact of New Technology on the International Media and Foreign Policy*. Norwich: HMSO.

Hurd, Douglas (1993a) 'War of the Words'. *The Guardian*, 17 September 1993.

Hurd, Douglas (1993b) 'Our Chance to End a Bosnian Winter of Suffering'. *Sunday Times*, 12 December 1993.

Jensen, K. B. (1990) 'The Politics of Polysemy: Television News, Everyday Consciousness and Political Action'. *Media Culture and Society* vol. 12 no. 1.

MacGregor, Brent (1995) 'Our Wanton Abuse of the Technology'. *Convergence* vol. 1 no. 1.

Schudson, Michael (1991) 'The Sociology of News Production Revisited', in J. Curran and M. Gurevitch (eds), *Mass Media and Society*, London: Edward Arnold.

PART FOUR

Comparing Coverage: TV News Coverage 16–21 May 1994

Introduction

ALISON PRESTON

In May 1994 the Research and Education Division at the BFI co-ordinated an international content analysis of the coverage of the Bosnian war on television news bulletins. During the week of 16–21 May 1994 all evening news bulletins on all national channels in the following countries were recorded: Algeria, Austria, Croatia, France, Greece, Italy, Macedonia, Russia, Serbia, Slovenia, Turkey, UK and USA. The evening news output from the all-news channels Euronews, CNN International and Sky News was recorded, as well as the items from Bosnia on the Reuters Television (RTV) World News feed during the week. From these recordings researchers from each country analysed the week's coverage of the war in a number of frameworks. The news output of the week was used as an axis along which to plot wider issues about the coverage of the war. The specialisms of the participants in the project mean that emphases shift in the following essays across a range of topics: close textual analysis of news reports; the logistics of journalism and news programming; news bulletin conventions; the relationship of news bulletins and journalism to government policy; and the relationship of governments to the conflict itself, as protagonists, neighbours, sympathisers or providers of UN personnel. Table 1 shows the main news stories that were covered during the week.

The emphasis given in these news stories varies from broadcaster to broadcaster and from country to country, as described in the essays below. For example, the visit of the Russian patriarch, Aleksei II, to the former Yugoslav republics, and the *hadj* (pilgrimage) to Mecca by Bosnian President Alija Izetbegović, both of which occurred during the week of analysis, were used by some broadcasters to make implicit and explicit connection between historic–religious references and the conflict. The Russian channel Ostankino emphasised the religious connections between Russia and Serbia, and the historical antagonism towards the Muslims. A description of the Serb St Simon mentioned that the Turks had burned him at the stake 400 years ago. Reports of the proposed meeting between the Croat, Muslim, Russian and Serbian religious leaders emphasised the lack of co-operation from the Muslim leader. These religion-based reports also documented the political nature of the Russian patriarch's visit – meetings with President Milošević and President Karadžić.

The Greek television bulletin on ANT1 connected the *hadj* ('expenses paid by the King of Saudi Arabia') explicitly with the refusal of the Bosnian Muslim religious leader to meet the Russian Patriarch, thereby implying Muslim unreliability: 'The

Table 1: Main events reported during the week 16–21 May 1994

Event	R	CN	EN	SN	AL	AU	CR	FR	GR	IT	MA	RU	SE	SL	TU	UK	US
Bosnian Muslim attack on Swedish convoy	✓	✓	✓	✓			*			✓		✓	✓	*	✓		✓
Clashes between Bosnian Serbs and Muslims near Tuzla	✓	✓	✓	✓		✓	✓	✓	✓	✓	✓	✓	✓	✓	✓		✓
Churkin–Milošević meeting	✓	✓	✓			✓	✓	✓	✓			✓	✓	✓	✓		
EU ministers meeting in Brussels to discuss Geneva peace plan		✓					✓	✓						✓	✓		
French 'List for Sarajevo' developments					✓			✓									
Serb shelling of Tuzla hotel	✓	✓					✓		✓	✓							✓
France to withdraw troops by end of year	✓	✓			✓		✓	✓		✓			✓		✓	✓	✓
Serb attack on Tuzla airport	✓	✓	✓		✓		✓		✓	✓					✓		
Pilgrimage to Mecca by Muslims from Sarajevo	✓	✓					✓					✓					
Meeting of Russian and Serbian Orthodox and Croatian Catholic church leaders	✓	✓				✓						✓		✓			
British Foreign Minister threatens to withdraw British troops			✓				✓	✓					✓			✓	
French aid workers freed by Serbs	✓	✓					✓	✓									
Karadžić meeting with Owen and Stoltenberg	✓		✓				✓					✓	✓				
UN plane lands safely at Tuzla airport	✓		✓										✓		✓		
French aid workers reunited with families								✓									
Heavy shelling on route between Sarajevo and Tuzla		✓															
British army officer apologises to Serb soldiers			✓													✓	
Opening-up of Croat and Muslim sectors in Mostar	✓						✓										
Sarajevo cease-fire lasted 100 days	✓			✓											✓		

Key:

R	Reuters TV	SN	Sky News	CR	Croatia	SE	Serbia
CN	CNN International	AL	Algeria	FR	France	SL	Slovenia
EN	Euronews	AU	Austria	GR	Greece	TU	Turkey
IT	Italy						
MA	Macedonia					UK	United Kingdom
RU	Russia					US	United States

* Both Croat and Slovenian television said that the attack was carried out by Bosnian *Serbs*

Muslim president ... left Sarajevo for a pilgrimage to Mecca. At the same time, however, the spiritual leader of the Bosnian Muslims, Mustafa Cerić, refuses to meet [the Serbian and Russian patriarchs]' (Tuesday 17 May, item 7). The Russian patriarch's meeting with President Milošević was also reported by ANT1, described in the Greek essay below as serving 'as a reminder of the cultural and religious proximity of the Serb and Greek nations'. On Russian Ostankino the *hadj* was reported as a sign of Serb generosity: '... the Serb army, controlling the approach to the airport, gave permission for the flight' (Tuesday 17 May, item 21). On Turkish television it was reported as a positive pro-Muslim story, for example TGRT reported that 'the UN, after resisting for a long time, finally decided to give protection to Bosnian Muslims who are on the pilgrimage to Mecca. Approximately 100 people have left Sarajevo and travelled to the airport under the protection of the UN. The convoy was cheered with people chanting ...' (Wednesday 18 May, item 5).

On Algerian television, the *hadj* was reported but not the visit of the Russian patriarch. Algerian television news generally emphasised the Algerian communality of experience with Bosnian Muslims, through the use of footage which portrayed the Islamic nature of the Bosnians: men-only public spaces, all women wearing the Islamic veil. Nevertheless there remained an element of distance in the tone of the reporting due to the non-Arab nature of the Bosnian Muslims.

The majority of bulletins in Western European countries in the analysis mentioned the *hadj* to Mecca but not the visit of the Russian patriarch to the former Yugoslav republics, even though there was a feed from RTV detailing it. This weighting exemplifies how the 'other' of Islam has more resonance in television news terms than the familiarity of Christianity, albeit Orthodox.

The emphasis by Greek and Russian television news bulletins on the visit of the Russian patriarch underlines the extent to which both countries were bound up in the conflict. They were connected to Serbia through religious history, which was then foregrounded in the visit. This resonance of domestic agendas and societal mores, which refracted the events of the week of analysis through particular prisms, was evident in a number of stories from other broadcasters. For example, French television news bulletins spent much time during the week covering the 'List for Sarajevo' – the intellectual Bernard-Henri Lévy's campaign to run for the EU elections on an intervention-for-Bosnia platform. What is of note here is not that there was coverage of this, but that the campaign fitted, almost stereotypically, a notion of 'Frenchness' – the abstraction of a conflict into a vehicle for philosophical/ intellectual discussion. As Taranger points out below, the actuality of 'Bosnia' disappeared, and the discussion was located instead in French domestic politics. In a similar way, the societal agenda in Italy was evidenced through the week's coverage. There was emphasis on domestic politics – Bosnia was reported via the speech by the Italian foreign minister in one report; and on the emotional – a report from a correspondent about his journey along the road to Goražde. In the USA, the longest report of the week was a local news item which juxtaposed the lives of Bosnian and American schoolchildren.

This desire to make the conflict more resonant for the viewer is both culturally specific (some cultures placing more emphasis on empathy and sympathy than others) but also *nation* specific. Broadcasters in countries very close to the war, for example Slovenia and Macedonia, exerted effort in making the conflict appear a distant event, whereas broadcasters in the 'far-away' Western countries attempted to draw their citizens' awareness to the humanitarian plight of Bosnian citizens by underlining congruence.

Many of the bulletin reports during the week of analysis began with the same raw material, but a number of factors served to modify them. In addition to the impact of historical, societal and political discourses outlined above, the presentation and production techniques of the journalists and of the newsroom also had an impact. A number of essays document the ways in which structural elements of the bulletin had an impact on the content reported: in particular, the *sourcing of information* and the *use of footage*.

The practice of giving to a viewer the source of a piece of information was able to imply either certainty or scepticism, depending on which source was quoted (reliable or unreliable; enemy or ally) and the verb used ('say' or 'claim'). For example Sky News reported one event as 'The United Nations says that Bosnian Serb soldiers failed to withdraw from Goražde' (May 20, item 6), and another as 'Serbs claim they [the British soldiers] failed to stop at a checkpoint' (May 21, item 3). The former implies certitude, the latter doubt. Giving the source either underlined the factual backing for the event, or imposed a barrier between the event and the journalist – he or she reported a claim but implied it was no more than conjecture. In this way journalists had a potential way of inserting their own opinion. The Russian news bulletin on Ostankino used 'verbal distancing techniques' to cast doubt on certain statements, for instance when reporting the freeing of French humanitarian workers by the Serbs: 'The French claimed that Première Urgence transported only human-itarian aid' (Thursday 19 May).

The source of news information was also given when one piece of information countered another. A Euronews item on the release of the French aid workers on Wednesday 18 May juxtaposed UN and Première Urgence claims: 'United Nations officials had claimed that Bosnian Serb leader Radovan Karadzic had released [the French aid workers] unconditionally. But their employers, Première Urgence, said they had paid $4000 each' (May 18, item 5). It is probable that the journalist was not able to ascertain the veracity of the statements and so presented both points of view, leaving it up to the viewer to decide which source to trust most (although using the 'claim' versus 'say' distinction to give some indication of the likely truth). In a similar way, the Sky News report about the town of Stolac on Monday 16 May made explicit the possibility that the information was partial, by giving its source: 'The blackened remains of a Catholic church *which the Croats claim* was shelled by the Serbs, burned by the Muslims' (emphasis added).

Likewise, the news bulletins on the Macedonian channel MTV highlighted the partiality of most of the information sources it used in its reports, except for information from the UN. The UN was also used in English-language bulletins as an objective source of news information. The problems with this were noted in the proceedings of a seminar attended by senior policymakers and news practitioners: '... the risk that the UN may have an agenda of its own, and that it may also be economical with the truth is not examined [by the news media]. The media fails to subject the international players, the UN as well as the peace mediators, to the scrutiny that their actions warrant' (Hopkinson 1993: 17).

Sourcing information did not have a uniform purpose. It provided insight into whether or not the journalist was able to assess a situation independently. It also implied that a journalist had assessed a situation and wished to signify that an event was true or false by giving the provenance of the information. It also implied that the journalist was unable to find out any more than that which the source had stated.

The second presentation issue concerns the use of footage. Although it is axiomatic that television news needs pictures, it is not the case, on the evidence of the week under analysis, that television news is picture-led. From 16–21 May, footage rarely provided the story. Of all the reports about Bosnia in this week there were only two with 'dramatic' footage – that is, footage of out-of-the-ordinary events. The first was a few seconds of footage showing a shell exploding near the main hotel in Tuzla on Sunday 15 May. The explosion happened at night, and the camera wobbled at the shell impact. This footage, from Reuters Television, was widely used by broadcasters the following day (see below). The second piece of 'dramatic' footage was of a British major's forced apology to a Serb commander (Friday 20 and Saturday 21, ITV and Sky News). The event was filmed by local Serb television, on low-quality video, and showed the officer's apology and the reactions of the soldiers grouped about him. However, most of the other new footage during the week had no pictorial resonance, consisting of talks, building damage or troop movements; illustrating rather than providing stories.

The week's analysis also revealed the problems that arose if words and footage were not synchronised. For example the 24-hour news channel Euronews rarely did this, and it was often unclear which side the pictured soldiers or civilians were on, or where the bomb damage was and how severe it was. On Friday 20 May Euronews reported that 'Muslim and Serb forces on the ground are continuing to jockey for territorial gains'. The statement was illustrated by a shot of a small group of soldiers sitting on a hillside. The commentary at this point did not refer to the pictures to explain which side these soldiers were on, and there were no overt visual distinguishing characteristics within the group. In such situations the viewer does not know, in a literal way, what is before his or her eyes. It can be argued that in this example the lack of naming in fact tallies with the way that the armies were 'jockeying'. There was attack and counter-attack with no overall significant breakthrough, and so precise documentation or labelling was irrelevant to the report.

However, the tendency is more widespread. Many of the bulletins analysed did not edit footage and voice-over precisely, as the essayists report. Turkish channels often used 'old and irrelevant' pictures, and there seemed 'to be a carelessness and at best an opportunism in terms of the use of footage'. Italian news bulletins were 'vague' in describing verbally the footage used, so that it was very difficult to know what the images were representing. Footage from Bosnia in French television bulletins was again characterised as 'unclear' and 'incomprehensible', acting more as symbols or ciphers of the war than as a detailed exposition of an event. Austrian television news in its authored reports did not always achieve congruence between what the images were showing (for instance evidence of food supplies) and the commentary given (that of the problems that lack of supply was causing). Slovene bulletins were 'non-visual' in their repetition of images over a number of days, their use of ubiquitous footage, and their cutting too quickly from shot to shot in a short space of time. The war footage of Croatian bulletins 'did not connect' with the verbal reports.

What images are evidence of depends upon the political standpoint of the broadcaster and the provenance of the footage and emerges in the voice-over commentary. The following example reveals again the degree to which footage was heavily dependent upon verbal explanation. The main hotel in the Bosnian city of Tuzla was shelled late on the night of Sunday 15 May 1994 and was documented by a Reuters Television World News report distributed on Monday 16 May. The footage of the night-time shelling showed lights in the distance, a wide-shot of people running as a siren went off and then a loud bang, which shook the camera as it zoomed in jerkily to try to pinpoint the explosion. This was followed by daylight shots of the damage done to the interior of the hotel, and shots from the window of the hotel. The Reuters TV text which accompanied the footage (see Appendix below) attributed the shelling of the hotel to the Serbs. The source for this was 'a police officer and a soldier standing outside the hotel' who said that the shells had been fired from the direction of the Serb stronghold. Particular images from this package were used by a number of broadcasters: CNN International, MTV (Macedonia), Algerian State TV, Show TV (Turkey), Croatian TV, Slovenian TV, Arte (France), Megachannel (Greece). Almost all of them selected the same images. Out of the shots collated by the feed, most used the two images of a close-up of a red telephone in the hotel surrounded by debris, and the footage of the explosion itself.

However, this unanimity over which images best conveyed the story was not matched by unanimity in attribution for the shelling. The Reuters Television text, as mentioned above, blamed the Serb side for the attack, albeit with some caution: 'Three tank shells, *thought to be fired from Serb positions*, hit the centre of Tuzla late on Sunday (May 15) evening, two of them slamming into the city's main hotel' (emphasis added). Croatian, Slovenian, Turkish and French bulletins went along with this analysis and described the Serbs as perpetrators, for example Show TV (Turkey): 'In the Serbian artillery attack mounted against Tuzla, by chance no one was injured'. CNNI and Algerian TV made the attack neutral. CNNI described the shelling almost as a natural phenomenon: 'Tank shells began falling last evening. Two struck the city's main hotel but caused no casualties according to UN officials.' Algerian Television News likewise: '… the situation continues to be tense in Tuzla where three shells fell on the town, on the central hotel.' Megachannel in Greece and the Macedonian MTV reported the shelling itself as a neutral attack, but by the position of the item the implication was that the shelling had been carried out by the Muslims. Megachannel announced at the start of the item: 'The situation worsens as Izetbegović's generals escalate their attacks against the Serbs, especially in Tuzla.' It then reported the meeting in Belgrade between Russian Special Envoy Churkin and Serb President Milošević. After this the anchor read: 'Clashes in Tuzla. A bomb fell on a hotel yesterday morning wounding four …' The earlier statement negated the possibility that the 'clash' might have been Serb-inspired. Similarly, Macedonian MTV positioned its neutral report of the shelling after the news of the Bosnian army attack on a UN convoy. All of these broadcasters subscribed to the Reuters World News feed, which meant that in addition to the footage they would have also received the textual information, logistics permitting. They could also have received information from other sources, either wire services or local media. Decisions to apportion agency for the attack therefore could have been logistical or political. But it is less important to discover which type of decision it was than it is to register the fact that most television news images have no intrinsic veracity. They are refracted, as all other information, through the prisms that have been discussed above.

A final prism is that of the presence or absence of journalists on the ground. During the week of analysis Sky News, ORF in Austria, TF1 and F2 in France, RAI in Italy and the BBC and ITN in Britain had reporters in Bosnia, evidenced by the transmission of 'authored reports' from Bosnia, in which some of the report is constructed by the correspondent rather than being solely a collation of items of news agency footage. However, Turkish broadcasters had few correspondents in Bosnia and were reliant on agency footage voiced-over in the studio. Macedonian

State TV sent only two crews to Bosnia throughout the conflict and relied on agency material. Greek TV channels occasionally put correspondents in Belgrade and Pale during the war, but not in other parts of the former Yugoslavia. Slovenian television news journalists were absent from Bosnia, as a result of Slovenia's attempt to distance itself from the conflict. The refraction of the foreign war event through a known correspondent makes the event easier to comprehend (although it then becomes an event limited by the domestic frame of reference). It brings events nearer to home. The reporting of the marketplace mortar attack of February 1994 in Sarajevo was a case in point. Having a journalist reporting from the scene made the report more forceful, as the reporter was an eyewitness to the aftermath. Having to quote from news agencies and other broadcasters immediately 'distanced' the report (see News World Conference, 1995).

The following essays describe the events in Bosnia during the week and their translation into bulletin reports. Each essay provides insight into what the war in Bosnia consisted of according to the bulletins in each country. They reveal the resonance of domestic agendas. As Gurevitch, Levy and Roeh (1991) concluded in their study of the globalisation of news stories: 'While the images may have global currency, the meanings given to them may not necessarily be shared globally. Television news in different countries, feeding on an increasingly similar global diet ... still speaks in many different voices' (214–15).

References
Gurevitch, M., Levy, M. and Roeh, I. (1991) The Global Newsroom: Convergences and Diversities in the Globalization of Television News', in P. Dahlgren and C. Sparks (eds), *Communication and Citizenship: Journalism and the Public Sphere*, London: Routledge.
Hopkinson, N. (1993) *The Media and International Affairs after the Cold War*, Norwich: HMSO.
News World Conference (1995) 'Broadcasting Without Borders', Saturday 11 November 1995, Berlin.

Appendix: Text of Reuters Television Feed from Tuzla, 16 May 1994
Three tank shells, thought to be fired from Serb positions, hit the centre of Tuzla late on Sunday (May 15) evening, two of them slamming into the city's main hotel.
One shell hit the fourth floor of the Tuzla Hotel, which houses European Commission monitors for the area. The second shell landed seven metres (23 feet) outside one of the hotel's main dining areas, where a reception was being held for two local basketball teams.
The third shell hit the outskirts of the town. There were no immediate reports of casualties. Aris Turkić, the technical manager of Zenica basketball team, said, 'We are very lucky, there were more than fifty people in there, we are very lucky.'
A police officer and a soldier standing outside the hotel said the shells were fired from the Serb stronghold on Mount Majenica, to the east of the town.
Bosnian army military expert Albhi Martinović, who surveyed the damage, said at least one of the shells that hit the hotel was an 85mm shell.
Tuzla has been the scene of fierce fighting for the past few days, even though it has been declared a 'safe haven' by the United Nations.

Algeria

Zohra Khandriche

The TV News Broadcasting Framework

The only Algerian television channel is a public channel under the direct jurisdiction of the Ministry of Information. The TV news bulletin is at 8 pm and lasts between 30 and 45 minutes. It is constructed in a standard way, alternating film reports with a studio-based news anchor. National and international news are separated into blocks, with a greater amount of national news. The bulletin ends with a series of short items. The language used is the official Arabic language, which is understood only by about half of the population. Nevertheless, most of the population watch TV news, even if they generally do not believe what is considered very official information.

TV News Coverage of the War in Bosnia

During the week of 16–21 May 1994 Bosnia was mentioned for the first five days. It generally was not mentioned in the headlines, but treated as a short item in the last part of the news, after other stories about foreign countries which were regularly reported on during the same period and often at greater length: Yemen, Egypt, Palestine and Rwanda. The topics that the news dealt with are laid out in Table 2.

There are three main features to notice about the presentation of the conflict. First, the information and footage chosen emphasised the fact that Bosnians were Muslims. The Bosnian people were represented as following the Islamic pattern closely: the public spaces (cafés and squares) were occupied by men only; all the women wore the Islamic veil and appeared in public only with their families or when they went

Table 2: Events reported on Algerian television, 16–21 May 1994

Monday 16 May	Negotiations and 'first light of hope'
	Serbs bomb Tuzla airport
	At Cannes Film Festival, Bernard-Henri Lévy's film *Bosna* is ridiculed
Tuesday 17 May	President Alija Izetbegović and a group of Bosnian people leave for Mecca on a plane provided by Saudi Arabia
Wednesday 18 May	Bombing of Tuzla airport
Thursday 19 May	French 'hostages' are released
	Serb bombing
Friday 20 May	Sarajevo celebrates the hundredth day of cease-fire

shopping. Only one item during the week, which showed the European dimension to Sarajevo, included interviews with people who were not visibly Islamic. Secondly, the Serbs were clearly marked as culpable. The bombing of Tuzla airport and several Bosnian cities was attributed to them (Wednesday 18 and Thursday 19 May), and more generally they were described as continuing to 'spread death and terror' (Friday 20 May). Thirdly, the television news presentation of the war made the conflict appear quite distant. This distance clearly contrasted with the way news about Egypt or Yemen for example was presented. Bosnian people, though they were Muslims, were Europeans and not Arabs. This distancing of the war was carried out in several ways.

First, although it mentioned Serb attacks, Algerian television did not emphasise the consequences of these attacks. Few pictures were shown and none were striking or dramatic. Very few details were given. On the contrary, it was prudently said about the Serb bombing of Tuzla airport on Monday 16 and Wednesday 18 May that 'the extent of the damage is not known'.

Secondly, in spite of a ritual formula which condemned the world for doing nothing about Serb crimes – the commentary on the hundred days of cease-fire in Sarajevo on Friday 20 May described how 'The Serbs continue to sow death and terror and the world helps by being content to watch and verbally condemn' – this accusation did not lead to a plea for, or any mention of, Algerian involvement in the conflict. On the contrary, the position of French philosopher Bernard-Henri Lévy, who advocated a clear involvement in favour of Bosnia, was ridiculed without being even set out (Monday 16 May).

On the whole, reports and commentaries appeared to be rather optimistic. Events that emphasised potential peace were highlighted. In this way, the release of the French 'hostages' was interpreted as showing rapprochement between the Serbs and the French. The most striking example was the item on Monday 16 May which several times mentioned a 'first light of hope' and prospects of peace, showing quiet, springlike pictures of Bosnia. The way that Bernard-Henri Lévy was insistently disparaged also discredited his pessimistic statement that 'Bosnian communities cannot live together' (Monday 16 May). To conclude, the Bosnian conflict was not treated by Algerian TV during the week of analysis as an important matter. The distance shown towards the situation was striking, in spite of the emphasis put on the Islamic aspects of the Bosnian people.

Austria

WALTER SCHLUDERMANN AND BRIGITTE HIPFL

The TV News Broadcasting Framework

The ORF (Österreichischer Rundfunk Fernsehen) is the Austrian public service broadcaster. It provides two national television channels, ORF1 and ORF2, which run complementary schedules. As a result of the development of cable and satellite television, the ORF no longer has a monopoly. However, in news coverage the monopoly still persists. Despite foreign competition, especially from Germany, the ORF news provides the only detailed coverage of domestic and foreign events from an Austrian point of view. The public obligations of the ORF – objectivity, balance and impartiality – give television news a semi-official character. Accordingly, its acceptance and credibility are high in all parts of the Austrian population. In spite of this, viewing figures have dropped: in May 1968 an average 2.3 million Austrians were informed of internal and foreign affairs via television news, compared to 1.6 million viewers in May 1994.

The main news is broadcast at the same time – 7.30 pm – on both channels. The length of the bulletin varies between 16 and 22 minutes. The average number of news items per programme is around fifteen, including a block of four or five items on economic news. The distribution of domestic and foreign affairs varies in accordance to what is in the news. In the week of observation from 16–21 May 1994, there were a lot of domestic events. Out of the ninety-six broadcast items, more than 70% focused on domestic affairs, compared to a usual average of 60% domestic affairs and 40% foreign affairs. There is no set order of presentation of domestic and foreign items. They are ranked according to importance. The news footage comes mainly from international agencies or from ORF correspondents. The ORF has permanent news agencies in the US, Russia, Germany, Great Britain, France and Italy. In the former Yugoslavia, there was a permanent ORF team which was changed regularly.

TV News Coverage of the War in Bosnia

In the week of observation from 16–21 May 1994, from a total of about a hundred news items, only two referred to the former Yugoslavia. There were two reasons for this below-average number of reports. First, there were two domestic issues that had a high profile: the forthcoming plebiscite on 12 June regarding Austria's entry into the European Community; and the intended deportation of a group of Kosovo-Albanians because of a controversial new law regarding foreign residency. Secondly, there was no spectacular and 'media effective' footage during this time, for example an attack on a UN vehicle, or a grenade thrown into a crowd of people. This was a week of 'normal' war which meant death, starvation, displacement, plundering and cruelty as part of everyday life in a war zone. However, these events were not extraordinary and therefore did not carry any 'noteworthy' news value.

The first report came on Tuesday 17 May and was entitled 'Partial Withdrawal' (see Table 3). It consisted of two separate thematic units. The first reported the intentions of the French and British governments concerning the possible withdrawal of their UN troops from the former Yugoslavia. This was not a report from the conflict area but a report which was related to it. Because the headline throughout the entire news item was entitled 'Partial Withdrawal', this section of the item obviously seemed to be more important in the view of the production editor. Another way to

Table 3: 'Partial Withdrawal', 17 May 1994, item 7 (from a total of 18), 6 frames, length 48 sec.

1	Time (seconds)	26
	Image	The anchor in the studio. Behind her on the right, a graphic of a UN tank with a few UN soldiers. Underneath this, the headline 'Partial Withdrawal'.
	Text	At the end of this year, France will withdraw 2500 troops from its 7000 UN soldiers stationed in former Yugoslavia. The partial withdrawal from Krajina in eastern Croatia, which is controlled by Serbs, and from the UN protective zone Bihać in northern Bosnia, is for financial and political reasons. Furthermore, Great Britain is considering withdrawing its UN soldiers if the warring parties in Bosnia do not approve a peace settlement.
2	Time	3
	Image	A group of soldiers – apparently officers who are not in a battle situation – walking through a sparse forest. It is impossible to tell to which army the soldiers belong.
	Text	No text
3	Time	5
	Image	A soldier stoops on a path surrounded by high grass and moves towards a position where some soldiers are waiting. He seems to be doing this more for the camera than out of military necessity.
	Text	The severe fighting between Serbs and Bosnian government troops continues. There are ...
4	Time	4
	Image	Trench with a bare-headed soldier. He holds an automatic gun.
	Text	... especially severe battles around the town of Tuzla in northern Bosnia. This region was ...
5	Time	7
	Frame	Close-up of a destroyed tank on a slight hill. The camera switches and zooms to the gun-barrel of the tank.
	Text	... declared a protected zone by the UN. The town's airport was fired on. The UN had planned ...
6	Time	3
	Frame	Meadow. To the right there are two soldiers crouching. The sound of a gunshot can be heard.
	Text	... to open it for some time in order to transport aid.

interpret this would be take note that the more important events for outsiders did not take place in the theatre of war within the former Yugoslavia, but took place in Paris, London or elsewhere.

The second unit of the news item attempted to give the impression of a direct report about the severe battles near Tuzla, but there was not the slightest reference in the images that severe fighting was going on. The fighting at or near the airport was not shown. The visual indicators were more symbolically presented: uniforms, guns and bullet-ridden tanks. The shot that could be heard in the sixth frame was presented as a dramatic highlight. These were images which could stand for any war situation, anywhere. The uniformed soldiers could not be assigned a party faction, neither from the text nor from the footage. The source of the images could not be identified.

The second report, broadcast on Friday 20 May (see Table 4), could be seen as a continuation of the previous story. This time a journalist was sent to the front lines of Tuzla, where heavy battles were raging, to provide a sense of authenticity. The impression of objectivity was increased by the distanced and unemotional language of the journalist. In her introductory commentary the studio anchor gave an overview of the situation in Tuzla which included references to severe battles and the

Table 4: 'Front-line Tuzla', 20 May 1994, item 11 (from a total of 17), 11 frames, length 1 min 51 sec.

1	Time (seconds)	23
	Image	Female anchor in the studio. On the right there is an insert with a still showing a destroyed building in a rural area and, underneath, the heading 'Front-line Tuzla'.
	Text	While France and Great Britain think out loud about whether to leave their troops in former Yugoslavia, severe battles continue to rage in the town of Tuzla located on the front lines. Serbian units tried again to disrupt the only supply line between Tuzla and the Bosnian heartland. Once again, an air drop of supplies was not possible today. Friedrich Orter reports:
2	Time	10
	Image	In the foreground there is a barbed-wire fence which surrounds an empty market with empty market stands. A woman enters the market through a hole in the fence while a man leaves through it. In the background an old woman can be seen.
	Text	The market is closed for now. Several days ago a Serb grenade was thrown into the market area injuring one person.
3	Time	8
	Image	Two multi-storied buildings. In the foreground, a clump of chives. The camera zooms back and shows a framed picture of the two multi-storied buildings.
	Text	Chives and parsley between multi-storied buildings. Self-reliance after a year of blockade.
4	Time	5
	Image	Improvised market. A group of men and women sitting and standing on the kerb of the road. They sell food which is laid on the ground in front of them. The camera pans the scene.
	Text	Housewives offer vegetables and herbs for sale.

5	Time	11
	Image	Close-up of a man in a shop. In the background, a shelf stacked with bread. The written insert: Enver Mujanović, Businessman.
	Text	The price has dropped drastically, says Enver Mujanović, a businessman. Previously a kilogram of flour cost about 140 schillings and now it costs about 10 schillings.

6	Time	9
	Image	Marketplace bustling with activity. A woman is weighing a sack of strawberries and gives them away. A close-up of hands.
	Text	A kilogram of strawberries from the region of Brčko costs 14 schillings. Formerly an area inhabited mostly by Muslims, it is now occupied by the Serbs.

7	Time	21
	Image	Close-up of the correspondent Friedrich Orter in front of a house holding a microphone with the ORF logo.
	Text	Since the armistice between Muslims and Croats, which was achieved under US pressure, the transportation of supplies from the Bosnian heartland to Tuzla is again possible. But there is the threat of another total blockade for the town if the Serbs succeed in achieving what they have planned to do, namely to establish a second corridor to the south of Tuzla.

8	Time	4
	Image	A street with many people, giving the impression of peace and normality.
	Text	Before the war Serbs accounted for 16 per cent of Tuzlá's population …

9	Time	9
	Image	Two old men are walking on a road, one of them is carrying an old backpack, the other one is pulling a small handcart with two sacks on it. The camera swings to the handcart. This image gives the impression of shortages and poverty.
	Text	… 10 per cent have moved away, the Croats stayed …

10	Time	10
	Image	Close-up of a man in an office. On the left hand is a small flag, in front is a microphone with an ORF logo. Written insert: Selim Beslagić, Mayor.
	Text	… says Selim Beslagić, the Muslim mayor. The Muslim–Croat battles in central Bosnia have never been a threat to the co-existence of these two ethnic groups.

11	Time	6
	Image	A place in town with a few people. In the background is a stand with some people. The camera pans up a minaret on top of which flies a black flag.
	Text	Here in Tuzla, says the mayor, we want to live and work in peace.

threat of supply lines being disrupted by Serbian troops. Yet no severe battles appeared in the images that were shown. The main part of the correspondent's report dealt instead with the supply situation of the population. The impression for the viewer was contradictory. Pictures of an empty marketplace and herbs growing between the multi-storied buildings connected with the reference for the necessity of self-reliance and projected an idea of poverty and shortages, but soon after this a marketplace bustling with activity was shown, and another image of loaves of bread on store shelves. These images, connected with the commentary that the price of flour had dropped to less than one-tenth its former value, gave the impression that supplies were adequate. But this impression did not last, as the next part of the report claimed that the supply situation was being threatened by an imminent Serbian military operation.

The second part of the report dealt with the behaviour of the Serbs, Muslims and Croats. Here there were obvious differences in the way their actions were evaluated and judged. The statement that the area of Brčko was 'formerly an area inhabited mostly by Muslims … now occupied by the Serbs' was a clear indicator that Muslims had been forcefully expelled by the Serbs. The commentary that 10% of the 16% of Serbs who occupied Tuzla had 'moved' gave the impression of a peaceful voluntary action. Furthermore, the conflicts between Croats and Muslims were understated given the fact that in the clashes between them there had been genocide and ethnic cleansing.

Conclusion

In general, detailed and lengthy reportage by all the Austrian media concerning the conflict in the former Yugoslavia could be expected because of the geographical proximity and the strong emotional involvement of Austrians based on shared histories. Despite the fact that the number of reports was atypical and below average during the week of observation, the two reports could be seen as good examples of the general tendency of ORF's reporting of the Balkan conflict.

The Serbs were presented in a more negative light than the Muslim and Croat opposition. This was manifest by the rhetoric chosen to describe each faction. The troops of the Bosnian Serbs were either called 'Serb units' or 'Chetniks', words which connoted guerrilla warfare and illegality, something outside the state order. In contrast to these pejoratives, their opposition was referred to as 'Bosnian government troops'. The military operations of the Bosnians were often labelled as 'offensives' and even 'liberating offensives', whereas the Serb attacks were described as acts of terrorism. In the case of winning land or 'ground', the Serbs were said to 'conquer' or 'capture' territory, whereas in the case of the Bosnians the term 'reclaiming' their land was often used. Through such rhetoric the Serbs were viewed as the aggressors while the other two parties automatically fell into the role of defendants, whose attacks were perceived as acts of justice. In reports about refugees and displaced people, Muslims and Croats were most often presented as the victims. Seldom were Serb refugees given the same status. The Serbs were better suited to play the role of the perpetrator which applied equally to the reports concerning their 'refugee camps'.

Such labelling conforms with public opinion in Austria, due in part to historical reasons. The Austrian prejudice goes back to the mid-19th century when nationalist strife intensified in the Balkans. At this time tensions increased between the Austrian–Hungarian Empire and the Serbian Kingdom. In 1914 Gavrilo Princip, a Serb, killed Franz Ferdinand, heir to the throne of the Empire, and his wife in Sarajevo. Since that time, Serbia has often been blamed by Austrians for initiating the First World War and the subsequent decline of the Austrian–Hungarian Empire.

France

MARIE-CLAUDE TARANGER

TV Coverage of the War in Bosnia

The news bulletins of the five non-subscription channels were examined: the three public channels (France 2, France 3 and Arte) and the two private ones (TF1 and M6). Although there are noticeable differences in style between the three main channels (TF1, France 2 and 3) and the minor ones (Arte and M6), their positions vis-à-vis the Bosnian conflict tended to be similar.

First, it is noticeable that there was a considerable quantity of coverage of the former Yugoslavia during the week under study. The subject was mentioned nearly every day on all channels and had more airtime devoted to it than any other subject. The information dealt mainly with three important events. The first was the campaign by Bernard-Henri Lévy and other French intellectuals in favour of Bosnia. It began on Sunday 15 May with Lévy's film *Bosna* being shown at the Cannes Film Festival and went on with the launch of a special electoral campaign for the European elections. This event was managed, both by its initiators and the TV channels, in such a way as to keep up the suspense as long as possible about whether or not Lévy would actually stand as a candidate. The second event was the release of eleven members of the humanitarian agency Première Urgence who had been detained for forty days by the Serbs. This event was treated as a big national story and produced extensive and emotionally charged coverage. The third event was the decision to withdraw some of the French troops from Bosnia, which was announced and commented upon as a political turning-point.

In addition to these 'spectacular' events, there were the everyday reports on the conflict: developments on the front line, the bombing of Tuzla airport, the breaking of the embargo, and preparations for the future reconstruction of Sarajevo. On the whole, even when there were no dramatic events, the former Yugoslavia remained present in the news. Such an emphasis on the duration of a conflict ('war goes on') is quite unusual for French TV news bulletins.

A further point to be noted is that most of the news about the former Yugoslavia was related to France. Bosnia at times almost seemed to disappear from view as the French focus of interest fell, for example, on the emotion of the families of the hostages, or on the French electoral campaign. Lévy's statement about his film *Bosna* is significant in this respect: 'The true subject of the film is us, is you, me.' This ethnocentrism cannot be considered as exceptional, however; it is arguably a general feature of TV news.

Overall, a complex position on the conflict emerged from the week surveyed. First,

133

almost every time something was said about aggression, for example in the reports about Lévy and about the 'hostages', the Serbs were presented as the aggressors and the Bosnians as the victims. Nonetheless, what was most often expressed was a refusal to take a stand in relation to the belligerant parties. This was the only acceptable choice indicated. The bulletins accentuated the extent of the difficulties, the inefficiency or failure of the current operations, and the general powerlessness. Most of the political figures expressed the same position, even if belonging to opposite political camps. Nuances appeared only between the more pessimistic or disillusioned statements and the more aggressive or optimistic ones. This dominant position of overall neutrality was expressed by various means. Often explicitly stated on the news by various political leaders, it was also transmitted in a more diffuse fashion, especially by government ministers who used, for example, neutral terms to designate the conflicting parties in Bosnia and so concealed their precise identity. The TV coverage itself used a range of means to express this same position: the remarks of the presenters, the voice-over commentaries, the images and the editing. It used the same neutral terms for the warring parties, the same tendency to present all belligerents in a symmetrical way and to be reticent about exactly who was responsible for the actions mentioned. The impression was sometimes given that the war was happening all by itself, impersonally. Even when those responsible for specific occurrences were mentioned ('The Serbs bomb Tuzla airport'), there was no emphasis or explicit condemnation of the act.

Similarly, footage and sound were most often from outside the areas of armed confrontation. The footage was often unclear, very rarely dated, and in general represented the point of view of the United Nations: either the logistics of the operations (trucks, movements, monitoring) or the consequences of fighting (ruins, destruction). The rare images that showed the war directly tended to be illegible and incomprehensible and served more as symbolic references (explosion and gunfire signifying 'chaos and confusion') than as actual descriptions. The violence was not emphasised. Instead there was an emphasis on technical and symbolic elements, which meant, in fact, that the images favoured the same peaceful values as the verbal discourse.

This general description can be underpinned by examining two particular items each dealing with an event in which the question of a real or symbolic commitment in the conflict came to the forefront.

The Launching of the 'Europe Starts at Sarajevo' Campaign for the 1994 European elections

The aim of this initiative was to obtain a commitment in favour of Bosnia, the principal consequence of which would be the lifting of the arms embargo in Bosnia. To this end, Bernard-Henri Lévy and his colleagues strongly denounced the acts and the crimes of the Serbs. The great majority of French political protagonists rejected this stance and thus dissociated themselves from discourse that denounced the Serbs. The television channels did the same.

The point of view in favour of Bosnia expressed by Bernard-Henri Lévy, André Glucksman and Bernard Kouchner was therefore never given the last word. It was systematically contradicted and counterbalanced by opposite viewpoints, which had all the more impact for being given by a variety of political personalities. There was excessive insistence on the 'isolation' of those designated as the 'intellectuals'. The way in which the position in favour of Bosnia was presented actually resulted in excluding Bosnia from the debate; only those consequences concerning French internal politics were retained. The remarks quoted in the news were very rarely those which really concerned the situation in Bosnia. The debate on the conflict, far from being developed, seemed on the contrary to be avoided. This was of course a result of an overall TV news framework that favours the proximate over the distant, the domestic over the foreign, but was also consistent with the political decision not to enter into the conflict.

The Release of the 'Hostages'

Eleven French citizens, who took part in humanitarian action in Bosnia, were victims of a Serb plot which accused them of arms trafficking. They were arrested in defiance of the law, imprisoned under very difficult conditions (at least psychologically) and finally released after a certain sum of money had changed hands. Admittedly, this story on the whole did no honour to the Serbs, who accumulated negative characteristics and who were unanimously presented as the 'baddies' of the story. It is notable, however, that these negative characteristics were never exploited. On the contrary, they tended to be minimised and relativised by other characteristics, for example that the prisoners were never mistreated.

The general treatment of this episode insisted in particular on the courage of the French, as well as the joy and the emotion aroused by their return. Two motifs dominated the accounts. The most common was the happy ending: we can come home and forget the Bosnian nightmare. But the humanitarian commitment was also reaffirmed: some of the released hostages were to continue their work in Bosnia; the suffering of the children must not be forgotten.

These two motifs embodied the dilemma often articulated on French TV about the Bosnian conflict: was it necessary to continue to act for the Bosnian population, against the war and the suffering, or should the French disengage and return home? Neither of these responses entailed taking a stand *within* the conflict, which was why neither of the two stories exploited the opportunity of condemning the Serbs.

Conclusion

Through their 'logic of peace' these stories taken from the conflict in the former Yugoslavia were clearly dissimilar to those portrayed on television during other conflicts. In the presentation of the Gulf War (1990–91), for example, a distinct 'logic of war' was discernable. The role of the Western powers was systematically highlighted and the confrontation was extremely personalised, with Saddam Hussein cast as the Devil. The restraint and moderation exercised in the presentation of the Yugoslavian conflict were rather atypical of television news, which at present tends most often to exaggerated and over-dramatic presentation.

Greece

ROZA TSAGAROUSIANOU

The Social-Historical Context

The end of the cold war led to major changes in the Balkans: the demise of state socialism, the break-up of Yugoslavia, the (re)construction and affirmation of national identities and the formation of new political entities. This led to a new climate in the region which did not leave Greece unaffected. The disintegration of the old order, combined with an economic and political crisis in Greece, has created a sense of societal insecurity[1] and instability.

To the traditionally uneasy Greek–Turkish relationship was added the mutual suspicion between the post-communist Albanian government and Greece, and the emergence of new post-Yugoslav states, especially of the Former Yugoslav Republic of Macedonia, which were perceived as a threat to Greece.[2] The situation became further complicated as, with the collapse of the state-socialist régimes of the Balkans, Turkish attempts to extend its influence over the area were perceived in Greece as a step towards the formation of an 'Islamic arch' extending from the Adriatic to the Black Sea and the geopolitical isolation of Greece from its European partners and the new economies of Eastern and Central Europe.

The uncertainty about Greece's position in the rapidly changing Balkans contributed to the emergence and intensification of processes of narrating, and thus constructing, the 'nation', and to the increasing 'nationalisation' of the universe of public debate in Greece.[3] The permeation of political and cultural life in Greece by nationalist discourse has affected the mass media, which has become one of the spaces where the construction of the Greek nation as a natural, homogeneous, organic community has taken place.

TV Coverage of the War in Bosnia

The coverage of the Bosnian conflict by the Greek media was not insulated from the impact of these changes in the geopolitical position of Greece and the sense of societal insecurity, as the following analysis of Greek television news coverage between 16 and 21 May 1994 indicates.

The television channels included in this study are the public service channel ET1, and three private channels, ANT1, MEGA and SKAI. ET1, the main public service broadcasting channel in Greece, broadcasts nationally. It has only nominal autonomy: since its foundation it has been subjected to government control and pressure, and its news bulletins are generally considered to express government views. ANT1 and MEGA are the two major private channels and attract a considerable national audience. ANT1 has consistently supported the centre–right forces of the political spectrum, campaigned against the recognition of the Former Yugoslav Republic of Macedonia and supported ultra-nationalist views regarding Greek–Albanian relations. Its news reports have stood out for their racist commentaries regarding Albanian migrants in Greece. MEGA has been generally more positive towards the centre–left and slightly more cautious in its approach to 'national' issues. It could therefore be argued that the two channels combined cater for a large audience supporting the major political parties in Greece.

SKAI, a less popular – although not insignificant – private channel, has extensive evening news bulletins and is thought, by its management as well as a part of the public, to provide a thorough analysis of the news. Its owner is also the proprietor of *Kathimerini*, a pro-centre–right quality daily, but the editors of the bulletins have been supporting PASOK (the Socialist Party) and this has been reflected in the channel's news.

Although there has not been any systematic research into audience use of news bulletins, the political affiliation of television channels in Greece indicates that viewers may select the news bulletins more likely to portray their own political views and positions.[4] However, one should also take into account other factors which may influence the choice of news bulletins, such as the general appreciation of a channel's other news and entertainment programmes. Finally, it should be pointed out that the news bulletins of ANT1, MEGA and ET1 are broadcast at different times, so that the viewer is in a position to watch and compare all of them.

The news bulletins selected for this analysis were the evening ones, mainly because of their larger audiences, longer duration and their comparatively more extensive coverage of the daily stories, and which might therefore reflect the views and objectives of the news editorial teams of the channels more clearly. The main evening news bulletin broadcast by ET1 starts at 9.00 and ends at approximately 9.30. ANT1 broadcasts its main bulletin between 8.00 and 8.30, MEGA between 8.30 and 9.00, and SKAI between 8.27 and 9.30 with the exception of Sundays when a shorter bulletin is broadcast between 8.27 and 9.00 approximately. Nevertheless, it should be said that, with the exception of SKAI, evening news bulletins rarely contain extensive analysis and commentary, as the time dedicated to each news item is usually between one and two minutes. They are effectively little more than a collection of headlines, based on footage received from international news agencies (although Greek television channels have occasionally used their own visual material from Serbia and the Bosnian Serb 'capital', Pale). As mentioned earlier, SKAI has a more extended news programme and presents itself as a channel with a commitment to news reporting.

During the period under study the conflict in Bosnia–Hercegovina was not very prominent in Greek television news bulletins, because it was overshadowed by domestic and regional events: the pressure to devalue the drachma after the decision of the Greek government to pursue a policy of convertibility in the international currency markets; the deterioration of Greek–Albanian relations; and developments in the Greek–Macedonian negotiations. In addition, the crash of a helicopter carrying a TV crew in northern Greece became the prominent news item during part of the period under consideration.

However, the situation in the Balkans, including the Bosnian conflict, was by no means neglected. All news bulletins featured short- to medium-sized reports on developments in Albania, Macedonia and Bosnia–Hercegovina during this period when these areas were not the main focus of attention internationally.

On Monday 16 May, when pressure for the devaluation of the drachma dominated the news, developments related to the Bosnian conflict were nonetheless covered by all four channels. The eighteenth item of the ET1 bulletin, which lasted a little over 45 seconds, focused mainly on the Russian peace initiative and the meeting between the Russian Envoy to former Yugoslavia Vitalii Churkin and Serbian President Slobodan Milošević, followed by a Russian TV clip from a meeting between the Serbian president and the Russian patriarch. In the last few seconds of the report on Bosnia, the Bosnian Serb offensive against Bosnian government-held Tuzla was also mentioned. In addition, the bulletin's twentieth item consisted of a 30-second report from Turkey which showed a meeting between Bulgarian and Turkish foreign ministers in Istanbul to discuss the Bosnian conflict.

The twelfth item in the ANT1 bulletin referred to the offensive against Tuzla, using international agency footage. In addition to that one minute of coverage, a little over 30 seconds were occupied by the bulletin's thirteenth item which referred to diplomatic initiatives for the resolution of the conflict; the EU foreign ministers meeting to discuss the latest peace plan and the Churkin–Milošević talks. The MEGA bulletin similarly dedicated approximately one minute to its eighth news item, a report on the Russian peace initiative and the Churkin–Milošević meeting, followed by a reference to the offensive against Tuzla. On the same day, the SKAI bulletin contained a one-minute report (item 11) on the peace plan discussed by EU ministers in Brussels, the Tuzla offensive and the Churkin–Milošević meeting.

On Tuesday 17 May the news reports from Bosnia were dominated by the visit/ pilgrimage of Bosnian president Alija Izetbegović to Saudi Arabia. The one-minute-long seventh item in the ET1 bulletin contained references to Western diplomatic efforts to reach a settlement of the Bosnian crisis; the meeting between Slobodan Milošević and the EU and UN envoys, Lord Owen and Thorvald Stoltenberg; the battles in the Tuzla area; and the Bosnian president's *hadj*, together with 300 other Bosnian Muslims, to Mecca. The report concluded with the newscaster mentioning that the pilgrims' expenses had been paid by Saudi Arabia. ANT1's report (1 min. 30 sec.) from Bosnia also referred to the Bosnian president's pilgrimage and the Saudi contribution towards the pilgrims' expenses, followed by a brief mention of the battles near Tuzla. It is interesting to note that the reporter covering the pilgrimage to Mecca represented it as a sign of the intransigent stance of the Bosnian–Muslim leadership by linking it to the refusal of the Muslim religious leader to meet the Serbian patriarch:

Main newsreader: With expenses paid by the king of Saudi Arabia, dozens of Muslims left Sarajevo for a pilgrimage to Mecca ...
Reporter: The Muslim President Alija Izetbegović and wounded soldiers left Sarajevo for a pilgrimage to Mecca. At the same time, however, the spiritual leader of the Bosnian Muslims, Mustafa Cerić, refuses to meet the Serbian Patriarch Pavle who is to accompany the Russian Patriarch Aleksei at a meeting in Sarajevo between the religious leaders of the warring sides.

Only the ET1 bulletins contained news items on Bosnia and former Yugoslavia on Thursday 19 and Friday 20 May: a one-minute report on the continuing clashes between Bosnian Muslims and Bosnian Serbs and on the Croatian political crisis after defections from the government party HDZ; and a one-minute report on the German 'mayor' to be sent to Mostar to help with the reconstruction of the city.

TV Discourses: A Brief Analysis

Owing to the geopolitical position of Greece, and the increased sense of societal insecurity among Greeks, I would argue that the significance of the coverage of conflict in Bosnia is much higher than in other European societies. In fact, the coverage of conflict in Bosnia should be seen as inextricably linked to the coverage of Balkan developments in general. Developments in Turkey, Macedonia, Albania and Bulgaria are equally important, usually perceived as interrelated and complementary to those in Bosnia.

Thus, for example, it could be argued that the participation of the Bosnian President in the *hadj* to Mecca became an important news item as it was interpreted to offer proof of 'common-sense' fears and suspicion regarding the situation in the Balkans. Its newsworthiness was due to the 'proof' it provided regarding the 'Islamic' character of the Republic of Bosnia–Hercegovina. By extension this was related to Turkish influence in the Balkans, represented in the popular imagination by the potent image of the consolidation of an 'Islamic arch' in the Balkans. It could thus be argued that, despite the humanitarian sympathy of the newscaster/audience towards the population of Bosnia–Hercegovina, the desired effect of this news report was to categorise, or reinforce the categorisation of, the Bosnian population into 'friend' and 'foe'. Thus, according to the news report, Bosnian Muslims (and, presumably, all those other Bosnians who have chosen to identify with the Bosnian government) are, at best, suspect because of their 'Islamic' credentials.

It is also interesting that in the discourses employed by the media in the coverage of the Bosnian Serb offensive against Tuzla, there is little reference to 'aggressors'. On most occasions, it is very difficult to discern who is the aggressor and who is not, as the commentary is brief, almost disinterested and emphasises the events as part of 'routine conflict'. This is in sharp contrast to the implicit disapproval (discernible in the ironic and surprised tone of the ANT1 news presenter) of the pilgrimage to Mecca of the Bosnian president to which I referred above, although the commentary does not present this as an act of provocation.

Of particular interest is the representation of the Serbian president, Slobodan Milošević, and by extension the Serbian nation, as a contributor towards peace and stability in the area. This was achieved by the reports of his meetings with the Russian Special Envoy to the Balkans, Vitalii Churkin, and the supporting visual material, as well as the reference in the ET1 bulletin of Monday 16 May to his meeting with the Russian patriarch. This strategy, which diverged from most international media treatment of Slobodan Milošević and the Serbs as international pariahs, is also complementary to the process of discrediting the Bosnian Muslims; not only is it a form of resistance to the internationally accepted mistrust and condemnation of the Bosnian Serbs and Slobodan Milošević personally, but also it offers a reminder of his international prestige, despite the adverse circumstances. In addition, the focus on his audience with the Russian patriarch serves as a reminder of the cultural and religious proximity of the Serb and Greek nations, reinforcing the recently cultivated popular belief in the cultural kinship and, by extension, common interests of the two nations.

The coverage of the Bosnian conflict during the week from 16 to 21 May 1994 reinforced existing popular fears, suspicion and views regarding the changing face of the Balkans. The presentation strategies in the news bulletins were based on the mobilisation of common-sense assumptions regarding the war, and the divisions between 'us' and the 'other'. Aspects of the news coverage served as a reminder of what is widely thought among Greeks to be at stake in the conflict in former Yugoslavia: a reminder of the identity of the opponents, the Bosnian Muslims and the Christian Orthodox Serbs, and of its political consequences.

The coverage of the conflict revitalised the potent image of the spectre of the consolidation of an 'Islamic arch' and offered a simplified outline of the political field in the Balkans as this is currently perceived by the majority of Greeks: if the Bosnian government is a Muslim government, and the population of Bosnia is Muslim, it is *ex definitio* not with 'us'. It is therefore posited as the 'other' in the highly polarised political field of the region. This reminder of where two of the participants in the Bosnian conflict stand reinforces the binary divisions between 'good' and 'bad' that prevail in popular consciousness and in the nationalist imaginary promoted and sustained by certain institutional actors in Greece, including the majority of the mass media.[5]

Notes

1. For a definition of 'societal security' see O. Waever et al, *Identity, Migration and the New Security Agenda in Europe* (London: Pinter, 1993).
2. Although only nationalist parties and some diaspora organisations have reservations about the current borders of the Republic of Macedonia, the general feeling in Greece is that Macedonia constitutes a threat to Greek security, because of specific clauses in its constitution regarding the protection of 'Macedonians residing in neighbouring states' and the perceived 'usurpation' of Greek history through the use of Greek 'names and symbols'.
3. For a discussion of these issues see S. Sofos and R. Tsagarousianou, 'The Politics of Identity: Nationalism in Contemporary Greece', in J. Amodia (ed.), *The Resurgence of Nationalist Movements in Europe* (Bradford: Department of Modern Languages, University of Bradford, 1993).
4. This is, at least, one of the factors of newspaper choice among Greek readers. See R. Tsagarousianou 'Mass Communications and Political Culture: Authoritarianism and Press Representations of Political Deviance in Greece', PHD thesis; University of Kent, Canterbury, 1994.
5. See Sofos and Tsagarousianou, 'The Politics of Identity'.

Italy

ANTONIA TORCHI

The TV News Broadcasting Framework

Six main evening news bulletins were analysed: RAI TG1, TG2, TG3, Fininvest's TG5 (Canale 5), TG4 (RETE 4) and Studio Aperto (Italia 1). The bulletins are broadcast between 6.30 and 8.30 pm, and usually summarise and enlarge the news given in the daytime. They all share some national characteristics that can be closely related to the coverage of the war in the former Yugoslavia.

The first characteristic is the importance given to words rather than images. For example, it is common for studio newsreaders to give long explanations at the same time as the interviewees themselves are speaking. In the coverage of the Bosnian war, reports on the peace talks in Geneva and Brussels would often show politicians interviewed by a correspondent in the background while the studio-based commentator summarised their words. Another example of the priority given to words is the way that even an event like a massacre would be verbally described, with no visual details except for a standard photo behind the newsreader.

The second characteristic is the repetition of the same news items many times a day. They are frequently kept for a few days. For example, in the week before 16–21 May 1994, the same report about Sarajevo under siege ran for three days on some RAI daytime bulletins.

The third characteristic is a general imbalance between national and international issues. National issues dominate while in the past political issues took definite priority (Agostini, Fenati, Wolf, 1989), now social issues come first. International issues, on the other hand, look incongruous. Even when they get the equivalent of television's 'front page', they are overwhelmed by the obsessive analysis of Italian society, Italian politics, Italian events, both major and minor. For example, notwithstanding the fact that the week under scrutiny was an atypical one, with the news bulletins mainly focusing on the new Centre–Right government led by Silvio Berlusconi, little time was given to Bosnia. Only the two leading news bulletins, TG1 and TG5, carried any news about Bosnia. TG1 had two items consisting of 4 minutes on Monday 16 May and 15 seconds on Tuesday 17 May, and TG5 had one item lasting 2 minutes on Tuesday 17 May.

There were notable exceptions to the general paucity of coverage about the Bosnian conflict. From time to time two news bulletins, RAI 3 (State Television) and Italia 1's Studio Aperto (Fininvest) tried unusual approaches to the subject. RAI 3 which often broadcasts foreign news sometimes carried out in-depth analysis of the war, looking at all the sides of the conflict. Italia 1 sometimes campaigned to shake people's consciousness, broadcasting live, for example, from the besieged Sarajevo for fifteen days, in an attempt to portray the city's multicultural life through 'non-Western eyes'.

TV Coverage of the War in Bosnia

As mentioned above, during the week of 16–21 May 1994 there was an overwhelming interest in Italian domestic politics. Nevertheless, the few references to the war in former Yugoslavia confirm the national characteristics already outlined, as well as showing others, such as the use of generic visual material (mostly from international news agencies as there are very few regular correspondents in the war regions), the use of particular sources for comments (almost always Muslim, seldom Croat and never Serb), and generous coverage of the diplomatic aspects of the conflict.

TG1 (RAI 1 bulletin) on Monday 16 and Tuesday 17 May reported the new Italian government's position on Bosnia as expressed by Antonio Martino, the Foreign Minister, at the EC summit in Brussels; the effects of the siege of Goražde; and the Serb attack against the Bosnian city of Tuzla. These three items followed particular patterns.

The official speech by Martino was aimed at reassuring both Italian allies and Italian public opinion about the continuity of the government's foreign policy, notably towards the former Yugoslavia, which was described as 'an aching pain in Italy's heart'. Martino reiterated that, 'the Italian government goes on supporting the plan to send new UN troops to Bosnia and confirms the reopening of the Italian embassy in Sarajevo ...'

The report on Goražde under Serb attack emphasised romantic and sentimental themes that symbolised the changes wrought on daily life by war conditions. The report showed footage of countryside taken from a camera on a van. The countryside then faded to a group of ruined houses around a church. The voice-over said: 'The 750 Muslims so far killed and 1000 injured are the result of Serb attacks. But the Serbs claim that ...' (close-up on ruined buildings and broken roofs) '... that is false. As one proof among many others, they point to this cemetery.' The reporter on his way to Goražde had reached a churchyard and was pictured looking at ruined tombstones, while explaining: 'This is a Serb [cemetery], destroyed by an integralist wing of Muslim forces who previously occupied this area.' The camera focused on details of flowers growing around the tombstones, and birds singing. The reporter continued: 'But if this is one of the Serbs' reasons, what about the Muslim reasons? It's difficult to know ...' The van then moved along a ruined road where injured people, mostly children, looked expectantly at the camera. Close-ups of head, leg and arm wounds, of sad eyes and cautious smiles. '... Especially now that the Serbs' latest decision is to banish all foreign journalists from Goražde. Goražde, secluded from the rest of the world, has finally become what the Serbs want: a ghost capital within a ghost state.' The report finished with a close-up on the reporter in front of a landscape (presumably the same as the beginning), with Goražde far in the distance, half hidden by trees.

The bombing of Tuzla was a very short item of 15 seconds, read to camera by the news anchor. Although not explicit in its condemnation of Serb action, disapproval was expressed through the tone and expression of the newsreader.

TG5 (Canale 5 bulletin) on Tuesday 17 May looked at the war in the former Yugoslavia from a rather different perspective, relating it to visual simulation and war games. Instead of news about Tuzla, it showed NATO troops in Sardinia on a training exercise, simulating an air attack and a landing. It described these manoeuvres of troops with reference to the war in Bosnia and made explicit the game/reality juxtaposition: 'For many "Top Guns" this has been a chance to practise their next missions in Bosnia. Not far from here, on the Italian borders, war is for real.'

The coverage of the week of 16–21 May 1994 suggests that footage is imprecise and adaptable to a broad range of comment. While there were plenty of official and political images from Brussels, Geneva and so on, there was a shortage of original images clearly related to specific contexts in dangerous zones. Goražde and Tuzla on TG1 were shadows in the distance when not just a small dot on a map. This lack of images was underlined by the fact that the TG5 news bulletin's only visible reality was a fake war outside Bosnia.

Instead of describing events neutrally, Italian journalists tended to make statements, to 'editorialise' the news. Audiences were bombarded with generic maps, confusing graphics, stereotypes of killed lovers and injured children and were not informed in any detailed way – either by words or by images – about the up-to-date military situation, changes in local politics, daily life under siege conditions, or the redefinition of borders. This vagueness was reinforced by the anonymity of information sources, especially for footage. There was no indication of production logos, or any other visual display such as date, origin, company or film-maker. So the source of the stories – and their validity – found their assessment mostly through journalists' statements.

This 'contempt' for images and the prioritisation of words have been described as a 'modern form of iconoclasm' (Vattimo 1994). It is as if dramatic situations can be 'cleaned' by speeches. As a result, Italian news bulletins often display two attributes which can be defined as standardisation and a lack of curiosity (Casadio 1993).

References

Agostini, A., Fenati, B., and Wolf, M. (1989) *Fatti nostri e fatti loro*, Rome: RAI-VQPT.
Casadio, G. (1993) 'L'eclisse dell'inchiesta', in P. Dorfles (ed.), *Atlante della radio e della televisione*, Rome: Nuova ERI.
Vattimo, G. (1994) 'Perche disprezzi le immagini?', *La Stampa*, 2 December.

Macedonia

Klime Babunski

The TV News Broadcasting Framework

In 1994 the main broadcasting outlet was Macedonian Radio and Television, which is a public broadcasting company. The director general and the directors of radio and TV are appointed by Parliament. Macedonian TV has three channels, with the majority of the second channel's schedule reserved for ethnic minorities. According to the State Bureau of Statistics, in 1993 there were seventeen private TV stations. At the time of analysis there were no networked private TV stations in Macedonia, nor was there cable television.

TV Coverage of the War in Bosnia

During the week of 16–21 May 1994 the coverage of the war in Bosnia and Hercegovina appeared in the middle of the bulletin. This was normal practice. Coverage was not insignificant: out of the 30-minute bulletin, the average time apportioned to coverage of the war was around 4 minutes.

The conflict in Bosnia was reported according to two main perspectives: either the daily tally of attacks and bloodshed, or diplomatic efforts for a cease-fire. During the week of analysis it can be argued that the accent of the coverage was on diplomatic efforts. For example, on the 20 May 1994 the Bosnia section of the bulletin was introduced in the following way: 'Despite all efforts of the international community to end the conflict ... the situation continues to be strained.' Great attention was given to Vitalii Churkin's visit to Belgrade and his meeting with President Milošević. The report from the correspondent in Belgrade stressed that the most important thing now was that, 'Milošević and Serbia are strongly supportive of the cease-fire ...', and that the renewal of the negotiation process was the beginning of the end of the war (Monday 16 May). As context for this news, the 'carrot and stick' approach was implicitly given. The carrot was 'the lifting of the sanctions' – the most important thing for Milošević – and the stick was 'the destiny of the political negotiations'. A particular 'stick' was the statement of the French Minister for Foreign Affairs about the possible withdrawal of French troops (Monday 16 May). Other diplomatic efforts were also framed positively: the talks between President Milošević, Lord Owen and Mr Stoltenberg were described as successful (Tuesday 17 May). But at the same time it was stressed that there were problems in Goražde and that the cease-fire in Sarajevo was not being obeyed.

The prosecution of the war was presented by short news items on Monday 16 May about Igman and Tuzla, and on Tuesday 17 May about Sarajevo. These items were based on reports from foreign news agencies, and on the statements of the UNPROFOR spokesman Rob Annink. On Thursday 19 May the war report came at the beginning of the Bosnia section of the bulletin. The Bosnian Serbs had launched a powerful artillery attack around Sarajevo airport. At the same time there was a report that the Bosnian army had started an offensive against Serb forces. The diplomatic efforts were in this instance reported second.

' On this day and on the next, particular attention was paid to the ordinary people in Sarajevo. The subject of the two reports was the destiny of the citizens in a partitioned Sarajevo. The first report included a church service of Orthodox Serbs and in the centre of the 'story' a young Serb girl and her hope that there could be an end to hate and intolerance, underscored visually by footage of traffic moving normally and people sitting out in cafés. The second report consisted of interviews with some Sarajevo citizens. The central points of the report were the feelings of fear that they felt, because of the 'Chetniks who surround Sarajevo ... and their daily shooting ... We believe in our victory, we will fight, because the world cannot, they do not want to help us.' Another person said, 'It is peaceful. There are no shells or anything. But there is fear, people are afraid, and a little scared. But it is good and I hope it will continue.' It was difficult to know which speaker was right: whether Sarajevo during the cease-fire was peaceful or whether there was daily shooting. The reporter did not indicate to the viewer which description of Sarajevo was more accurate.

The only 'army' in the war, according to news bulletin description, was the Bosnian army; the Serbs and Croats were called 'military forces'. This naming of soldiers was linked to the naming of territories: Croat and Serb forces were always described as entering 'Bosnian' territory, i.e. foreign territory. However, Macedonia was not a side in the war and the Macedonian media did not report according to the 'us and them' formula. The contradictions and differences between pieces of information generated were usually stressed. The only source which was not questioned was UNPROFOR and its official press officers.

Russia

MILENA MICHALSKI

The TV News Broadcasting Framework

In 1994 there were seven terrestrial television channels in Russia. The main state-owned channel was called Ostankino (it has since become ORT, Russian Public Television). The main news programme *Vremiia* (Time) was usually on at 9 pm and lasted 50 minutes, including 20 minutes of sports coverage. *Vremiia* retained a similar structure to its Soviet format: opening with headlines in brief, followed by more detailed domestic news, then news from the 'near-abroad', that is, those states which used to form part of the Soviet Union and still had close links with Russia. This was followed by 'international' news from the rest of the world.

TV Coverage of the War in Bosnia

The former Yugoslavia, in the week 16–21 May 1994, always formed the transition between news from the near-abroad and the rest of the world. Of approximately thirty items covered in each bulletin, the former Yugoslavia always came about twentieth. The coverage of events in and concerning the former Yugoslavia was fairly comprehensive in the period examined here. It ranged from military matters, in other words accounts of the fighting, through political issues, such as reports on attempts at arbitration and on the UN, to religious matters, which were closely, indeed explicitly, tied in with political issues. The main body of news during the week revolved around the visit of Aleksei II, Patriarch of Moscow and All-Russia, to the republics of former Yugoslavia. This can be explained by the desire to emphasise the religious bond between Orthodox parts of former Yugoslavia, such as Serbia and Montenegro, and Russia. Patriarchs from the two countries were reported to have discussed the question of the Orthodox religion in countries liberated from totalitarian regimes. On-the-spot reports from Belgrade on Monday 16 May were eloquent on the impressive nature and significance of the Orthodox church St Sava, describing it as 'grand', 'the largest in the world' and 'majestic'. Aerial views included in one of the reports supported the suggestion that it was impressive. The joint service held by the Russian and Serb patriarchs was said to be attended by several thousand and was broadcast over the whole of Yugoslavia. Its political importance was shown by President Slobodan Milošević of Serbia and Aleksei II shaking hands outside. Aleksei II was then metaphorically canonised, through camerawork which used a dissolve from a mosaic of St Simon's face to the patriarch's face. Further political links were made to this religious visit when Radovan Karadžić, president of the self-styled Republika Srpska, was shown presenting Aleksei II with a traditional stringed instrument, and when the Bosnian Serb military commander, General Ratko Mladić, met the patriarch. Similarly, the patriarch visited a Russian battalion in the Serb quarter of Sarajevo, indicating that the army and the Church were not only no longer incompatible, as they were under communism when religion was taboo, but were even on the same side.

In contrast to the good relations indicated between those of the Orthodox faith, there were some veiled comments relating to the Catholic Croats and the Muslims. One such comment was an aside explaining the history of St Simon, who is 'the most beloved Serbian saint' and who was 'burnt at the stake by the Turks' 400 years ago. This was an allusion to the 500 years of Turkish occupation of the area during which some Slavs converted to Islam. There was a clear anti-Muslim implication here, which stretched to the present day, despite being disguised as history.

A pro-Serb bias was also evident in a report three days later, on Thursday 19 May. Although it had just been stated that 'the conflict between the Serbs and the Muslims continues in the Bosnian town of Tuzla', the next sentence continued: 'The leader of the Serbs, Radovan Karadžić, called for world co-operation to exert pressure on the Muslims to stop the offensives.' There was no indication here that the Muslims were not the only side committing such offensives; the fact that it was a (Bosnian) Serb who was said to be calling for peace seemed intended to suggest that the Serbs had peaceful intentions, but were being thwarted by aggressive Muslims.

There were further implications that it was the Muslims in particular, but also the Croats, who were to blame for the lack of peace in former Yugoslavia. This could be seen in the Russian and Serbian patriarchs' joint invitation, on Monday 16 May, to the Croatian Cardinal Kuharić and the Muslim Reis Ul-Ulema (spiritual leader) Cerić to meet the following day to make a bid for peace. The next day's report on the meeting, due to take place at the airport, revealed that it was less than successful, as the Reis Ul-Ulema refused to participate. The visual elements were used here to maximum effect, with lengthy shots showing the conference tables at the airport deserted except for the Russian and Serb patriarchs. There was much emphasis in the commentary on the lack of co-operation from the other religious leaders: 'The Russian and Serbian patriarchs waited ... for the Croatian and Muslim religious leaders to turn up' and 'the Muslim leader declined to take part. After the two Orthodox patriarchs had waited a long time, Cardinal Kuharić arrived.' In contrast to this, the report that 360 Bosnian Muslims, including the president of Bosnia–Hercegovina, were going on a pilgrimage to Mecca, suggested by the tone of the voice-over commentary a generosity of spirit on the part of the Serbs, as 'the Serb army, controlling the approach to the airport, gave permission for the flight to take place'.

Coverage of international and political meetings was neutral, including the meeting between Russian Special Envoy Vitalii Churkin and Serbian President Slobodan Milošević, to discuss an earlier Geneva meeting between ministers for foreign affairs. This meeting between Churkin and Milošević did, however, serve to underline links between the two countries. The meeting in Zagreb between Lord Owen and Thorvald Stoltenberg, respectively the EU and UN mediators, in which they insisted that a cease-fire must be a condition for future talks with contact groups was similarly neutrally reported, featuring an interview with Owen. In contrast, footage of freed French humanitarian aid hostages arriving in Paris was accompanied by a statement expressing the French humanitarian aid workers' protestations of innocence regarding the supplying of arms to Muslims. Doubts were cast upon the veracity of this statement by the employment of a verbal distancing technique: 'The French claimed that Première Urgence transported only humanitarian aid', and 'According to the French the Serbs themselves planted [the arms]'. Once again, the implication was that the Serbs might be innocent of the accusation.

As far as the coverage of the prosecution of the war was concerned, a 'video review' was used, which included footage of fighting. Although fighting around Tuzla after an alleged Bosnian Serb attack was shown, on Monday 16 May, a distancing technique was used again in reporting the destruction of the centre of Tuzla by Bosnian Serb tankfire: '. . . according to information from the Muslims'. This could have been intended to suggest an element of unreliability on the part of the Muslims. Otherwise the war damage was shown neutrally, using footage of a moving tank, shells being fired and unidentified soldiers scurrying around in darkness, filmed with a hand-held camera. To add a human factor, a solider and a person in civilian clothes were shown picking up a shell. In a report about the patriarch's visit to Trebinje, in Hercegovina, it was stated that fighting was continuing there, implying that he was courageous to go. He was also said to have been to Sarajevo, but that it had been impossible to send a report to Moscow as the Muslim army had blown up the radio relay station, severing all links from Republika Srpska. This comment was emotionally charged, putting yet further blame on the Muslims with no explanatory context.

Overall, it is clear that despite attempts to appear neutral and objective in their reporting, it remained the case that the accumulation of details evidencing unilateral sympathy, as well as the religious historical references to the Turkish occupation, coupled with emphasis on an exaggerated Orthodox fraternity, conveyed *Vremiia*'s pro-Serbian bias.

Serbia

ZDENKA MILIVOJEVIĆ

TV Coverage of the War in Bosnia

The main evening bulletin on Serbian television's (RTS) Channel 1 was analysed. The bulletin starts at 7.30 pm and has a reach of 4.5 million (the size of the electorate) throughout the territory of the Federal Republic of Yugoslavia (FRY). Unlike other types of media in the FRY, the bulletin is the only source of information that reaches all types of audiences.

During the week of analysis the bulletin varied in length from 40 to 50 minutes, and had an average of 30 stories in any one bulletin. The main items relating to Bosnia are set out in Table 5.

The very first item in the bulletin on Monday 16 May, of seven and a half minutes, set the political tone. The camera filmed the meeting between President Milošević and Aleksei II, zooming in on Milošević while the newscaster read the key parts of Milošević's speech from the presidential office release: 'Regardless of the difficulties, the Serbian nation is determined to defend its legitimate, national and state rights and interests. Serbia has always supported a just peace, which is only attainable with the full respect of the parties in the conflict. The Serbian nation in war-torn areas does not wish to attain its rights to the detriment of the rights of other nations, but rather to defend the same rights which have been acknowledged for others and to preserve its freedom and its country.' This statement was in no way related to the meeting that Milošević had had with Aleksei II. No matter who Milošević talked to, such statements were regularly found in the releases from his office and were intended to 'affirm' the policy of the Serbian leadership.

The next item was indicative of the manner in which RTS portrayed the war in Bosnia. It showed the meeting of the FRY President Lilić with Aleksei II, while the newscaster read the presidential release: '... The current refusal by the Islamic leader to attend this meeting [of religious heads in Sarajevo] only indicates that the Muslims still believe the war option to be the solution to the Bosnia–Hercegovina crisis. ... The experience acquired thus far demonstrates that whatever compromise the Serbs in this former Yugoslav republic make, the Muslims are always the ones to renege on agreements, and in decisive moments stage tragedies resulting in innocent civilian victims. ... Their main purpose is, as the patriarch agreed, to continue the practice of demonising the entire Serbian nation by most of the world's media, which the patriarch himself noted, are financed from sources well known to all the world.' In fact, the Islamic leader did not refuse to come to the meeting, as he himself informed

Table 5: Main RTS News Items 16–21 May 1994 relating to Bosnia

Item number	Length min:sec	Subject
		Monday 16 May
3	0:26	Metropolitan Kiril of the Russian Orthodox Church stated yesterday that Cardinal Franjo Kuharić and the Reis Ul-Ulema Mustafa Cerić had responded positively to the invitation of the Russian and Serbian patriarchs to meet them in Sarajevo to talk about peace.
4	5:50	Serbian president Slobodan Milošević received Russian Special Envoy Vitalii Churkin.
8	1:10	Yugoslav Minister of Foreign Affairs Vladimir Jovanović made a brief visit to Sofia on his return from Zimbabwe, stating that each day of sanctions against FRY doubled the duration of the war in Bosnia.
9	1:13	One of the topics of today's EU Council of Ministers meeting in Brussels was the crisis in the territories of the former Yugoslavia.
10	1:05	Reactions of the conflicting parties [in Bosnia] to the Geneva declaration aroused hopes, since neither side fully rejected it, stated the Russian Foreign Minister Andrei Koziyrev on his return to Moscow.
13	1:35	In a rather lengthy article in the newspaper *Pravda*, a well-known Russian academic Paelo Volouev and scientific associate of the Russian Academy of Sciences Ludmilla Tiabunienko sharply criticised the policy of the USA and the Russian attitude towards the conflict in Bosnia.
14	0:44	In the German newspaper *Süddeutsche Zeitung* Jens Snider wrote that Serbs in Croatia who, before the present war, accounted for about 12 per cent of the population according to estimates from human rights groups, live in villages and smaller towns, especially close to the front lines, which are extremely dangerous.
17	0:33	The battlefields in the former Bosnia–Hercegovina, on the front line between the Muslims and the Serbs, were not quiet again today.
18	0:49	Intense fighting on the Majevica battlefield substantially subsided today, compared to previous days.
19	0:24	At the Mostar front, according to a communication from the so-called Bosnia–Hercegovina Army, provocations from the Croatian Defence Councils became increasingly frequent over the past twenty-four hours.
		Tuesday 17 May
1	4:12	Serbian President Slobodan Milošević met with co-chairmen of the conference on the former Yugoslavia, Thorvald Stoltenberg and David Owen, today.
12	1:45	In Paris, the French Minister of Defence Francois Léotard said that about 2,500 French soldiers would be withdrawn from the territories of the former Yugoslavia by the end of the year.
13	0:58	Offensives against Republika Srpska (RS) continued.
		Wednesday 18 May
12	0:15	Eleven members of the French humanitarian organisation Première Urgence were released from detention, as confirmed to Tanjug by the Serbian military authorities in Lukavica.
13	0:19	In Washington it was announced that the Contact Group for Bosnia would consider tomorrow and the following day the plan for ending the hostilities and territorial delimitation in Bosnia–Hercegovina, on the basis of the ministerial meeting in Geneva.

Item number	Length min:sec	Subject
14	0:31	Madeleine Albright, US Ambassador to the UN, stated that the USA believed that the territorial division of Bosnia–Hercegovina in the ratio 49 per cent for Serbs and 51 per cent for the Muslim–Croat federation was acceptable.
15	1:45	On the eve of the Contact Group meeting in Washington, the *New York Times* uncovered a sharp conflict developing between Washington and Moscow despite their apparent unity.
17	0:13	In New York, countries belonging to the Islamic Conference organisation at the UN were again preparing a draft resolution to end the arms embargo for the Bosnian Muslims.
18	1:35	Paris indicated the possibility of withdrawing 2,500 'blue helmets' from the territories of the former Yugoslavia by the end of the year. This caused numerous reactions.

Thursday 19 May

6	0:30	The Patriarch of Moscow and the Whole of Russia Aleksei II left Belgrade this evening for Sofia, thus ending his six-day visit to the Serbian Orthodox Church (SPC).
9	1:29	The Contact Group meeting began in Washington
10	1:00	The French Minister for Foreign Affairs Alain Juppé stated that the ministers of the US, Russia and Europe would meet again on 13 June so as to consider the progress of the agreement on the resolution of the Bosnia conflict.
12	0:30	The British Foreign Office Minister Douglas Hogg warned that the conflicting parties in the former Bosnia–Hercegovina have a deadline of only two months to reach an agreement or face the withdrawal of the UN troops.
13	0:11	The Spanish Defence Minister Julio Garcia Varga stated that Spain intends to reduce the share of its troops in Bosnia over the next few months.
14	0:51	The Japanese newspaper *Yomiuri Shimbun* wrote that the withdrawal of a part of the French contingent from UNPROFOR would jeopardise the entire operation in the field and bring about a change of situation.
15	0:22	Co-chairmen of the conference on the former Yugoslavia, Lord David Owen and Thorvald Stoltenberg; spoke to President Franjo Tudjman in Zagreb last night.
17	0:43	UNPROFOR representative in Sarajevo Rob Annink stated that the Muslim army has, over the past few days, pursued simultaneous offensives against Serbian forces in the eastern and western fronts of Central Bosnia.
18	2:50	Muslim forces have again started war operations in the vicinity of the television station in Stolice.
19	0:15	Serbian civilians left places in central Bosnia under Muslim control, complaining that they are being ill-treated by the Muslim authorities, stated UNHCR representative Chris Janowski.
20	0:25	A UN aircraft landed at Tuzla airport this morning, escorted by two NATO fighter planes.
21	0:27	President of the Dutch Government Ruud Lubbers visited the Dutch 'blue helmets' in Tuzla and other regions, and has today stated in Sarajevo that The Netherlands will not give up peace efforts, and that the Dutch 'blue helmets' will remain in Bosnia.

Friday 20 May

6	1:10	In Washington the Contact Group is about to conclude its two-day meeting to formulate a common view on the resolution of the Bosnian crisis.

Item number	Length min:sec	Subject
7	0:20	The White House repeated that it would not send troops to Bosnia before a peace agreement is reached.
8	2:24	The Bosnian crisis was the subject of discussions between the French Minister for Foreign Affairs Juppé and his hosts in Moscow, but no details have been made public.
9	0:45	British military and political analysts claimed that UN forces could, before the autumn, be withdrawn from Bosnia unless the warring parties start negotiations and provide reliable guarantees of their readiness to accept peace within three weeks.
16	0:29	Muslim forces in Bugojno fired tank projectiles at civilian targets in Srbobran.
17	0:45	The leadership of the Muslim army in Mostar claimed that HVPO units have today opened sniper fire on Muslim positions.

RTS after it had broadcast the above story, which indicates that the item was either a case of misinformation, or intended to show that the Serbs were always right. 'Demonisation', 'foreign media' and their 'finances' were frequent subjects of RTS, used to explain why the world did not understand the Serbs.

Bosnia was explicitly mentioned in the third item, about the meeting between Milošević and Russian Special Envoy Vitalii Churkin. The newscaster in the studio read from a presidential release: 'During the talks it was indicated that Russia would bear in mind the indisputable fact that from the very outset of the crisis Serbia has supported a peaceful solution, and would discontinue further application of economic sanctions against our country, thereby making the largest step towards ending the war in the former Bosnia and Hercegovina, since the economic embargo of the international community directly encourages the Muslim leadership to seek the attainment of its objectives through war.' The release did not state who 'indicated' this during the talks. Such phrases as 'undisputable fact' were often used in official communications so as to present the view of the Serbian authorities as something generally recognised and incontestable. This particular statement reflected the position of the Serbian leadership and was presented as the joint conclusion of the meeting.

RTS regularly selected articles from the foreign press to enable it to present the attitude of the official authorities or convey what the political leadership of Serbia could not say aloud. For example, on Monday 16 May, next to a *Duma* still and a photo of Lilić, the newsreader read: 'The newspapers *Duma* and *Continent* have placed special emphasis on the statement by Lilić that any idea on the resolution of the conflict in Bosnia, including the federation between Muslims and Croats, is acceptable unless it is aimed against the third party which did not take part in the negotiation ... The *Standard* specifically underlined the words by President Lilić that there has never been a true arms embargo for the Muslims in Bosnia–Hercegovina ...' The television news in this way took from the foreign press only those statements which were in line with Serbian interests in the crises in the former Yugoslavia.

Reporting on the war in Bosnia was mostly done without quoting sources for information. The Muslims, in all news from the battlefield, were always 'attacking'. The reports made no mention of military units, only of the national affiliation of soldiers. In RTS reports on the Muslim–Croatian conflict, however, the source of the information was always stated, sometimes even repeatedly.

One of the linguistic rules of RTS, as well as the Serbian authorities, was to refer to the war in Bosnia always as a 'civil' war. For example, Vice-President of the Federal Government Željko Simić was reported saying that, 'We have informed Minister Jerensky [the Hungarian Head of Diplomacy] of all the important steps undertaken by the Yugoslav policy since his visit, as a contribution to the faster resolution of the civil war in the former Bosnia–Hercegovina, the establishment of peace and finding the ways for equal negotiations of all parties to the conflict ...' (item 7, Monday 16 May).

The first item on Tuesday 17 May 1994 reiterated the peace-policy narrative of RTS: 'The President of Serbia Slobodan Milošević received the co-chairmen of the Conference on the Former Yugoslavia, Lord Owen and Thorvald Stoltenberg. In his talks with the co-chairmen the Serbian president pointed out, "Peace is in the interest of all people and nations in the Yugoslav space."' This classic RTS item emphasised the peace policy of Serbia, while the key interest was defined in the connected report about the press conference. The camera focused on Owen and the reporter in the studio translated Owen's statement: 'We have focused on the issue of ending the hostilities. This is obviously the highest priority. But the largest problem is Goražde, where there are still some violations of the agreement. ... We have made our position very clear ... if a solution is found to include the withdrawal of the Bosnian Serb forces to the agreed lines, then the sanctions will be relaxed ...'

The report after this one confirmed the importance of the need to terminate the sanctions: 'The visit of the Patriarch of Moscow and the Whole of Russia to Yugoslavia has been followed with exceptional attention by the Russian public and media ... the media transmitted the statement by the Russian patriarch that the sanctions against Yugoslavia were unjust and that Russia supported the lifting of sanctions, as evidenced by the decision of the state Duma.'

At the time of analysis RTS was still transmitting statements by Serbian officials affirming the negotiating position of the Republika Srpska leaders, a practice it discontinued after the introduction of Serbian sanctions against the Bosnian Serbs. For example, the seventh item was a lengthy (two and a half minute) report of the Serbian Prime Minister Mirko Marjanović's message in a Russian radio interview. Against a still of Moscow and a photo of Marjanović in the bottom left corner, the newscaster in the studio quoted his words: 'From the very outbreak of the Yugoslav crisis we have been supporting a just solution which must protect the interests of Serbs in the same way as the interests of Croats and Muslims are protected. ... The sanctions have become meaningless, because Yugoslavia has complied with the UN requests.' Speaking of the extent to which the Serbian leadership could influence the Bosnian Serbs, Prime Minister Marjanović stated that Serbs in Bosnia decided on all issues of their survival: 'This is one nation ...' Once the Belgrade policy towards Pale had changed however, Bosnian Serbs no longer existed for RTS.

The bulletin of Tuesday 17 May included an RTS report from Mount Majevica. There was footage of the regional television station there, and a (seen) reporter who described how 'the Muslim forces have kept coming at the Serbian forces for days, and a special target of their attacks is the television and communications relay on Majevica ... which is under UN protection.' He continued: 'While media attention was focused on Brčko, they tried to attack. ... Their daily attacks are to no avail ...' The Head of General Staff of the East Bosnia Corps of the RS Army Budimir Gavrić was then shown saying, 'The enemy used a few scout-raider groups to attack a wider area around the Stolice facility. These groups numbered twenty to thirty soldiers each and attacked from a number of directions. ... On this occasion there were ten to fifteen such groups, and they had strong artillery and mortar support. ... To the best of our knowledge they do not have tanks, but this time they used them from a few directions ... there is something fishy about it. ... Our observers noted UNPROFOR vehicle movements. ... During a period of calm the Serbian soldiers rest reading the Muslim papers found with the captured Muslim fighters ...' This was a rare instance of a war report which was not illustrated by library footage or photos, but by new images. It remained the case, however, that only one source of information – the Serb military – was used. There was no statement by UNPROFOR to either confirm or deny the report.

Selected quotations from the foreign press emphasised disagreement between Washington and Moscow. For example, the news anchor reported in an item on Bosnia on Wednesday 18 May that, 'On the eve of tomorrow's meeting of the Contact Group in Washington, the *New York Times* reveals that behind an apparent unity, a sharp diplomatic conflict is taking place between Washington and Moscow. ... The possibility indicated by Paris that it could withdraw some 2,500 French soldiers from the territories of the former Yugoslavia by the end of the year provoked numerous reactions and activities in certain countries. ... French commentators stress that the threat made by Paris is in the first place addressed to the Americans. ... British analysts believe that this particular move by France is intended as a kind of pressure, primarily on the USA, for its military involvement in the Bosnia crisis. ... The Italian Foreign Ministry has officially confirmed today that this country would be prepared to send its soldiers to Bosnia if so requested by the UN. ... Official Moscow sources state that it is a subtle diplomatic manoeuvre compelling the three warring parties to consent to the division of Bosnia in the ratio 51:49 ...' The news from Paris does merit reaction, but as seen from the above extract, RTS focused primarily on criticising Washington.

The particular running order of items on Thursday 19 May reveals how news was selected according to the criterion of the 'political suitability' of an event, rather than on the basis on any evaluation of its topicality. The sixth item in the bulletin documented the speech of the Russian patriarch, with the report of the Washington meeting of the Contact Group placed after this. The patriarch's speech was chosen for its proximity to the views of the Serbian authorities. A studio journalist translated: 'We have signed the Sarajevo declarations inviting all the believers of the world to pray for peace in this region which has been bleeding and suffering human casualties for quite a long time ... the sanctions have to be abolished. They are unilateral. The state Duma has, too, expressed the will of the Russian people that the sanctions are unilateral and have to be cancelled. We do hope that they will be abolished ...' The camera focused first on the Russian patriarch making the statement and then on the Serbian patriarch saying: 'The meaning of the declaration is to end the bloodshed which brings misfortune to Serbs, Croats and Muslims ...' RTS gave a great amount of publicity to the visit of Aleksei II to Yugoslavia, and specifically his visit to Kosovo. Although Aleksei II did not represent secular authorities, his statement was nonetheless used for local political purposes.

The next item on Thursday 19 May dealing specifically with Bosnia was a phoned-in report from the Tanjug correspondent Dejan Lukić in Washington. The on-screen still was of the White House: 'Today in Washington, the Contact Group for Bosnia is starting a debate on ending the hostilities and territorial delimitation between the Muslim–Croatian Federation and the Bosnian Serbs precisely at the moment when US diplomacy indicates precious little signs of readiness to apply pressure on the Muslim side. ... According to estimates here, the current tactical line of American diplomacy is, at least, controversial.' The report, brimming with statements of views, did not quote the source of 'estimates here', nor did it specify who 'officially presented the US attitude'.

The next item consisted of Juppé's statement read by the newscaster in the studio: 'The chief of French diplomacy announced a new ministerial meeting and repeated the intention of his country to withdraw the French 'blue helmets' from Bosnia unless an agreement among the warring parties is reached. ... Judging by the estimates of the Paris analysts it is a very clear signal addressed primarily to Sarajevo and Washington. Paris claims that if the Americans wish to arm the Muslims and encourage them to wage the war, which would mean a war with Serbia, they can do this without France'. Juppé's statement here served RTS only as the opening line for a series of views, barely substantiated, since they referred only to unidentified 'Paris analysts'.

The next item showed footage of Juppé and Russian Foreign Minister Kozirev, at a press conference in Moscow and was accompanied by a phoned-in report from the RTS Moscow correspondent Jasmina Pavlović-Stamenić: '... Moscow has made it clear to Paris that it does not agree with the announced possibility of withdrawing the British and French 'blue helmets' from Bosnia if the peace agreement is not signed. Moscow calls this move a subtle piece of diplomacy which applies indirect pressure and influences the parties to the conflict not to prolong their acceptance of political solutions ... The communication from the [Kozirev–Juppé] talks was not available at the time that this report was made ...' It is therefore difficult to see how the RTS reporter could have known what 'Moscow made ... clear to Paris', since the official communication had not been distributed to the journalists when the RTS journalist was making her report. The problem of truthful reporting in this case becomes even greater bearing in mind that RTS screened the footage from the press conference by Juppé and Kozirev. This could mean that the RTS correspondent did not attend the press conference, or that nothing stated at the press conference agreed with the official policy of Belgrade, or that the report had been sent before the press conference, which is why RTS had only the authentic pictures of it rather than knowledge of what was said there.

Bosnia and Hercegovina is an internationally recognised state. Although Mr Hogg definitely did not use the attribute 'former' himself, on Thursday 19 May the newscaster read: 'The Minister at the British Foreign Office Douglas Hogg warned the warring parties in the former Bosnia–Hercegovina that they have a deadline of only two months to reach an agreement or else face the withdrawal of UN troops and the discontinuation of foreign assistance.' The next item, however, did not use the term 'former' with Bosnia–Hercegovina: 'In Madrid the Spanish Defence Minister Julio Garcia Varga stated that in the next few months Spain intended to decrease the share of its troops in Bosnia.' This difference in labelling can be interpreted either as a lack of professionalism, or as a result of an explicit calculation about when and when not to use the term.

The next item on Bosnia on Thursday 19 May revealed RTS's preference for comments in the foreign press favouring the Serbian side in Bosnia. The Japanese newspaper *Yomiuri Shimbun* was quoted as being critical of the proposed withdrawal of the French from UNPROFOR, and by extension of US policy: 'The French decision is directly related to the American insistence on a sharper stance towards the Serbs and the decision of the US Senate to recommend that the arms embargo for the Muslims in Bosnia be unilaterally lifted.' RTS regularly portrayed the USA as a negative force within the conflict and sought to indicate 'differences' between the

Europeans and the Americans in their approaches to the war.

A block of news from the Bosnian battlefield on Thursday 19 May began with a statement from the UNPROFOR representative, which said that: 'The Muslim army has, over the past few days, engaged in simultaneous offensives against the Serbian forces at the eastern and western fronts of Central Bosnia.' This was rare: RTS did not transmit statements by UNPROFOR representatives speaking of Serbian attacks on Muslims or Croats in Bosnia. Statements by UNPROFOR officials were mentioned only if they referred to a threat for the Serbian side in Bosnia.

This item was followed by a phoned-in report: '... over a hundred destructive projectiles. ... This time again they were not deprived of the assistance of the NATO planes which, flying at rooftop level, broke the sound barrier and carried out continuous provocation above Serbian fighter positions ... At Muslim strongholds around the relay other provocation has been observed such as the burning of car tyres, so as to give the impression of Serbian units attacking their positions. The objective is the same as in other media-forced battlefields to bring the NATO planes into the conflict to bomb Serbian positions ...' This report and comment did not describe what actually happened, but rather explained to the spectator what allegedly was in the 'background' of the event.

The first item dealing with the Bosnian war on Friday 20 May reported that: 'The Federal Government has today considered the proposals for the resolution of the Bosnia–Hercegovina crisis broached at the Geneva meeting. ... Full support to a document of this kind was stated by the Yugoslav side and especially to the agreement on the four-month cease-fire.' The RTS reporter from the press conference made the usual generalisations. The news that the 'Muslim forces from Bugojno last night fired tank grenades at civilian targets in Srbobran ...' was given without mentioning the source, and came far down in the bulletin. The next item was read by the newscaster in the studio: 'The leadership of the Muslim army in Mostar claims that units of the Croatian Council of Defence (HVO) have today opened sniper fire on Muslim positions at the Mostar front line. Croatian Radio, however, quoting military sources, claims that the Muslim forces attacked and shot at the positions of the HVO Travnik Brigade which refrained from responding to the provocation.' This example shows how when conflicts of 'enemy' armies were concerned, even the names of units were mentioned, along with the source.

The last news item on the war in Bosnia in the bulletin on Friday 20 May was a lengthy phoned-in statement by Goran Perčević (Vice-President of the Socialist Party of Serbia) who said that 'there will be no success to the negotiations unless all three parties in Bosnia are treated equally. As for the proposal for territorial delimitation in the ratio of 49:51 we believe that as far as Serbia and the FRY are concerned any agreement on this must be reached with the consent of the representatives of the Republika Srpska.' This piece took four minutes, which was unusually long for the bulletin. The broadcast included almost everything Mr Perčević had said. This RTS practice not to cut or interpret statements by 'important' political personalities of the ruling party was one example of the established thesis of politicisation within the bulletin.

Conclusion

The results of the analysis indicate that the well-known journalist rule stating that the highest political personalities and institutions have priority as sources of information was brought to the fore by the bulletin. All the items of news had the same overall context – that of positive propaganda for the policy of the ruling party. This was, first of all, reflected in the selection and order of the news, which was entirely dependent on the bulk of daily activities of all officials of the Socialist Party of Serbia, regardless of the fact that these were on occasion unimportant. The findings also indicate that the news sought to reflect the attitude of the Serbian rather than the Yugoslav official policy towards the war in Bosnia and the crisis in the formerly Yugoslav territories. The propaganda of the official policy was pursued in a number of ways. The selection of events to become news was not always based on the importance of the event itself, but rather on the possibility of using it to substantiate an official political position. An example of this was the piece broadcast on Tuesday 17 May: 'The Party of the Russian Unity and Concord stated yesterday that Russian diplomacy had made a number of mistakes in the former Bosnia–Hercegovina, primarily in terms of the recognition of Bosnia–Hercegovina and introduction of sanctions against Yugoslavia.' It was a common practice of RTS to emphasise marginal political groups and their 'initiatives' if they coincided with the policy of Belgrade, and thus give them much more publicity than they actually deserved. Even when RTS broadcast a news item in a 'correct' manner, it nevertheless tended to (ab)use it as an 'opening line' for a political-propaganda comment. Thus RTS always transmitted statements by Yugoslav politicians to foreign media, in great detail. Foreign media were critically reviewed, domestic media never.

Such terms as 'indisputable fact', 'it is said', 'point out' and 'emphasise' were often used in official communications so as to present the attitudes of Serbian authorities as generally recognisable, incontestable, correct and unique. Statements which were quoted or transmitted directly were almost always presented as the attitudes of the Serbian leadership disguised as the common conclusions of official meetings. Reporting on Bosnia served the purpose of reflecting the day-to-day political orientation of the authorities, rather than imparting to the public of the FRY (i.e. Serbia) information about the war in Bosnia.

Slovenia and Croatia

SANDRA BAŠIĆ-HRVATIN

The TV News Broadcasting Framework

As a centralised and federal state, the Yugoslav media space was composed of several 'national' media systems which were subordinated to the centre primarily on an ideological level – a level which was an important source for the reproduction of homogenised ideology. The production of news was a central point in constructing this consensus about the existing social order. This ideological subordination was achieved through the definition of what were (or were not) important or newsworthy events, who was allowed to speak in the name of political structures, and in the political control over the appointment of editors and journalists. If the press was the first medium to be placed under the pressure of pluralisation, television was the last medium to be democratised. It was the last medium to allow opposition speakers on the screen.

At the end of the 1950s, television studios in Zagreb, Belgrade and Ljubljana came on the air as the common Yugoslav broadcasting system (JRT). During the 1960s each of the national studios, Ljubljana and Zagreb, produced 30 per cent of their own programmes for the common JRT exchange. The television centre in Belgrade produced 40 per cent of all broadcast programming because it produced news for all the other centres. By 1975 all the other national television centres were on air. Except for the centres in Kosovo and in Macedonia, which were financed directly from the federal budget, all the other centres were under the financial control of their own national governments.

Slovenia

From the very beginning, Slovenian television had an unique position among all the other national studios. Because of its geographical closeness to Italy and Austria, whose television signals were receivable within the borders of the Slovene territory, Slovenia never had the complete informational blockade as did other parts of Yugoslavia. Slovenia also had the first (and the only) regional television centre (Koper/Capodistria) which was set up to inform both the Italian minority in Slovenia and the Slovene minority in Italy.[1]

From the beginning of television broadcasting, then, news programming was given the status of being the most important element in television production, as the most important way of disciplining the audience. According to a primary recommendation of the federal government, the central news programme had to be produced uniformly for all states and subtitled into national languages. However, at the end of the 60s, the television centre in Ljubljana started broadcasting its own national news programme, a national production in a national language. From that point, it could be said that Slovenia had a national broadcasting system.

From the 70s onwards the broadcasting systems were decentralised.[2] All the television centres produced their own news programmes which were broadcast on the first (national) channel. On the second channel, according to a 'national key system', alternate news programmes were broadcast, with a different centre producing the bulletin each day. From the beginning of the 80s each republic/province had the right to broadcast their national programming on the first television channel, while the second was under the control of JRT.[3]

In the 80s when the print media was opening up or extending the space for public discussion, uncovering various economic and political scandals, news programming on television continued to portray (primarily on a visual level) the dominant symbolic universe of a homogeneous state. In other words, while the former Yugoslavia was 'falling apart' in newspapers, the television screen continued to reproduce unproblematic public rituals. The first television pictures of Yugoslav army tanks on the streets of Priština (Kosovo) and the first pictures of brutal beatings by federal police against demonstrators in Kosovo were a real visual shock for most viewers, hitherto used to library footage.

With the establishment of new national states, the regional television systems of the former republics became national/state systems, organised as public service broadcasting. Today, the Slovene media space is a kind of 'paternalistic-commercial' system 'with a tendency towards privatisation and commercialisation of the media (particularly the press) on the one hand, and of 'examining and/or exercising state power over the media (television in particular) on the other' (Splichal 1995: 99). In the period of transition, print media was driven completely by market regulation because the new government abolished all kinds of state subsidies. The new Media Act adopted in 1994 allowed the establishment of private regional and local commercial television stations. From 1995 Slovenia has had two national public channels, one national commercial channel, one national religious channel, four regional channels and twelve local channels. Slovenia is also covered by three external channels: Croatian Television 1 and 2 and Hungarian Television. At the time of this analysis in 1994, there were two national public and one national commercial channels. More than 30% of households (on the borders with Italy and Austria around 80%) were able to watch at least fifteen satellite and cable channels.

According to a national opinion poll carried out in 1994 the main news programme on Slovene television was watched by a daily average of 75% of the available audience. If we exclude language as the biggest obstacle for watching foreign programmes, most Slovene viewers are still highly loyal to the national news programme. This loyalty is explained by the 'greater objectivity of news' on national television. Among foreign television channels, Croatian television has the biggest audience share. One third of Slovene viewers regularly watch Croatian news bulletins. Slovene viewers can also watch (on a different local cable system) Serbian television programmes transmitted by satellite.

Croatia

Croatian television (CRT) is almost completely under state control. CRT has three national channels; the first is exclusively devoted to news, politics and national culture. It is broadcast by satellite to cover the whole of the territory of former Yugoslavia. CRT has a studio in Široki Brijeg (Bosnia and Hercegovina) which covers news relating to events in the parts of Bosnia and Hercegovina under the control of the Croatian army. On CRT the biggest audience share (80%) goes to *TV Dnevnik*, the main news bulletin. Almost 40% of viewers believe completely in the objectivity of its information, while only 15% think that its news information is not trustworthy.[4]

TV Coverage of the War in Bosnia

The main news bulletins of Slovene and Croatian public television were broadcast simultaneously on all their respective public channels. During the week of 16–21 May 1994 there were important events related to internal politics in both countries. In Slovenia, the main news was connected with changes in the Italian government, the beginning of an open diplomatic conflict between Slovenia and Italy about Italian refugees after the Second World War and information related to political scandals connected with arms smuggling (arms for government forces in Bosnia found in packages with humanitarian aid) and money laundering (money from casinos which was used in the previous regime for financing the Yugoslav secret police and now for financing certain political parties).

In Croatia, the week of analysis coincided with a period of political conflict between factions inside the ruling party. Some months after this, two leaders of the biggest Croatian party resigned. The cause for the political attacks was a letter they had sent to the American Congress about the Croatian involvement in the Croatian–Muslim military conflict in Bosnia and Hercegovina.

There were differences on Monday 16 May between the reporting of STV and CRT. STV started its news bulletin with the meeting between Russian Special Envoy Vitalii Churkin and Serbian President Slobodan Milošević in Belgrade, and the common Croatian–Muslim military command in Bosnia. The next item was about the shelling of Tuzla, the Serbian attack on the Swedish humanitarian convoy near Sarajevo,[5] and the statement of the UNPROFOR press spokesman about this attack. Further information was connected with the 'refugee problem' in Slovenia and the humanitarian aid sent by the Iranian and Italian governments.

On the same day, CRT started its bulletin with the funeral of the mayor of the town of Bjelovar (Slavonia) who was killed by a mine ('Again the Serbian evil-doers use violence against innocent Croatian people'), the start of common military command operations in Bosnia, the Tuzla bomb shelling, the Serb attack on the Swedish humanitarian convoy, the conflicts between the Bosnian army and the Serbs, and the Churkin–Milošević meeting. After that there followed information from Mostar about humanitarian aid sent to the Catholic church in Mostar, a protest by mothers, wives and children of twenty-six missing Croats near Bugojno, the Mass marking the third anniversary of the death of a well-known Croatian military officer in Bosnia, and finally a press conference of the Serbian liberal forum held in Zagreb which 'wants to inform the world about crimes by the Karadžić army'.

On the one hand, Slovenian television followed the characteristic viewpoint of the Western media, that of the distant observer. On the other, and particularly with regard to stories about refugees, it also presented a vantage from inside the war, the view of the involved insider – simply because of the fact that these 'others' who are

160

involved in the war are so close to 'us'.[6]

Croatian television used a much more complicated matrix to explain the war. It was based on the comparison of the cruelty of the other side against 'our' system of civilised values. Defining the 'other', that violent other, which endangered the very existence of its community was the strongest mechanism used. As Klaus Theweleit (1993) remarked, the first thing you lose, when you lose a war, is your memory. At this point, CRT, with its 'closed' narrative operation, tried to win a new war, which it played out on the television screen, trying to reconstruct (recollect) a new collective memory.

Slovene television: The Balkans are somewhere else
The war in Bosnia and Hercegovina on Slovene television was covered in two distinct news blocks: news relating to Slovene domestic politics (problems with refugees, possibilities of economic co-operation between Slovenia and Bosnia–Hercegovina, commentaries about different topics which expressed the opinions of the Slovene government), and news exclusively devoted to daily events on the battlefield. The latter news block was usually broadcast as an introduction to the part of the bulletin devoted to foreign news. It was composed as a visual bricolage of ten to fifteen very short news items lasting no more than one or two minutes, functioning as a kind of instant picture of a war which could happen anywhere in the world.

Slovene television did not have its own correspondent in Bosnia–Hercegovina and textual material was taken from international television sources. A primary source of information was the official Bosnian government in Sarajevo, a very clear signal that in Slovene eyes the Serbian side was the aggressor in the war.

There were two dominant tendencies on Slovene television news. The first was the discrepancy between news information and visual presentation. There was a non-illustrative use of television in reporting from Bosnia and Hercegovina, which included using the same footage for different items of news and ubiquitous shots of soldiers on the battlefield and destroyed and burned landscapes. Footage sequences were so short that the viewer could not follow the pictures of the event, so that the war in Bosnia–Hercegovina became, in a sense, invisible. For example, on Thursday 19 May, the fourth item on STV was the round-up of news from Bosnia: 'So, let's look at what happened today in the Balkan region.' This remark by the anchor is the first step in the process that we may call 'The Balkans are somewhere else'. In not more than a minute it was said that the cease-fire had been violated once again; that on Mt Majevica Muslims and Serbs were fighting again (with footage of a soldier on the ground); that a UN aeroplane had landed at Tuzla airport, with a statement from the UNHCR spokesman explaining that the plane would evacuate wounded civilians (to counter Serbian accusations that the Tuzla airport was being used for military purposes); and finally information about the French UN soldiers released from the Serbian detention camp, after the French government paid $44,000 to the Serbs for their release.[7] On Friday 20 May, most of the visual material was identical to the previous day's. The STV anchor narrated, to camera, the statement of the British foreign minister that 'Muslims have to accept military defeat'. This was illustrated at points by footage of Lord Owen and Radovan Karadžić in a very friendly and relaxed conversation. (This footage was used by CTV several times as a 'silent comment' on the foreign minister's statement.)

The second major tendency on Slovenian news was the use of refugees as symbols for the war. This enabled both an understanding of the war and a way of disconnecting from it. At the beginning of the war stories about refugees functioned as a method of achieving solidarity with the suffering of others, through empathy. When it became clear that Slovenia was definitely out of the war, this solidarity deteriorated. The refugees became strangers, 'other'. This was the starting-point of a process of national exclusivism. All the irrational violence witnessed on-screen became something that happened in 'those' Balkans, that part of former Yugoslavia away from the principles and values of 'our' (Slovene/European) civilisation:

> Every actor in the blood-play of its disintegration endeavours to legitimise its place inside by presenting itself as the last bastion of European civilisation ... in the face of oriental barbarism. For the right-wing nationalist Austrians this imaginary frontier is Karavanke, the mountain chain between Austria and Slovenia; beyond it, the rule of Slavic hordes begins. For the nationalist Slovenes, the frontier is the river Kolpa, separating Slovenia from Croatia: we Slovenians are Mitteleuropa, while Croatians are already Balkan, involved in the irrational ethnic feuds that really do not concern us. We are on their side, we sympathise with them, yet in the same way one sympathises with a Third World victim of aggression. For Croatians, of course, the crucial frontier is the one between civilisation and the eastern Orthodox collective spirit, which cannot grasp the values of western individualism. Serbians, finally conceive themselves as the last line of defence of Christian Europe against the fundamentalist danger embodied in Muslim Albanians and Bosnians. (Žižek, 1992: 39–40)

This tendency towards nationalist exclusivism can be seen in the results of a public opinion poll about dominant values in society carried out in 1994 in Slovenia and Austria (National Public Opinion Research, Slovenia). Eighty per cent of Slovenes did not recognise themselves as Yugoslavs. Most thought that Slovenes were most similar to Austrians. They saw Turks, Serbs, Bosnians and Russians as nations completely different from their own.[8] Most Slovene respondents thought that Austrians and Germans were most friendly to Slovenes, and that Serbs were the most hostile to the Slovene nation. It is hardly necessary to point out that in the Austrian part of the research the results were different. Austrians felt almost no affinity with Slovenes. Interestingly, however, both Austrians and Slovenes felt the same degree of distance from Serbs and Bosnians, even though Slovenes, until 1990, had lived in the same state with the members of these two nations.

Croatian television: The eyes do not see
The main news bulletins on Croatian television during the period of analysis started with headline news, then information related to internal affairs, then information about events in occupied Croatian territory and, finally, foreign policy. The first news item in this last section related to the war in Bosnia–Hercegovina and was divided into news and commentaries. The news section was brief, usually only a few minutes long. The footage shown did not connect with the verbal reports. It changed every ten seconds or so and was composed mostly of foreign material from CNN, Sky News or Reuters.

At the end of the 'war news' there was news from Herzeg Bosna, the part of Bosnia–Hercegovina controlled by the Croats. Although the newsroom in Zagreb was following Croat policy of trying to restore the historical friendship between Croats and Muslims, the newsroom in Herzeg Bosna continued to denote the

Muslims as the enemies.[9] As we said before, media coverage of the war in Bosnia on both television channels used stereotypical visual material which followed a particular pattern. The main goal was to simplify the pictures of the war, to make them easy to watch for the audience. Following this visual homogenisation, it was possible to predict what kind of pictures would support the text.

The war in Bosnia was constructed as both spectacle and ritual. It was impossible to represent the war in its totality; it could be shown only in fragments, reduced to small details that could be easily understood. How did this happen in practice? The following is an example of a 'spectacular' way of seeing the war. On 17 May CRT broadcast an item about the killing of civilians in one small village in the western sector (Slavonia). There was a close-up of tortured bodies, with hands tied with barbed wire and crushed heads. These pictures exemplified both the identifying and distancing value of using war victims in footage. Close-ups of a mutilated body do not say anything. The body could be anyone's, anywhere. The journalistic 'human interest' paradoxically created a distance – it ushered the viewer into the most horrible scenes of violence and destruction and then enabled him/her to say: 'Not me!'. Such imagery allowed viewers to see death, while at the same time the closeness of the focus made death 'disappear'. It made viewers immune (Lotringer 1992: 85). This report was followed by another about the building of a new bridge near Varaždin. Croatian journalists had been allowed, for the first time, to visit territories under Serbian control (this sector was under the control of Russian UNPROFOR soldiers). This item was an example of the 'ritual' way of presenting the war. Viewers could see a big Serbian flag, and the unseen reporter described how he saw, in the car of a Russian UNPROFOR soldier, a book and a video-cassette titled 'Ustashas' Genocide against Serbs'. This statement functioned as a starting-point for a ritualisation of the war. It was extremely personal (as distinct from the impersonal aspect of the dead civilians), as it allowed each viewer to recollect his/her own memory about his/her understanding of the war.

There were other mechanisms that Croatian television used to cover the war. The first was a result of the lack of real ('live') pictures about the news events. These 'missing' pictures were replaced by the dramatic use of voice or sound. Croatian television often used this mechanism at the time of the siege of the town of Vukovar, when the director of Vukovar Central Hospital reported the atrocities and destruction of the town via radio. Most viewers did not notice that instead of live pictures they were 'watching' live sound from Vukovar. The first real pictures of Vukovar were broadcast by Serbian television, when the Croatian audience could put together the sound and the picture, and see the reality of the suffering (lines of refugees leaving the town).

The second mechanism was connected to the viewpoint of the televisual 'eye', particularly evident in the reports from Sarajevo. Whereas Serbian television used pictures of the town seen from a distance ('the eye of the artillery') and therefore avoided showing the reality of the destruction taking place, Croatian television used pictures of Sarajevo from inside the town, from below ('the eye of the target'), in which the viewer could see destroyed houses and people running from snipers.[10] It might even be said that there were not just two different narratives, two different visual presentations of the war, but actually two different wars: 'ours' and 'theirs'.

Another mechanism was related to the process of reducing the guilt felt towards the other side during the war – the distinction made between things done to 'us' and things (however similar) done by 'us' to the 'other' (Judt 1992: 89). The projection of guilt on to the other side and the identification of the enemy as pure evil was a highly efficient way of simplifying the war. The first step was to organise a mythological structure to be used for the interpretation of events when one's own side was using 'unacceptable' methods: violation of civil rights, destruction of civic buildings and spaces (hospitals, monuments, cemeteries, etc.), killing, rape or ethnic cleansing. In this case the mythical structure functioned as an alibi, as an empty space.

This mechanism is present, for example, in the Serbian 'metaphysical fear' of Croats and Muslims based on experience from the Second World War, and in the Croatian mythical fantasy about its thousand years of belonging to Western (Christian) civilisation, as a 'cordon sanitaire' against the despotic, irrational East (the Balkans). A particular example of the resonance of mythology occurred in April 1993, when Serbian television broadcast information that the Croatian army had destroyed the Jasenovac monument (for the victims executed in the Jasenovac concentration camp by the Ustashas during the Second World War), which was at the time of the report in territory controlled by the Serbs. This news caused deep offence and bitterness in Serb communities. Subsequently, after the Croatian military operation in May 1995 in western Slavonia, CRT was able to broadcast pictures of diplomats accredited in Zagreb standing in front of the monument, as visual proof that the monument was still there and that the Serbian side had in fact lied. Serbian television did not broadcast this information.

How did these imperatives work, if at all, on the Muslim side? In a newspaper article ('Lebanon in Europe', *Danas*, 19 February 1993) about Mujahadin fighters in Bosnia and the reasons why young Muslim boys take up Islam, the journalist points out that the existence of the troops was related to the lack of a Muslim national tradition, to the lack of historical heroes and myths that might contribute to national identification. It was because of this that Muslims were forced to embrace Khomeini, Saddam Hussein and other Islamic leaders. Even before the Muslims took on an Islamic identity, they were branded in the Serbian media (and partly in the Croatian media during Croatia's conflict with Bosnia) as 'Islamic fundamentalists', 'Mujahadins', 'Jihad fighters' or 'green berets'. Out of all the other nations in the territory of former Yugoslavia, Muslims tied their national identity to a multinational and multicultural Yugoslavia for longest. It was the war in Bosnia and Hercegovina and the Serbian violence against the Muslims which gave birth to this identification with Islam, and gave Muslims the idea of something worth sacrificing their lives for – an idea which they did not have before the war – the idea of homeland.

Conclusion

The analysis of media coverage of the war in Bosnia and Hercegovina on Slovene and Croatian television shows that techniques and ways of interpretation in both countries shared some similarities. Television in both countries used closed symbolic worlds, which could only be understood by members of the same national community. They appealed to a 'hidden' collective historical background, which for the most part consisted of meanings and experiences from the Second World War.

The major difference was that while for Slovene television the Balkans and its war were 'somewhere else' (because Slovenia was somewhere else, i.e. not in the Balkan region), for Croatian television, even though viewers saw some of the war on-screen, much of it remained hidden.

Notes

1. During the 60s Slovene television broadcast for their national audience TV news from Italy (RAI). The federal government demanded that the Slovene government stop this 'ideologically

unacceptable Western information'.

2. That is, decentralised on a geographical level, while remaining centralised at the level of content. In reality, although the broadcasting system of former Yugoslavia was divided into eight different regional television centres, the content of their broadcasts was the same.

3. However, disregarding these conditions of decentralised television production and programme exchange between national studios, programmes made in Zagreb and Belgrade prevailed on both channels. In 1986 every seventh hour of broadcast programming on Slovene television was 'imported' from Belgrade. By contrast, Belgrade television did not broadcast any programme produced in Ljubljana in the same period.

4. This poll was carried out by the weekly tabloid *Globus* which in 1994 was a very influential political opinion former. The tabloid put discussions about Croatian war crimes in Bosnia and political and economic scandals related to the ruling party on the public agenda.

5. All other broadcasters, except for Croatian television (see below), described the attack as a Muslim one (Ed.).

6. This 'distant' media coverage of the war in Bosnia was based on the presumption that the war in Bosnia could be explained only through the historical, ethnic and religious background of the conflict. In other words, it was only explicable if we knew (or understood) the entire history of the Balkan region. For those who did not understand, it was just a savage spectacle, simply terrifying to watch. A further point is related to the category of media stories dealing with children in war, to enable easier identification with the suffering of others. On one level of identification we are 'touched' by the pain of other human beings. On a second level, we share a communality of experience with all the other viewers.

7. All other broadcasters in this study described the released hostages as members of the humanitarian organisation Première Urgence (Ed.).

8. The construction of the Turks as the primary 'other' is a good example of this national exclusivism. In everyday social interactions most Slovenes do not have any experience of living with Turkish people. So the mental picture of the Turk is just another symptom, an 'ideal other' which functions as a way of closing the community against strangers.

9. For example, on Tuesday 17 May CRT reported President Izetbegović's press conference at Zagreb airport before his departure on a pilgrimage to Mecca, and his friendly conversation with President Tudjman. The next item, on the other hand, referred negatively to the Muslims. It was a piece from the Herzeg Bosna newsroom and documented the blockade of a humanitarian convoy near Bugojno: the wives, mothers and children of twenty-six missing Croats (supposedly killed by Muslims) were demanding information about their fate.

10. A further example of the 'eye of the target' was a CRT report from Srebrenica (8 March 1993). When American humanitarian aid was sent by parachute, CRT reported: 'And when they [the Americans] try to help the suffering people of Bosnia, Serbs are helping like this' (the sound of 'live' shelling); and further, 'When artillery does not destroy the town and when people in Sarajevo could go into the streets, walking in the street looks like this' (pictures of people hiding behind a wall and a mother with a little girl saying to her: 'Don't be afraid, everything will be fine, don't cry'), followed by the sound of sniper shooting.

References

Bugarski, Ranko (1994) *Jezik od mira do rata* [Language from peace to war], Belgrade: Krug.

Čolović, Ivan (1994) *Pucanje od zdravlja* [Healthy as hell], Belgrade: Krug.

Judt, Tony (1992) 'The Past Is Another Country: Myth and Memory in Postwar Europe', *Daedalus*, Fall, pp. 83–118.

Lotringer, Sylvere (1992) 'Stroj za ubijanje: Fotografija in smrt' [This killing machine: photography and death], *Likovne Besede*, no. 21/22, pp. 84–6.

Mueller, Claus (1973) *The Politics of Communication: A Study in the Political Sociology of Language, Socialisation and Legitimisation*, London: Oxford University Press.

Salecl, Renata (1994) *The Spoils of Freedom: Psychoanalysis and Feminism after the Fall of Socialism*, London: Routledge.

Splichal, Slavko (1995) 'Slovenia: The Period of "Capitalist Enlightenment"', *Javnost/The Public* vol. 2 no. 3, pp. 97–114.

Theweliet, Klaus (1993) 'The Bomb's Womb and the Genders of War (War Goes on Preventing Women from Becoming the Mothers of Invention)', in M. Cooke and A. Woollacott (eds), *Gendering War Talk*, Princeton: Princeton University Press, pp. 283–314.

Zimmerman, Warren (1995) 'The Captive Mind', *The New York Times Review* vol. 2 no. 2, pp. 3–6.

Žižek, Slavoj (1992) 'Eastern European Liberalism and its Discontents', *New German Critique*, no. 57, pp. 25–49.

Turkey

ASU AKSOY

The TV News Broadcasting Framework

Broadcasting has been open to commercial competition in Turkey only since 1990. In the ensuing four years until 1994, the year of the period under analysis, it moved very quickly from being a state-controlled system to being one of rampant, and often lawless, commercialism, with the dominant newspaper groups extending their ideological and political agendas into the broadcasting arena.

Until 1990 the broadcasting regime of Turkey was characterised by a monopoly of the state broadcasting system. The state-run TRT held a monopoly over national radio and television broadcasting. The break-up of the state system worked to bring about the insertion of the voice of the 'real Turkey' into the broadcasting environment. While it had previously only been possible to see programmes that conformed to official ideology, in 1994 it was possible to see and hear virtually anything. Given the low circulation of newspapers in Turkey, television had always attracted heavy viewing. With the introduction of commercial stations, it became the predominant medium for the expression of popular sentiment.

The consequences of the new commercialism were complex: private channels were driven by a desire to gain market position, but also by pressure to promote the political and ideological agendas of their parent companies (reflecting the interests of the new elite groups in the economy against the 'official', statist outlook). Private channels turned everything that the state channel TRT had been doing upside down. They introduced new and more popular kinds of magazine programmes, game shows and quiz shows. Different ways of reporting the news were introduced, and, as competition started to heat up, anything and everything became potential material: the Turkish public was exposed to the quarrels between the private TV companies regarding the dirty deals of shareholders. Yet, what the private channels never gave up was the promotion of their own opinions and interests, and news was one of the best vehicles to put this into practice. The search for popularity and power was the context in which the distorted reporting of the bombing of Goražde in April 1994 took place (see below), and, indeed, all consequent reporting of Bosnian events. This kind of distortion in the commercial media scene led to growing scepticism about the virtues of a free media – a fertile ground for authoritarian positions regarding the regulation of the media.

166

The attack on Goražde

On 9 April 1994 it became apparent that Turkish coverage of the events in Bosnia was capable of being marred by self-interest and irresponsibility, with potentially devastating consequences. Two of the nationwide commercial television channels, TGRT (known for its conservative and pro-Islamic stance) and Interstar (known for its fierce competitiveness), broadcast throughout the night, starting with the main news programme, the news that the Serbs had attacked Goražde with chemical weapons, causing a massacre with thousands dead. Picking up the story much earlier than the other channels, these two broadcasters clearly used this occasion to promote their own causes (the one ideological, the other commercial). The 'news' was used to galvanise public opinion. Both channels used old library footage of atrocities to 'illustrate' the massacre. In addition, they called on their audiences to participate in public rallies in Ankara and Istanbul to protest against the massacre. At 2.30 am that night, the Turkish Prime Minister Tansu Çiller issued a written declaration of protest against the massacre. Later in the day she had to radically change her position, admitting that there was not, in fact, evidence to support the case that chemical weapons had been used on Goražde.

These broadcasts by two influential Turkish television channels helped to bring about the events of what some commentators dubbed 'Bloody Sunday'. After the transmissions by Interstar and TGRT, protesters, mostly from religious factions and from the Nationalist Movement Party (MHP, the pro-fascist party), gathered in Taksim Square in Istanbul (where it is illegal to hold such meetings) and in Ankara, waving their religious and nationalist flags and shouting slogans. Protesters in Ankara stoned the buildings of the UN, TRT (Turkish State Broadcasting Company) and the DYP (Tansu Çiller's True Path Party), causing a lot of damage.

It was only towards the evening of 10 April that it became clear that the news had been greatly exaggerated and that there was no proof of a massacre. Other commercial channels then started getting into the picture, interviewing Bosnian officials who denied the use of chemical weapons. By the following day, it became clear that no such incident had taken place in Goražde.

Investigations were carried out by the Istanbul Attorney General and by the Ankara State Security Court to examine the Interstar and TGRT broadcasts. The executives of these two channels acknowledged that they used old footage of atrocities, but claimed that all they had really done was to relay material that they had received from foreign sources before anybody else did. They claimed that this was just 'good journalism'. The prosecutors, wanting to use the event to justify restrictions of the media, argued that the broadcasts of both channels were a clear example of 'irresponsible' and 'provocative' broadcasting. Alarmed by the possibility that commercial television might be used as a vehicle for mobilising public support in favour of the Islamic Refah Partisi (Welfare Party), or in favour of any unwanted ideology, the government was propelled into supporting what turned out to be an authoritarian broadcasting bill, passed within ten days of these events.

The TV news coverage of the war in Bosnia

The news broadcasts of the major nationwide commercial television stations between 16–21 May 1994 should be read within this context of growing scepticism about the benefits of a free media, especially among those concerned about the increasing power of the Refah party. The Broadcasting Act, which was criticised for being open to censorship and political manipulation, was finally passed on 20 April 1994, giving considerable powers to the prime minister to intervene. TRT kept its status and the

Table 6: Events reported on Turkish TV news bulletins, 16–21 May 1994

Date	Channel	Item No.	Length (min. sec.)	Topic
17 May	Show TV	13	1:00	Fighting around Tuzla
	Interstar	13	0:09	Bombing of Tuzla airport
	ATV	13	1:00	Serb attacks on Sarajevo
	TRT1	10	1:00	Serb attacks on Sarajevo
	TRT1	10	same item	Repositioning of French army
	TRT1	10	same item	French withdrawal
18 May	TGRT	5	1:00	Pilgrimage to Mecca
19 May	Interstar	10	0:42	French withdrawal
	Show TV	13	1:00	Bombing of Tuzla airport
	TRT1	8	2:00	Government forces push back Serbs in Olova, Vareš and Kladanj
	ATV	11	0:30	UN plane lands at Tuzla airport
20 May	ATV	12	1:27	'Europe Starts at Sarajevo'
21 May	ATV	9	0:20	Serb attacks around Tuzla
	TGRT	6	0:15	Bombing of Bugojno
	TRT1	8	1:30	Bombing of Bugojno

commercial channels were given time to clean up their act. For this reason, the private channels became much more cautious in dealing with sensitive issues like that of Bosnia.

When examining the news broadcasts of the period between 16–21 May two factors should be borne in mind. First, this period was an unfortunate one for monitoring the news in Turkey, because it coincided with two of Turkey's most important public and religious feasts: Thursday 19 May (Day of Youth, in remembrance of the beginning of the 1923 revolution) and Friday 20 May (the religious Feast of the Sacrifice). Because of these two holidays, the period from 19–25 May was a long holiday period and news programmes were lighter compared to normal periods. The second important factor to bear in mind is that unless something exceptionally 'newsworthy' happened in Bosnia, Bosnian issues were overshadowed by pressing local debates and developments. One such development was the announcement of the 'Democracy Package' by the prime minister, another the military operations in south-eastern Turkey and in northern Iraq, and the third was the visit by IMF officials to evaluate the 5 April Economic Stabilisation Programme introduced by the Çiller government.

Five nationwide channels were subjected to content analysis: TRT1, which is a state-run television channel with a wide appeal; Show TV, ATV and Interstar, all commercial channels; and TGRT, a conservative and nationalist private channel.

The events reported are set out in Table 6.

There were three days when most of these five channels broadcast reports on Bosnia (17, 19 and 21 May). None of the channels reported anything on Bosnia on the 16th. Two of the channels, TGRT and ATV, reported items on dates that the other channels did not, and on topics which were not picked up by the others: on Wednesday 18 May, TGRT reported on the *hadj*, or pilgrimage, to Mecca of a group of Muslims from Bosnia, and on Friday 20 May ATV reported on the 'Europe Starts at Sarajevo' campaign.

Tuesday 17 May was the day when news about the bombing of Tuzla airport reached Turkish channels. It is interesting to note that three of the channels (TRT, Interstar and ATV) were precise about the location of the attack, whereas the other channel, Show TV, reported the event as simply an attack on Tuzla (it gave its full report of the event on 19 May). The Tuzla airport bombing was reported as only the tenth item in the news broadcast in the case of TRT1, and thirteenth in the case of others. There were no pictures of the event. All channels used stock footage; although the bombing happened in May one channel used pictures from the winter, although the news was all about the airport bombing, all of the channels used pictures of soldiers walking through a forest.

On Thursday 19 May coverage by the different channels varied a great deal in terms of content. TRT1 gave two minutes to Bosnia (item 8), describing how the government forces had pushed back Serbs. Show TV reported the Tuzla airport bombing (1 min., item 13), accompanied by library pictures of the city being bombed. It is interesting that none of the channels, other than Show TV, reported on NATO's decision not to bomb Serb positions after the bombing of Tuzla airport. Coverage on Thursday 19 May shows how news coverage of a topic can vary from channel to channel. While Interstar noted that 'England has called upon the Muslims to accept defeat and pressed them to sacrifice more on the peace table', none of the other channels mentioned this point. There were factual differences, too, between the reports. Interstar and TRT1 disagreed on the number of French soldiers in the former Yugoslavian territory: in one case it was 6,000, in the other 2,500.

On 20 May only the ATV news reported on the 'Europe Starts at Sarajevo' campaign (1 min. 30 sec., item 12). The coverage of the campaign was accompanied by newsreel clips from Bosnia, mostly of the wounded and of children. Strangely this item was presented as a French domestic problem. It was said that the decision of a number of prominent intellectuals to enter the European Parliament election under a separate list had caused a stir in French political circles, and that Bosnia had now become an internal problem for France.

On Saturday 21 May three of the channels reported the same event – the bombing of Bugojno – in more or less similar ways, though their pictures were all different. On this occasion, Bosnia-related news appeared in a more prominent position in the bulletins, though it was given much less time. TRT1 devoted one and a half minutes to footage of a woman wounded in the head, including close-up shots; this did not appear on any of the other channels.

Conclusion

Several main characteristics emerge from the news coverage of Bosnia by these five Turkish channels. First, the state channel, TRT1, tended to allocate more time to the events, but was selective in terms of its coverage. It did not, for instance, report on the pilgrimage of the Bosnian Muslims, nor on the French appeal. As a result of its newly cast role as an independent and public channel, TRT1 tried to devote equal time to its news items and to carry those news items which clearly had informational content rather than speculation. Second, the commercial channels were unpredictable both in terms of the time they allocated and in terms of the topics that they handled. They seemed to be motivated more by the appeal of the news items for their audiences. Third, it was impossible to tell if the channels were using up-to-date footage or not. In most cases, the news was accompanied by old and irrelevant pictures. There seemed to be a carelessness and at best opportunism in terms of the use of footage.

On the whole, coverage of Bosnia was rather played down during this period in Turkey. This was partly because of the backlash against the 'proactive' broadcasting of TGRT and Interstar in April regarding the bombing of Goražde, and partly because of the holiday then taking place in Turkey. Bosnia was treated by all channels as part of their 'tour of foreign affairs', and no special emphasis was placed on Bosnian affairs.

United Kingdom

ALISON PRESTON

The TV News Broadcasting Framework

The main evening news bulletins on BBC1, ITV, Channel Four, Sky News, Euronews and CNN International were analysed. They are all English-language channels that could be received in the UK (which is why BBC World Service TV News was not included in the study): the first three on terrestrial television, the second three through cable or satellite. The Reuters Television news agency reports from Bosnia for the week were also documented. The two British 'flagship' bulletins are those of 9 pm (BBC1) and 10 pm (ITV), both lasting approximately 30 minutes. Channel Four has a 50-minute bulletin *Channel Four News* at 7 pm, which combines long reports with shorter summaries. Sky News, Euronews and CNN International all have hourly bulletins throughout the 24-hour cycle lasting approximately 10 minutes. Sky News and CNN also broadcast more lengthy bulletins of which this study examined Sky News' *World News Tonight* programme at 9 pm, and CNN International's *International Hour* bulletin at 8 pm GMT. Appendix A details the characteristics of the bulletins and their viewing figures.

TV News Coverage of the War in Bosnia

There was little coverage of the conflict on the terrestrial British main television news bulletins (BBC1, ITV and Channel Four) during the week in question. From 16–21 May there were two 2-minute items on BBC1; one 2-minute report on ITV; and one 18-second report on Channel Four. There was no obvious reason for the lack of coverage. The domestic news agenda was not significantly turbulent to push foreign events or policy from the news bulletins. Indeed, the threat of UN withdrawal by the British Foreign Minister Douglas Hogg on Wednesday 18 May, described by the BBC1 report as 'undiplomatically blunt' and 'unusually clear', might have been expected to be of particular interest to British viewers. Yet this was reported briefly only by the BBC1 bulletin, although it was covered on Serbian, Turkish, Austrian, Slovenian, Croatian and Macedonian television news. There were correspondents in Bosnia for BBC and ITN, as seen by Kate Adie's report on Saturday 21 May for the BBC, and Paul Davies' report on 19 May for ITN, shown on Macedonian TV, so there was no personnel reason for a lack of coverage. In any case, two of the reports for the week were compiled from the domestic studio: the ITV report shown on Saturday 21 May was introduced by the studio anchor as being from 'James Boyce [who] has been looking at pictures of the incident'; and the BBC1 report on

Wednesday 18 May was by Brian Hanrahan, the BBC's diplomatic correspondent, based in London. Rather, the terrestrial bulletins at this time did not cover non-crisis events in Bosnia. There was no 'Bosnia slot' in which to document the ebb and flow of the prosecution of the war.

In contrast, there was more coverage on the European or international channels of Euronews, CNN International and Sky News. These channels tend to provide a round-up of Europe-wide events, with their viewers perhaps more likely to take a greater interest in the conflict and to require an update of developments. Sky News had six stories about Bosnia from Monday 16 to Saturday 21 May (although three of these were in fact on the Saturday breakfast programme rather than the evening programmes); Euronews, thirteen from Monday 16 to Friday 20, three of which led the bulletin on Tuesday 17; CNN International, thirteen from Monday 16 to Friday 20. To set these numbers in context, the Reuters news agency carried fifteen stories from Bosnia from Monday 16 to Saturday 21 May. Table 7 summarises who reported which events.

The BBC1 report on Wednesday 18 May focused on the British government's threat to withdraw its UN troops. No action in Bosnia was reported. In other words, the conflict was mediated through the UN's diplomatic and humanitarian effort. The BBC1 report on Saturday 21 May, from its correspondent Kate Adie, used as its focus the hundred-day cease-fire in Sarajevo, with a context of visual and verbal description of the privations of a Bosnian village: combining news of diplomatic development with the particular difficulties of inhabitants. The brief *Channel Four News* item on Tuesday 17 May dealt with the French announcement of troop withdrawal. France was reported to be 'frustrated by the international failure to negotiate a settlement for the conflict'. This phrasing highlighted the involvement of countries other than those directly fighting in the war. The ITN report on Saturday 21 May for ITV focused on the capture and release of a group of British UN soldiers by the Bosnian Serbs, an event which took place in Bosnia yet had British interests as the main 'hook'.

Sky News took the conflict as an event in its own right, in addition to it being a UN/British involvement story. On Monday 16 May its first item on Bosnia highlighted the increased fighting 'between Serbs and Muslims', and the meeting between the Russian Special Envoy Vitalii Churkin and Serbian President Slobodan Milošević. The second item was a report about a town in eastern Hercegovina and the problems facing its inhabitants. On Saturday 21 May its breakfast news focused on the UN protest over the holding of the British officer, but also showed a report from Dubrovnik, Croatia, about the rebuilding of the city and its attempts to redevelop its tourist trade.

Euronews reports during the week used as their organising focus a variety of subjects. Most items were organised around the intervention of either the UN or foreign personnel, although there were some that focused primarily upon Bosnian citizens and soldiers.

CNN International reports gave round-ups of the day's events both in terms of diplomatic initiatives and war events. They overtly stressed the inevitable, prolonged nature of the conflict: 'A mortar bomb exploded near Sarajevo airport today, *yet another* violation of the no-weapons zone' (CNN International, 18 May, item 3; emphasis added).

The focal positions taken by these reports reveal one of the tensions that was present in reporting the war in former Yugoslavia. The tension was between whether the organising focus of a report was the actuality of war (with diplomatic efforts to

Table 7: Events covered by UK/English-speaking television news bulletins, 16–21 May 1994

Event	RTV	Euro	Sky	CNN	BBC	ITV	C4
Bosnian army attack on Swedish UN convoy	✓	✓					
Clashes between Bosnian army and Serbs near Tuzla	✓	✓	✓	✓			
Churkin/Milošević meeting	✓	✓	✓	✓			
EU ministers meeting to discuss Geneva peace plan				✓			
Serb shelling of Tuzla hotel	✓	✓		✓			
French threat to withdraw troops by end of year		✓		✓	✓		✓
Serb attack on Tuzla airport		✓		✓			
Pilgrimage to Mecca by Sarajevo Muslims	✓	✓		✓			
Bosnian Army take 7 miles of ground	✓						
British Minister's threat to pull out British troops					✓		
Serb attacks on Tuzla	✓	✓		✓			
French aid workers freed		✓		✓			
Meeting between Lord Owen, Thorvald Stoltenberg and Radovan Karadžić	✓	✓					
UN plane lands safely at Tuzla airport	✓	✓					
French hostages reunited with families		✓					
France gives Bosnia a 13 June deadline	✓			✓			
Heavy shelling on road between Sarajevo and Tuzla				✓			
UN protest over Serb treatment of British officer	✓		✓			✓	
Opening-up of sector in Mostar dividing Muslims and Croats	✓	✓					
Summary of continued conflict		✓					
Sarajevo: 100-day cease-fire	✓			✓			
Bosnian army show UN peace monitors their gained ground	✓						
Cease-fire in Goražde near agreement	*	*	*		✓		

Key:

RTV Reuters Television World News Bosnia Feed   Sky Sky News
Euro Euronews   CNN CNN International

* Data for these channels not collected for Saturday 21 May

get a cease-fire a secondary by-product) or whether the diplomatic effort was the crucial narrative (with the prosecution of the war reported only when its events served to tweak diplomacy in one direction or another).

In other words, definitions of what constituted 'event' and what constituted 'context' were not universal. Some UNPROFOR commanders in Bosnia advocated a tougher approach and stated that they used the media to further this aim. General Lewis MacKenzie after his tour of duty in Bosnia commented that 'the media was the only major weapons system I had' (quoted in Hopkinson 1993: 17). The British government, however, consistently preferred to avoid military intervention by the UN and publicly regretted the way that television coverage 'forces foreign policy makers to give one of the current twenty-five crises in the world greater priority' (Douglas Hurd, British Foreign Secretary, speaking in September 1993). Many

UNPROFOR commanders wished to make the actuality of war the primary focus of media attention, while the British government preferred there to be a focus on diplomacy. This polarity is the reverse of the more usual positions that military and government take at time of crisis in their relationship with the media. In other conflicts, especially the Gulf War of 1990–91, the military have tended to be secretive and governments more willing to court media coverage in order to gain popular positive public opinion (see Hopkinson 1993: 10).

The decision to focus either on diplomacy or on the prosecution of the war is also dependent on the role that the television news bulletin is given. A bulletin is either a 'journal of record', as the BBC *Nine O'Clock News* sees itself,[1] and so concentrates on events of political rather than humanitarian importance, or it is more concerned to provide for its viewers an arguably more straightforward and accessible, even entertaining, round-up of specific acts of war.

During the week of analysis it was noticeable that, on the terrestrial bulletins, reference was explicitly made to British and UN interests. The conflict was thus refracted through these domestic, or in the case of the UN, proximate, concerns. The war itself was reported directly only when major events happened. The relatively minor events of the week under analysis were reported, when at all, in the oblique way described above.

Conclusion

British media coverage of the war in former Yugoslavia was marked by confusion and disagreement over the legitimacy of what to report and how to report it. Among the major difficulties were how far to 'humanise' the war, and whether the organising focus for TV news reports should have been the prosecution of war and its casualties, or the search for diplomatic peace. There was an overall tension between journalists and government over the response that Britain should be making. Many journalists advocated for some sort of intervention, and government ministers the opposite. For all the complaints – or boasts – that television news sets the policy agenda, the results in this situation of conflict – non-intervention – actually point to a lack of journalistic power. Additionally, as can be seen from the week's content analysis, television news was not a consistent witness to events. There were periods when coverage was minimal, as well as periods when there was maximum coverage.

The tone of reports during the week of analysis was typical of the general thrust of television news portrayal of the war. Journalist condemnation or emotion was evident only in terms of response to the human tragedy of a particular situation rather than an explicit articulation of blame. The balance in favour of the position of Bosnian Muslims came with the predominance of documentation of their difficulties rather than any overt 'siding' by journalists.

Note

1. 'The *Nine O'Clock News* tries to take a serious news agenda, like one of the broadsheet newspapers. ... And what we try to do is take what we believe to be the twelve to fifteen most serious and important stories for our viewers that day and explain them' (BBC editor in interview with author, 1991).

Appendix A: Characteristics of Bulletins

The BBC1 *Nine O'Clock News* has an average of 9 to 12 stories. The news is packaged into items combining a reporter and footage and graphics. It is rare for there to be an interview in the studio, although live 'two-ways' are often conducted between reporters on location and the news presenter in the studio. The items last for an average of 2 minutes, ranging from 1 to 4 minutes. The bulletin was watched by around 6 million viewers at the time of analysis.

ITN *News at Ten* has an average of 11 to 14 stories. It has a similar set-up and agenda to the BBC news, although the BBC *Nine O'Clock News* sees itself as a 'journal of record' and ITN is more aware of its need to package news attractively. Its items range in length from 10 seconds to 4 minutes. It had an average of about 7 million viewers a day during the period of analysis.

Channel Four News has an average of 9 to 14 stories. It acts as an alternative news programme in prime time. It mixes in-depth, long reports, often with studio interviewees, with a shorter middle section which provides a round-up of the day's events. It attracted around 800,000 viewers daily at the time of analysis.

Sky News *World News Tonight* has a varying number of stories, ranging approximately from 12 to 20. It mixes in-depth 'serious' news with lighter stories. For example, on 18 May 1994 it spent 6 minutes on the Princess of Wales' shopping habits and followed this with 4 minutes on the Mongolian economy.

Euronews has between 13 and 16 stories per bulletin, none of them lasting longer than a minute. There is no studio, and the footage is voiced-over by a series of narrators.

CNN International's *International Hour* has an average of 17 stories in its bulletins, ranging in length from 15 seconds to 7 minutes.

References
Hopkinson, Nicholas (1993) *The Media and International Affairs after the Cold War*, Wilton Park Paper 74. Norfolk: HMSO.
Hurd, Douglas (1993) 'War of the Words', *The Guardian*, 17 September 1993.
MacKenzie, Lewis (1995) *A Soldier's Peace*. Transmitted 7 January 1995, BBC2.

United States of America

ANANTHA BABBILI

The TV News Broadcasting Framework

The dominant channels of television news in the USA are: ABC (American Broadcasting Corporation), NBC (National Broadcasting Corporation), CBS (Columbia Broadcasting System) and CNN (Cable News Network). Although the MacNeil/Lehrer NewsHour is an additional source of information on PBS (Public Broadcasting System), it is not viewed as an equal competitor for news and information.

A 1994 survey showed that between 70 and 80 per cent of Americans said they received 'most of their news from television'. On an average weeknight, roughly 30–40 million people tune into the network newscast at any given moment. Roughly half of all adults over the age of eighteen are regular viewers of the network newscast (cited in Freedom Forum 1995). A 1995 study also found that ABC, CBS and NBC have strikingly similar newscasts in terms of both structure and content. Each runs for 30 minutes of which about 20 minutes is actually devoted to news reports. Each broadcast is typically divided into five segments, between which it airs commercials. Each devotes the first segment to the top story or stories of the day. A typical broadcast will feature about fifteen news items, some of which may deal with different aspects of the same story. Most stories are very short, often less than 60 seconds (Freedom Forum 1995).

TV News Coverage of the War in Bosnia

This analysis must be seen in the context of the US foreign policy toward the region. Even though the war in the former Yugoslavia erupted in June 1991, the issue was conspicuously absent from political debates and from the presidential campaign of 1992. By 1994, however, the Clinton presidency made its concern for developments in former Yugoslavia known. President Clinton vocalised active support for conflict resolution in Bosnia through strengthening the role of the UN and the deployment of US troops. Republicans opposed active and direct US involvement in Bosnia but advocated arms supply to the Bosnian Muslims by lifting the UN embargo.

All regular news programmes were videotaped during 16–21 May 1994. The networks and local stations studied were *ABC World News Tonight*, *NBC Nightly News*, *CBS Evening News*, CNN 1 and CNN 2 *Headline News*. The local television stations included the ABC affiliate, WFAA-TV Channel 8; the NBC affiliate, KXAS-TV Channel 5; and the CBS affiliate, KDFW-TV Channel 4, all in the Dallas/Fort

Worth metropolitan area. The week's sample yielded 1,440 minutes of newscasts on five national networks and three regional/local television stations. Out of the 922 minutes of news during the week (excluding adverts) only 4 minutes 30 seconds were devoted to the news in Bosnia and for reporting of the conflict in former Yugoslavia. Out of 740 news items during the week on five national networks and three local/regional affiliates, only five items were devoted to events in Bosnia. Out of the five items relating to Bosnia, the most in-depth news story was generated locally in the Dallas/Fort Worth area. It dealt with Dallas school children sharing their lives with Bosnian children by sending school supplies and art work. Out of the 4 minutes 30 seconds of total Bosnia airplay during the week, this story from Dallas took 3 minutes. The following is a breakdown by day of the stories reported.

On 16 May the only news item about Bosnia among the eight news outlets studied was on the local/regional channel of the ABC affiliate in Dallas/Fort Worth. The news story was the seventh item in the newscast. It was preceded by stories relating to controversy on security at the World Cup Soccer Stadium in Dallas; a corporate merger in telecommunications; the murder trial of two teenage girls in Dallas; remembrance of a Dallas police officer killed in the line of duty; convicts in Texas jails using taxpayers' money to file excessive lawsuits against the state; and a federal court case declaring a Dallas school district desegregated. Since the news item about Bosnia was locally generated, the video source was the local television station itself. The reporter began the story with a voice-over of a typical day in a school in America while introducing a video clip of a day of school in Bosnia. This included shots of war, with the noise of artillery making a child look nervous. Fighter planes dropping missiles in Bosnia were contrasted with schoolchildren in colourful surroundings in a Dallas school. The reporter asked schoolchildren questions that elicited responses pointing to the good fortune of living in America. The story thus portrayed US citizens as caring, humanitarian and altruistic.

There was no story about Bosnia in any of the eight news outlets on 17 May.

On 18 May the ABC *World News Tonight* had a 13-second story as its eleventh item out of fifteen news stories. The story dealt with eleven French aid workers set free by Serbs in exchange for $44,000 paid by a French aid organisation, and was narrated in an ironic tone by the news anchor straight to camera: 'In Bosnia today a classic case of blackmail. Eleven French relief workers ... were set free today ... only after a French aid organisation paid $44,000 for their release. The Serbs called it bail.' As with the usual, although not universal, practice of US television news, ABC did not identify Serbs or Bosnians or other ethnic groups in the conflict by religion. If any reference to religion was made, it was to 'Bosnian Muslims'.

On 19 May there were two items relating to Bosnia on Thursday 19 May: one on CBS and the other on CNN 2. The CBS *Evening News* item lasted 20 seconds and the CNN 2 item 18 seconds. The CBS news story on Bosnia was sandwiched between the serious illness of Jacqueline Onassis Kennedy and Clinton's fierce defence of his administration's foreign policy. The CBS story dealt with the flaring-up of war in Bosnia again, described as the Bosnian government's refusal to take part in peace talks while Bosnian forces gained ground. This story was placed quite high in the CBS newscast, third out of fourteen news stories. The story had no correspondent and was read entirely by the news anchor, over shots of troops on their way to the battle lines. Bosnians were referred to as 'Muslims'.

The CNN 2 news story was a report of a UN flight bringing radar equipment to Bosnia amid heavy fighting. The item was placed as the eighth story out of twenty-two, with President Clinton meeting the Indian prime minister in the nation's capital as the preceding story, and the continued killings in Rwanda as the succeeding story. The footage, of an aeroplane landing, was not sourced.

On 20 May there were no stories relating to Bosnia broadcast on any of the eight television news outlets.

On 21 May the only story on Bosnia appeared on CNN 1 and lasted 41 seconds. The story was an update on life in Bosnia–Hercegovina and was placed as the fourth item out of twenty-two in the newscast. It was sandwiched between the airport shelling by rebels in Rwanda and the US international trade review in Washington, D.C. Since the preceding story dealt with the crisis in Rwanda, the Bosnia story implicitly portrayed the theme of Europe meeting its own Rwanda in Sarajevo. The report consisted of a series of shots of Sarajevo voiced over by the studio anchor.

Conclusion

As Walter Lippmann noted in 1922, the accurate and more complete portrayal of events abroad has remained elusive in US democratic discourse in this century. The emphasis on speed, artificial censorship of news and views by the gatekeeper, and the tendency to simplify complex global issues within limited vocabularies act as barriers to healthy public awareness and democratic debate. We contend that the prevailing news values, regulatory climate, criteria for selection and rejection of foreign news, lack of a sustained debate on ethics of pedagogy, economics of correspondents and the very nature of American journalism in a marketplace of ideas, all impinged upon the extent to which Bosnia was rendered visible.

References

Lippmann, W. (1922) *Public Opinion*, New York: The Free Press.
Freedom Forum Media Studies Centre (1995) *Headlines and Sound Bites: Is That the Way It Is?*, Research Series Preliminary Report, April 1995.

Index